Grahams o' the Mearns

An Investigation into my Graham Family Roots

David L. Graham

© 2011 David L. Graham, All Rights Reserved
Version 1.1
ISBN 978-1-105-29603-1

Table of Contents

Introduction – Ne Oublie 1

The First Explorations 4

"The Brickwall" – Alexander Graham, Tailor 6

Grahams o' the Mearns - A Detailed History 13

    First Three (and Highly Speculative) Generations 13

    Second Generation – And Still Speculative 15

    Third Generation – Getting Closer 17

    Fourth Generation 20

    Fifth Generation 26

    Sixth Generation 33

    Seventh Generation 40

    Eighth Generation 53

    Ninth Generation 59

    Tenth Generation 65

    Eleventh Generation 75

Where We Came From – Places of Origin 78

    The Mearns – St. Cyrus, Marykirk and Surrounding Parishes 78

    Forfar 80

    Dundee – Migration to the Big City 81

    Brooklyn NY – The Starting Point for Grahams in America 84

Grahams Down Under 91

Trades and Professions - How Grahams Supported Themselves 97

    Military Service 98

Who Were We, Really? – Personal Essays on Our Family and Ourselves 100

    Sheila (Graham) Rattray 100

    Charles IB Graham 101

    Maureen Graham-Graham Family Memories 103

    Donald Charles Graham 103

    Barbara (Graham) Pate 105

    Robert Schwarz 105

    Jeanine Graham 108

    David Alma Graham 109

Auntie Nan	110
Don Graham	114
Ethel (Eccleston) Graham	126

The Tale and Trail of Minnie Watson, Half-Sister 128

Loose Threads - Mysteries to Be Solved 133

The Grahams By Archie McKerracher 138

Odds and Ends 154
- Table of All Grahams Baptised in St. Cyrus, Old Parish Registries 1696-1852 154
- List of Grahams 157
- Most Popular Given Names 161
- Online Resources – Places I've Posted 161

Selected Maternal Lines 162
- The Wilkies 162
- The Cuthberts 165

On Fevers, Fate and Family History 173

Epilogue 180

4 Jun 2006 Graham Reunion in Auchterarder Scotland. L to R: Ronald Rattray, Donald Graham, Gavin Rattray, Jeanine Graham, Craig Barclay, Nanette (Graham) Holroyd, Georgia Rattray, Dave Graham, Nancy (Graham) Hamilton, Sheila (Graham) Rattray, Maureen Graham, Ros (Rattray) Barclay, Wilma (Gibbs) Graham, Steve Simon, Howard Rattray, Rona Barclay, Willie Campbell, Joy (Rattray) Campbell, Sonia Campbell, Claire (Graham) Simon, Rachel Campbell.

Introduction – *Ne Oublie*

November 2011

It is not without some irony that I began this Graham family history compilation after gazing upon the motto found on the Graham crest – Ne Oublie -- the French phrase for Do Not Forget. It is with this attitude that I embarked on this journey which has proven fascinating and miraculous.

Family history is a virulent bug. If never exposed, one can proceed through life blissfully ignorant of one's ancestry, and quite happy I'm sure. Prior to 2001, I counted myself in this group, faintly aware that I had Scottish ancestry and that the Graham name was one of the renowned Scottish clans. But then I took a trip to Scotland and spent part of a day perusing family history in the General Registry Office in Edinburgh. Within hours, I had discovered three generations of Graham ancestors that little had been known about or

The Graham Crest

passed down. I had been exposed, and in my case the family history bug was indeed an infectious strain. Since June 2001, I have spent countless hours researching my family history on both paternal and maternal sides.

As one of two Graham males of my generation, I have always felt the subtle pressure of carrying on the Graham line, at least as it has existed in the American branch. Consequently, I have been particularly keen to extend my knowledge of our male or paternal Graham lineage. Like many, I had hoped to uncover some royal or noble connections. Alas, at this juncture, I can only chuckle when I realize that James Campbell GRAHAM and his father Alexander GRAHAM both appear to have been illegitimate children born out-of-wedlock. Note however, that both were given their father's surname and that this name stuck. It raises more questions than I have been able to answer, thus far.

The journey began in 2001 with a stop at the Scottish National Registry Office in Edinburgh during a family vacation trip to Scotland. I knew very little about our Graham roots. My paternal grandfather – David Alma GRAHAM – had died the year before I was born. My own father passed away from an untimely heart attack in 1990 at the age of 61. My great grandfather – the first David Alma GRAHAM – had died when my father was only 4 years old. Not much family information had been handed down. But my father's brother -- Bob GRAHAM -- provided me with a bit of knowledge that David Alma Graham and his wife Agnes Robb CUTHBERT had come to New York from Scotland in the mid-1880's. These, my great grandparents, had six children, four of whom survived, all born in Brooklyn. The surviving children were Jennie Francis, followed by the second David Alma, then Agnes Cuthbert and finally George Forbes. The women never married but the two boys did and had two children each. David Alma (2) had two sons – my uncle Bob and my dad, Charles James Graham, often called Chuck. Though Bob was older by eight years, the two brothers were quite close. I know that Bob was pleased in his last years to learn what I had begun to discover and I think my own father would have greatly enjoyed this family history research process, or certainly the fruits of my labor. I know I certainly have.

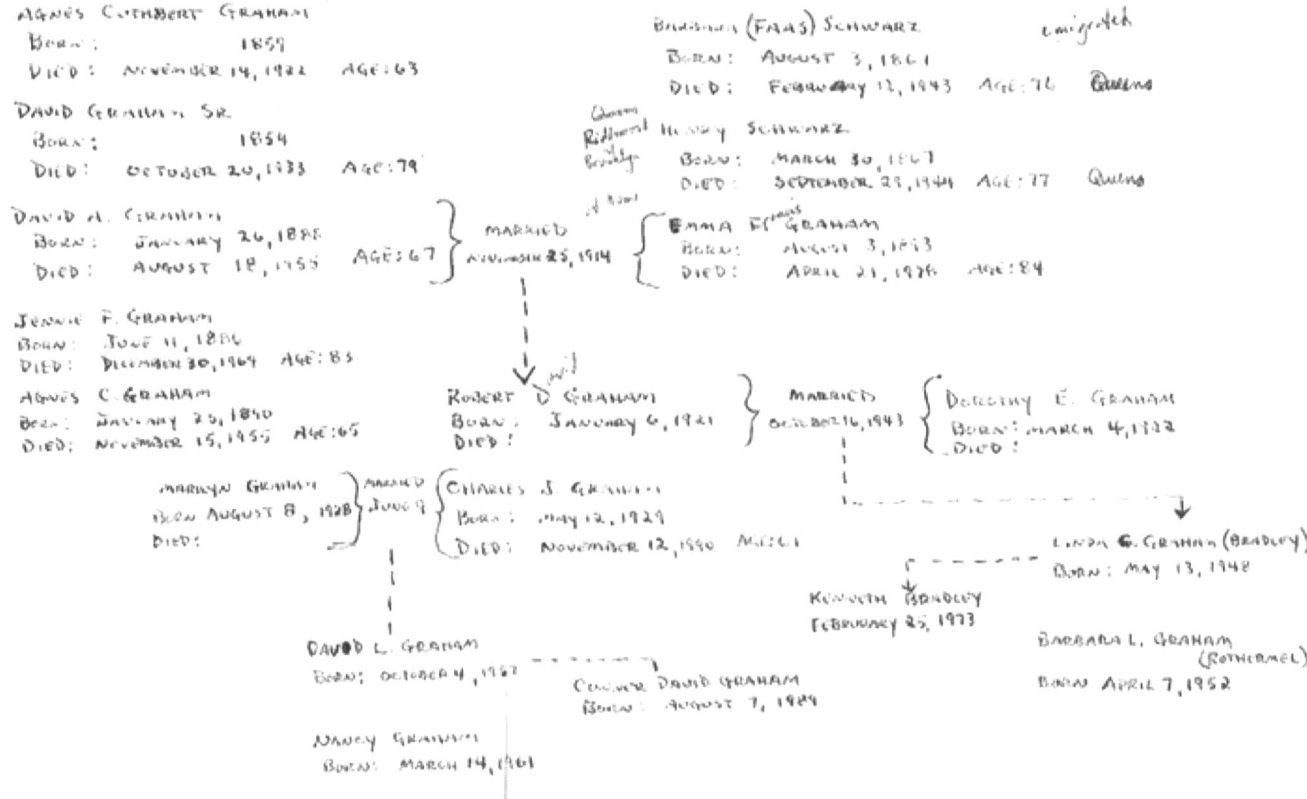

Original Graham Family Tree provided to me by Robert D. Graham, ca 2001

In the following pages readers will find a compilation of our research, findings, musings, speculations, and family history stories provided by several living relatives. These latter contributions are for me the most enjoyable and rewarding. The stories bring the extended Graham family history to life in the first person. They add depth and color. Readers will see that my extensive research into our earliest ancestors is intriguing but lacking real knowledge of who these people were, what their lives were like, and what their beliefs and values may have been. It seems easy to speculate that our Graham ancestors neatly fit the common Scots stereotype – taciturn, dour, self-reliant, thrifty, but this no doubt misses the mark for most if not all those who have lived before us. This Graham family history is my attempt to link the past with the present and offer future generations a detailed understanding of who they are in the broadest sense. Ne Oublie.

I wish to thank the many family members who have contributed to this work. First, Robert D. Graham (Uncle Bob) was the person that helped start me on this journey by giving me what he remembered about his grandparents. Second, I have been absolutely delighted to make an electronic connection with Sheila (Graham) Rattray and her daughter Ros (Rattray) Barclay and all the Scot Grahams related to Charles I. B. Graham. Their interest in Graham family history mirrored my own and together we have 're-built' the Graham family on both sides of the Atlantic after recognizing our common ancestor James Campbell GRAHAM and his wife Catherine WILKIE. I also wish to acknowledge Isobel (Cuthbert) Martin in Australia, and Margaret (Wright) O'Connor and Clive Rowe in New Zealand for helping establish connections to Grahams and Cuthberts 'down under.' Finally, my 2nd cousin George Graham has offered a number of wonderful photos, artifacts, and information from his family archives that have built an even more detailed picture of the American Grahams. To all of you, my deepest thanks and gratitude.

Maureen and Donald Graham, ca 1945

George C and David A Graham, ca 1925 Brooklyn

Ne Oublie -- Do Not Forget!

The First Explorations

Who knows why one's heritage suddenly becomes important? While being related to kings or queens, artists or warriors might make for an interesting cocktail party conversation, statistics suggest that most of us come from rather common stock. But it is in the stories of these 'common folk' that we begin to understand the romance of our lineage. Why would someone immigrate to this country? What was life like for this family in the 1880's, the 1770's or perhaps earlier? Perhaps it's just a genetic thing – an urge to find out how our DNA became what it is, even if, on a daily basis, we can't quite comprehend why our DNA does what it does to us and for us.

So it was with me as I reached my forties. Dad passed away from an untimely heart attack in 1990 at the age of 61. His father, a first generation American, survived a heart attack at 62 but couldn't beat the next one at age 67. As I began to contemplate my own mortality I also began to gain a curiosity about my roots, just what stock was I derived from? It just so happened that I have been a life-long golfer, pretty fair as a teenager but less so in middle age. I also had a small but burgeoning interest in single malt whiskies. Perhaps it was a genetic thing, or it could simply have been fate. But whatever the reason, I got my wife Jane interested in a trip to Scotland in the summer of 2001.

After months of preparation reading tour books, websites, talking to friends, we finally set upon dates and a general plan of attack. Having two boys nearly 12 and 10 also had to be accounted for in the planning. No 'one-stop-a-day' racing from city to city. Youngsters meant picking and choosing a few choice spots where we could hang out if the weather or the energy level wasn't up to snuff.

We flew in and out of London spending five days there to begin our trip and then trained up to Edinburgh. After five nights in Edinburgh we rented a car and headed to a self-catering cottage in Banchory, twenty-five miles east of Aberdeen. Along the way we drove along the south coast of the Fife and around to St. Andrews stopping to pay homage to the home of golf and then on through Dundee and on up to Banchory. This proved a good base of operations for the Dee Valley and gave me the chance to take the family on driving tours, hikes, distillery visits, castles, amusement parks and even an afternoon at the beach. After this we headed north to Inverness and then on to Skye before swinging back down toward Ft. William and then on into the suburbs of Glasgow. Alas, the weather did not cooperate on this last stretch and diminished the obvious beauty of the western Highlands. After three and half weeks we were all done in from the touring. Our last few days and nights were casual and less frenetic than the early portions of the journey, but no less rewarding. A stop at the Balloch Highland games, followed by a driving tour of the Trossachs, some golf for Dad and a trip to the new Glasgow Science Center made for an enjoyable conclusion to this Scottish adventure.

As with most vacations, this one had its share of special moments, events, sights and experiences. And rarely are they part of the planned itinerary. Perhaps the biggest occurred during our last full day in Edinburgh when I left the family to stop by the Scottish Registry Office and do my first genealogical explorations. By way of my Uncle Bob, I knew only that my great grandparents (David Graham and his wife Agnes Cuthbert Graham) emigrated to the U.S. in the 1880's from Scotland, he thought from Glasgow. We knew very little about them or their origins and consequently couldn't go back very far in the GRAHAM family lineage. I had no idea what I might learn, if anything, but I plunged into the registry office, paid my day-use fee and began exploring my roots. Before going inside, I expected to be one of two or three people rummaging around a dark musty old building comprised of rows upon rows of paper files and such. Instead, I was assigned one of 60 odd stations in one half of the building and by the time I arrived at 9:30 am, most of these were occupied. Genealogic searching was a more important pastime than I thought!

Scotland's foresight to begin formal record keeping in 1855 has proven a boon to family history detectives like me. A computerized database of names, births, marriages and deaths along with Old Parish Records that predate the 1855 records proved to be an interesting and wonderful resource. After a few minutes to familiarize myself with the query rules, I was off and running in my attempts to find out about David Alma Graham and Agnes Cuthbert Graham.

What I found amazed, delighted and energized me. The original plan had been to stay for two hours but that stretched into three and then, after meeting Jane and the boys for lunch and a Scottish National Gallery tour, I went back for another hour. Searching computer records led to microfiche copies of birth, marriage and death certificates. My efforts would have been slower and more cumbersome if not for the help I received from an elderly volunteer. Occasionally, he would pass by my seat in front of the screen and in hushed tones suggest different search strategies or prevent me from pursuing blind alleys.

I began the search without expectaction but hoping to get more information about David and Agnes prior to their immigration to the U.S.A. But, with the help of the kindly docent, I went back two earlier Graham generations. It was exciting to think that I had just discovered something that no other living Graham relation knew. And there was clearly more to discover. What I didn't realize in that very first foray was that I had run into my very first 'brickwall.' The discoveries stopped abruptly and I had run out of time that day. David's grandfather was one Alexander Graham who had James Campbell Graham with Christian or Christina Doig. However, no marriage entry could be found. Thankfully, the internet as a genealogy research tool was emerging quickly. Though I traveled a long way to Edinburgh in 2001 my journey was just beginning.

"The Brickwall" – Alexander Graham, Tailor

After returning from our month-long sojourn to Scotland, I began to use the internet to learn what I could about family history research and our Scottish Graham ancestors. What started as a few short hours in General Registry Office exploded into a time-consuming passion to investigate my Scottish roots. I certainly didn't realize it that late June day in Edinburgh but Alexander Graham, my great-great-great grandfather had immediately become a 'brickwall' the ancestor at which conclusive evidence of parentage stops or cannot be identified or overcome.

In the fall of 2001, after writing for copies of death, marriage and birth certificates, I obtained a death certificate for one Alexander Graham that died in Dundee 17 Jun 1871 whose occupation was listed as tailor, journ(eyman).

Death registration for Alexander Graham

The biggest disappointment was that no Christina Doig was listed as wife but several clues presented avenues for exploration. First and foremost, Alexander's parents were listed as Robert Graham, ploughman (deceased) and Mary Nicholson farm servant, deceased. What was particularly interesting was that Alexander was illegitimately born and that this was recorded on his death registration. This information also led to a new avenue. My early internet research focused on Alexander Grahams in the Angus area, but a quick search of the LDS site (www.familysearch.org) showed that an Alexander Graham was christened in Marykirk in the lower Mearns of Kincardineshire. Another finding was that his death was witnessed by a daughter, Margaret Watt (who's signature appears in the top right) from Keithbank, Rattray. She must have known about and disclosed his illegitimate status. It would be two years before I figured out the significance of this finding.

Another noteworthy finding was that Alexander Graham could not be tied to Christina Doig but instead was listed as the widower of Ann Lindsay and Barbara Fettes. These marriages were easy to find. Alexander married first Ann Lindsay in Marykirk on 22 Sep 1821 in the parish of Marykirk. I had learned this very early on in the research, but it was several years before I made the effort to look at the actual entry. By the time I did, the mystery had been solved, at least to my satisfaction, but the entry did offer more confirmation about 'our' Alexander. Note that the entry states that he was from the Parish of Glammis. This area proved to be the place where Alexander Graham met and had a relationship with Christina Doig.

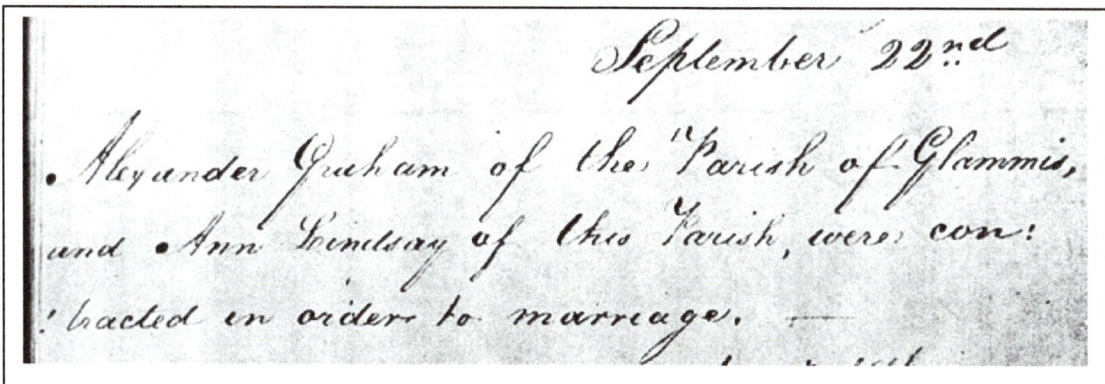

Marriage entry for Alexander Graham and Ann Lindsay dated 22 Sep 1821; source: LDS microfiche for Marykirk OPR.

According to the LDS data, Alexander and Ann Lindsay had two children: (1) Alexander Graham, born 3 Nov 1821, registered in the Marykirk parish and likewise (2) Mary Ann Graham, born 20 Dec 1822, Marykirk. No other children were born that were listed to this couple, at least in the Old Parish Registries in Marykirk or the surrounding towns. At first, I thought that daughter Mary Ann changed her name to Margaret and was the witness to her father's death in Dundee in 1871, but a new revelation occurred when I located a Margaret Nicholson Graham born to Alexander Graham and Elizabeth Sharp on 8 May 1821 in Marykirk.

Birth entry for Margaret Nicholson Graham dated 8 May 1821, illegitimate daughter of Alexander Graham and Elisabeth Sharp.

The notation, Natural Daughter as opposed to Lawful Daughter indicates that the child was illegitimate, born out-of-wedlock. This finding offered another in a long series of "Aha" moments. Records show that Margaret Graham married Charles Watt in Montrose 27 Dec 1846. They had one son, John, whose birth or baptism was not recorded but who does appear on many census entries.

Marriage entry for Alexander Graham and Barbara Fettes dated 31 Dec 1848 from Blairgowrie OPR.

Alexander Graham married Barbara Fettes on 31 Dec 1848 in Blairgowrie, Perth. But by 1851 this couple was located in Dundee on Doigs Entry off Overgate, an address that no longer exists. No children were born to Alexander and Barbara, this despite the fact that she was thirty years younger than our Alexander!

What do we know of this Alexander Graham, an illegitimate journeyman tailor? Though records document important milestones, they offer few insights into the quality and character of his life. However, peruse these records more carefully and one can begin to paint an interesting portrait.

Born illegitimately to Robert Graham and Mary Nicol, he must have been close to his mother, otherwise, why name his first born daughter – also illegitimate – Margaret Nicholson Graham? The fact that his death certificate was witnessed by this daughter strongly suggests that father and first (illegitimate) daughter had a long and abiding relationship. It is also possible that Margaret became the matriarch of the family after Ann Lindsay died. Earlier in my investigations I was perplexed that his birth mother was listed as Nicol but that his death registration indicated Nicholson, but since his daughter provided the details to the Registrar, it is no wonder that she assumed that his mother was indeed Mary Nicholson and not Nicol as the records show.

Alexander's father Robert Graham (the ploughman) actually had a lengthy career in the Royal Regiment of Artillery before returning to the Montrose area and remarrying. After siring Alexander in 1796 at the age of 19, Robert went on to marry Henrietta Law 14 Jul 1798 in Fordoun. This marriage occurred just one month after Alexander was baptized in the Marykirk church on 3 Jun 1798. Robert joined the Angusshire Militia before accepting a post in the English army and he and his young wife soon found themselves stationed in Kilmarnock, Ayrshire south of Glasgow. It was here that they had their one and perhaps only child, a son named Archibald Douglas Graham who was born 10 April 1799. No further trace of Henrietta or Archibald Graham has yet been found. I suspect that they may have been camp followers and died of illness at some point during Robert Graham's twenty one year career (1803-1824) with the Royal Regiment of Artillery, but this is speculative.

Thus, Alexander Graham was probably raised by his mother Mary Nicol although we can only guess as to where. Perhaps Mary did marry and move to some other town or parish. In his adult life, Alexander's trail took him from Marykirk to Glamis to Tannadice to Blairgowrie and finally to Dundee. Who taught him the tailoring trade? His early life is lost to us as there are no records from 1798 until 1821, but when he does re-emerge, young Alexander Graham does so with great fanfare, at least as a progenitor. Note the cluster of children he sired within a nineteen month timeframe.

It's quite puzzling to realize that, when one thinks about the timing of the births and therefore the likely dates of conception, Alexander moved between Marykirk and Glamis with great facility. Could his mother have been in the Glamis area, or even Blairgowrie where he would later reside at least for a short time? Even if so, why did he have a connection to Marykirk? He must have had relations with Elisabeth Sharp in August or September 1820. But then he went on to have relations with Ann Lindsay some time around February 1821 before they would marry 19 Sep 1821 in Marykirk. And to complicate matters, he must have had a tryst with Christina Doig in Glamis that occurred in April, May or June of 1821 as evidenced by the Glamis Kirk Session minutes transcribed below.

Transcript of Glamis Kirk Session

"2nd Dec 1821 Session Met & Constrd

Christian Doig appeared and acknowledged herself to be guilty of a relapse in fornication. She declared that she was with _child to Alexr Graham who lately removed from this_ place & was now residing in Aberdeen. The woman_promised to get a letter from him to the Kirk Session_acknowledging him to be the father of her child, which_would serve till he returned to make his confession_before the Kirk Session. Christian Doig after being warned of her danger & suitably chastised was dismissed for the_present.

L.N. (?) Closed with prayer"

Two items from this entry are noteworthy. First, Christina Doig acknowledges 'a relapse in fornication.' This comment helped establish that the Christina Doig, mother of James Campbell Graham, was born to Robert Doig and Isabell Neaves in the parish of Glamis 10 Jan 1784. Christina was one of a set of twins born to this couple. The relapse being referred to helped us pinpoint this woman as having had one earlier son, also born out-of-wedlock, to a William Donaldson in Glamis in 1812. While there was no birth or baptism entry for James Campbell Graham he was probably born in January or February of 1822 which suggests a conception date of April or May 1821. The second point is that Christian Doig told the Kirk Session that Alexander Graham, who would have been 23 or 24 and about thirteen years younger, was residing in Aberdeen. Perhaps this is what he told her or perhaps she simply gave the Session a location that was far enough away to remove the chance of any further investigation. Whatever the case, it seems a very unlikely relationship that led to our common ancestor James Campbell Graham.

At this point in the narrative, some six years after my earliest efforts in 2001, I thought I knew everything that could be known about Alexander Graham. My genealogical detective work had run its course and I suspected that Alexander's wife Ann may have died in child birth or shortly after the birth of Mary Ann in 1823. But on the spur of the moment I decided to see if I could locate an 1841 census entry for Margaret Nicholson Graham. What I found in late July 2007 astounded me and opened up entire new avenues for exploration. Using Scotland's Peoples website, I uncovered evidence that Alexander and Ann Lindsay had four other children prior to 1841, none of which were recorded in the Marykirk Parish Register. Either they weren't recorded because Alexander and Ann chose not to, or because the records were not well kept or lost. I presume the former and suppose that Alexander and Ann were not religious or willing to conform to the Church of Scotland.

The entry for Ann Graham in the lower right offers many interesting facts that had not been known to me prior to July 2007. First, Margaret Nicholson Graham, the step daughter is living with her stepmother in Logie Pert at Logie Works, a small village about 3 km southwest of Marykirk. Second, the family of Alexander and Ann Lindsay comprised:

- Margaret, age 20, flax spinner
- Alexander, 19, flax dresser
- John, 16, flax dresser
- Andrew, 13, flax dresser
- Renwick, 11
- Elizabeth, 9
- Rachel Low, 3

Another intriguing question - why was Alexander not in this household but rather in Tannadice, a village about fifteen miles from Logie Pert? Using the first census of 1841, we found Alexander listed as age 40 and living with a young apprentice in the village of Tannadice, Angus. The English Parliament commissioned the first national census and it was executed in 1841. The information collected was minimal and ages were rounded down to the nearest five years. So, although Alexander was actually 44 when it occurred, he was listed as age 40. It also indicated whether the person was born in county or not, and in this entry, Alexander Graham, Tailor, journeyman was shown as not being born in Angus which fits with his Marykirk, Kincardineshire birth. Was he an itinerant tailor, moving from town to town as business dictated? Or was he already estranged from his wife and family? Was he an 'absentee' father perhaps influenced by his own lack of a father figure? Obviously, Alexander is not around to explain or defend, but we might be seeing the origin of a pattern that seemed to befit Graham fathers for the next two or three generations.

1841 Census Entry for Alexr Graham, Tannadice

1841 Census

Parish of _Tannadice, Village of_   24

PLACE	HOUSES		NAME and SURNAME, SEX and AGE, of each Person who abode in each House on the Night of 6th June.			OCCUPATION	WHERE BORN	
Here insert Name of Village, Street, Square, Close, Court, &c.	Uninhabited or Building	Inhabited	NAME and SURNAME	AGE Male	AGE Female	Of what Profession, Trade, Employment, or whether of Independent Means.		
			Alexander Graham	40		Tailor J.	N	
			William Cummin	15		do Ap.	Y	

Another intriguing finding was the entry of Rachel Low age 3. Typically, a youngster in the household with a different name suggested some relation between the families; however, I was unable to find a conclusive link between this youngster and other family relations.

There are many intriguing discoveries and implications from this 1841 census entry. Readers will find in subsequent pages that numerous descendents of Alexander Graham1798 and Ann Lindsay continued on and migrated southward down to Dundee, Dunblane in the Perthshire area and beyond to Australia, New Zealand and the USA. The re-connection of Graham relations in Scotland (descendents of Charles IB Graham) and America (descendents of David Alma Graham) was perhaps the greatest consequence of my research and good fortune. But it is equally marvelous to contemplate that there may be other Graham relations still in Scotland or elsewhere stemming from our common ancestor – Alexander Graham, the journeyman tailor.

Timeline for Alexander Graham (#55)

Date	Event	Place	Details	
Feb 1797	birth	Marykirk	born to Robert GRAHAM and Mary NICOL	
3 Jun 1798	baptism	Marykirk	witness were James Cowie and James Gove, both of Thornton	
May 1821	birth	Marykirk	birth of Margaret Nicholson Graham by Alexander and Elizabeth Sharp	
22 Sep 1821	marriage	Marykirk	Ann Lindsay	
3 Nov 1821	birth	Marykirk	lawful son Alexander Graham	born to Alexander and Ann Lindsay
Dec 1821	Kirk Session	Glamis	recognition of fornication btw Alexander and Christine Doig	
~Feb 1822	birth	Glamis	natural son James Campbell Graham	born to Alexander and Christina Doig
10 Dec 1822	birth	Marykirk	lawful daughter Mary Ann Graham	born to Alexander and Ann Lindsay
1824	birth	Marykirk	lawful son John Graham	born to Alexander and Ann Lindsay
1828	birth	Marykirk	lawful son Andrew Graham	born to Alexander and Ann Lindsay
1830	birth	Marykirk	lawful son Renwick Graham	born to Alexander and Ann Lindsay
1832	birth	Marykirk	lawful daughter Elizabeth Graham	born to Alexander and Ann Lindsay
1841	census	Tannidice	Alexander Graham, tailor journeyman with one apprentice	
31 Dec 1848	marriage	Blairgowrie	marriage to Barbara Fettes	
April 1851	census	Dundee	Alexander & Barbara located at Doigs Entry Overgate, Dundee	
April 1861	census	Dundee	Alexander & Barbara located at 2 Park Entry, Dundee	
21 Jun 1869	death	Dundee	death of Barbara (Fettes) Graham at 2 Park Entry	
17 Jun 1871	death	Dundee	death of Alexander Graham, Tailor, journeyman at 2 Park Entry	

Composite of Charles IB Graham family. Back row: Charles, William and David Souter. Front row: Agnes "Nan", Charles IB, and Agnes Dickson Soutar Graham.

Grahams o' the Mearns

Grahams o' the Mearns - A Detailed History

Once it became clear that our Graham ancestors could be traced back to St. Cyrus in the lower Mearns, I began a detailed analysis of all Graham marriages and baptisms in that and nearby parishes. The earliest Graham marriage entry in St. Cyrus is for James GRAHAME and Isoble HILL. Using Scottish naming traditions, I speculate on many of the potential GRAHAM offspring recorded shortly after this marriage. Let me be absolutely clear – everything I present in the first three generations is <u>highly speculative</u>. Confounding the analysis is the fact that many baptism entries listed only the father with no mention of the mother. However, having reviewed microfilm records of the Old Parish Registers for many of the areas in and around St. Cyrus, I can confidently say that our ancestry can be traced back to Alexander GRAHAM and Jean/Jane MITCHEL. This Alexander GRAHAM was probably descended from GRAHAMs already living in the area and working the land as farmers or fishermen. He may have been a grandson to the James Graham we begin with below. Or, perhaps not.

Editor's Note: The style and structure of the information in this section was generated by the LDS software FamilySearch Personal Ancestral File version 5.0, however, I made some editorial changes to improve readability. The report begins with the first male Graham. Every person in the file has number but is also designated M for male and F for female. A + sign means that the person has issue (i.e., children). The notation NFR is my own addition and means No Further Records have yet been located although I have not used this notation consistently.

First Three (and Highly Speculative) Generations

1. **James GRAHAM(E)** .

IGI contains marriage records between James GRAHAME and Isoble HILL in 1698 with possibly seven offspring all born in St. Cyrus, Kincardineshire just a few miles north of Montrose on the eastern North Sea coast. Further study is required for confirmation, but assuming that families in that day and age stayed close to their lands, it appears that our Graham lineage can be traced back to this area of Scotland.

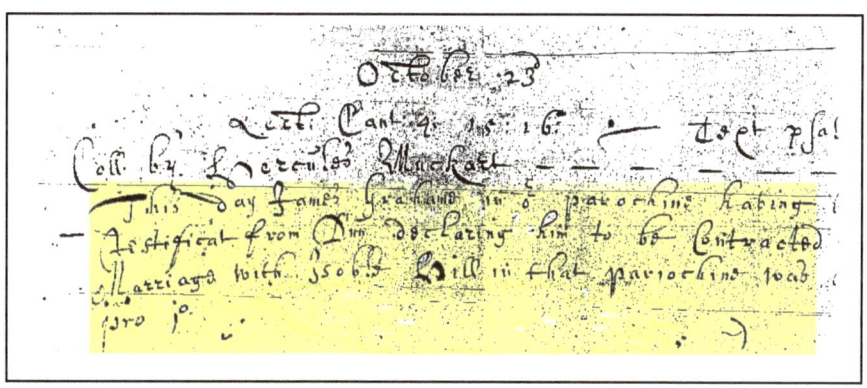

James married **Isoble HILL** daughter of John HILL and Barbara CUTBERD on 23 Oct 1698 in St. Cyrus, Kincardine, Scotland. Isoble was christened on 6 Jun 1680 in Dun, Angus, Scotland.

> After reviewing the St. Cyrus OPR, it reads "This day, James Grahame in o(ur) parochins (parish) having Aestificat from Dun declaring him to be contracted in marriage with Isoble HILL in that parochins was pro(claimed)." Dun in Angus (on the other side of Montrose basin). Dun OPR records report a christening of Isobell HILL to John HILL and Barbara Cutberd (Cuthbert?).

James and Isoble <u>may</u> have had the following children:

2   Mi. **Robert GRAHAM** was christened on 30 Aug 1696 in St. Cyrus, Kincardine, Scotland with father listed as James Graham but whether this Robert was born to this James Graham(e) is purely speculative. It may have been this James with a different mother or a completely different James altogether.

3	Mii.	**John GRAHAM** was christened on 15 Sep 1700 in St. Cyrus, Kincardine, Scotland.
		John may have married **Margaret NICOLL** on 26 Jun 1729 in St. Cyrus, Kincardine, Scotland.
4	Fiii.	**Janet GRAHAM** was christened on 20 Sep 1702 in St. Cyrus, Kincardine, Scotland.
+ 5	Miv.	**James GRAHAM** was christened on 8 Oct 1704. He was buried on 27 Feb 1785 at Brownhill in the parish of St. Cyrus.
+ 6	Mv.	**Robert GRAHAM** was born on 14 Dec 1707.
+ 7	Mvi.	**Alexander GRAHAM** was christened on 23 Jul 1710.

Emma (Schwarz) Graham, Charles J. Graham, David Alma Graham, and Robert D. Graham, ca 1929

Second Generation – And Still Speculative

5. **James GRAHAM** (James) was christened on 8 Oct 1704 in St. Cyrus, Kincardine, Scotland. He was buried on 27 Feb 1785 in Brownhill, St. Cyrus, KCD, Scotland.

> Burial date is speculative but there is a burial entry for a James Graham, Brownhill on 27 Feb 1785. Old parish maps indicate that Brownhill was farmland very near the Hill of Morphie.

James married **Isobell NICOLL** on 16 Jun 1732 in St. Cyrus, Kincardine, Scotland.

They may have had the following children:

+ 8   Mi. **James GRAHAM** was christened on 23 May 1735.

   9   Fii. **Margaret GRAHAM** was christened on 13 Mar 1737 in St. Cyrus, Kincardine, Scotland.

  10   Fiii. **Mary GRAHAM** was christened on 5 Aug 1739 in St. Cyrus, Kincardine, Scotland.

  11   Miv. **John GRAHAM** was christened on 5 Jun 1742 in St. Cyrus, Kincardine, Scotland.

  12   Mv. **Alexander GRAHAM** was christened on 15 Jul 1744 in St. Cyrus, Kincardine, Scotland.

  13   Mvi. **David GRAHAM** [1] was christened on 18 Oct 1747 in St. Cyrus, Kincardine, Scotland. He died on 17 Sep 1820 in Montrose, Angus, Scotland. He was buried[2] in Montrose, Angus, Scotland. David married **Mary BRAND** on 16 Jun 1781 in St. Cyrus, Kincardine, Scotland.

6. **Robert GRAHAM** (James) was born on 14 Dec 1707 in St. Cyrus, Kincardine, Scotland.

SPECULATIVE. While there is IGI data on a birth of Robert GRAHAM with a father James and a marriage to Janet WHITE (or WHYTE), I cannot confirm that this Robert Graham is the same as that born in 1707. Likewise, the children listed born to this Robert GRAHAM only have a listing of their father and not their mother. Scottish naming tradition point in favor of my hypotheses but this NEEDS CONFIRMATION.

Robert married **Janet WHITE** on 28 Jun 1739 in St. Cyrus, Kincardine, Scotland. The marriage entry above states that Robert and Janet were both from the parish of St. Cyrus, however there are no records of a Janet White/Whyte birth in Kincardineshire in the early 1700's.

They may have had the following children:

  14   Mi. **Robert GRAHAM** was christened on 30 Mar 1740 in St. Cyrus, Kincardine, Scotland.

+ 15   Mii. **Alexander GRAHAM** was christened on 28 May 1743 in St. Cyrus, Kincardine, Scotland.

  16   Fiii. **Ann GRAHAM** was christened on 7 Apr 1745 in St. Cyrus, Kincardine, Scotland.

  17   Miv. **James GRAHAM** was christened on 17 Feb 1748 in St. Cyrus, Kincardine, Scotland.

  18   Fv. **Mary GRAHAM** was christened on 1 Apr 1750 in St. Cyrus, Kincardine, Scotland.

  19   Fvi. **Margaret GRAHAM** was christened on 21 Jun 1752 in St. Cyrus, Kincardine, Scotland.

  20   Mvii. **John GRAHAM** was christened on 2 Jun 1754 in St. Cyrus, Kincardine, Scotland.

  21   Fviii. **Helen GRAHAM** was christened on 27 Jun 1756 in St. Cyrus, Kincardine, Scotland.

22 Mix. **Andrew GRAHAM** was christened on 17 Feb 1760 in Benholm, Kincardine, Scotland.

This fellow can be confirmed as the child of Robert GRAHAM and Janet WHITE as the Benholm Clerk of Session recorded the names of both parents. Why he was born and baptized in Benholm, a village just north of St. Cyrus, whereas the remaining children were baptized in St. Cyrus remains a mystery.

23 Fx. **Jean GRAHAM** was born on 16 May 1762 in St. Cyrus, Kincardine, Scotland. She was christened on 16 May 1762 in St. Cyrus, Kincardine, Scotland.

7. **Alexander GRAHAM** (James) was christened on 23 Jul 1710 in St. Cyrus, Kincardine, Scotland. Alexander may have married **Mart. SMITH** on 25 Jun 1749 in St. Cyrus, Kincardine, Scotland. They had the following children:

24 F i. **Jean GRAHAM** was christened on 23 Jul 1749 in St. Cyrus, Kincardine, Scotland.

25 Fii. **Janet GRAHAM** was christened on 21 May 1750 in St. Cyrus, Kincardine, Scotland.

26 Fiii. **Helen GRAHAM** was christened on 13 Oct 1751 in St. Cyrus, Kincardine, Scotland.

27 Miv. **Charles GRAHAM** was christened on 26 Apr 1752 in St. Cyrus, Kincardine, Scotland.

28 Fv. **Ann GRAHAM** was christened on 28 May 1754 in St. Cyrus, Kincardine, Scotland.

+ 29 Mvi. **Alexander GRAHAM** was christened on 14 Jul 1754. He died after 1841 but before 1851.

30 Fvii. **Mary GRAHAM** was christened on 17 Apr 1757 in St. Cyrus, Kincardine, Scotland.

31 Mviii. **William GRAHAM** was christened on 13 Jun 1762 in St. Cyrus, Kincardine, Scotland.

Robert D. Graham, Emma, David and Charles, ca. 1943

Dave, Nicole and Don Graham, Mar 2007

Third Generation – Getting Closer

8. **James GRAHAM** (James GRAHAM, James) was christened on 23 May 1735 in St. Cyrus, Kincardine, Scotland. James married **Ann DORRAT** though the marriage is not listed in Old Parish Records. However, baptismal listings of their two children provide both parents' names.

They had the following children:

32 F i. **Helen GRAHAM** was christened on 27 Oct 1754 in St. Cyrus, Kincardine, Scotland.

33 M ii. **John GRAHAM** was christened on 4 Mar 1759 in St. Cyrus, Kincardine, Scotland.

15. **Alexander GRAHAM** (Robert GRAHAM, James) was christened on 28 May 1743 in St. Cyrus, Kincardine, Scotland.

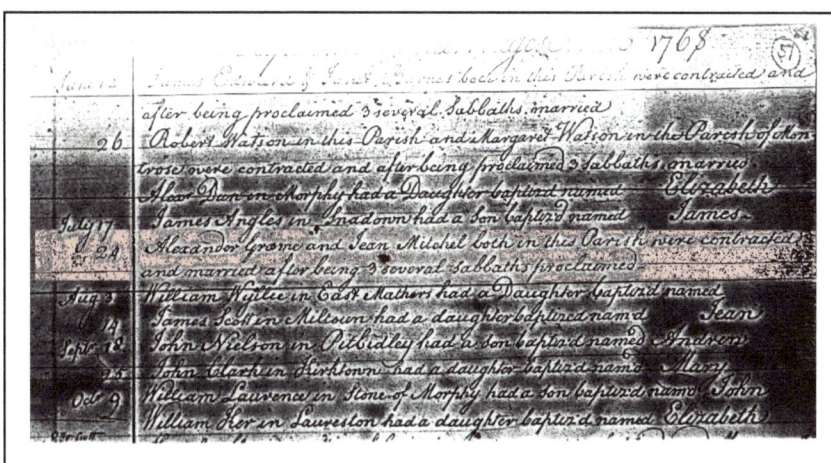

IGI lists a marriage between Alexander GRAHAM and Jean/Jane MITCHEL, however, the first five children below are assumed to be theirs. The birth/christening sources only list Alexander as father, no mother listed, not an uncommon practice in Old Parish Registries. Further research by Caroline Makein (Dec 2005) showed that Robert Graham was born to Alexander GRAHAM in Hill of Morphie. Helen GRAHAM (ch 26 Jun 1783) was born to Alexander GRAHAM and Jane MITCHEL in Hill of Morphie, the first time the mother was recorded in the church records. From this we can be confident that this Alexander GRAEME/GRAHAM and Jean/Jane MITCHEL are (thus far) our earliest confirmable GRAHAM ancestors.

IGI data lists two Alexander GRAHAMs born in St. Cyrus, one in 1743 and another in 1744. The first Alexander GRAHAM (ch. 28 May 1743) was probably born to Robert GRAHAM and Janet WHITE. Based upon Scottish naming patterns, this fellow is likely to be the one to have married Jean MITCHEL. For example, the first child born to this couple was named Janet after Alexander's mother, a fairly common approach to naming. The second Alexander Graham candidate (ch. 15 Jul 1744) was likely born to James GRAHAM and Isobell NICOLL.

Alexander married **Jean or Jane MITCHEL** on 24 Jul 1768 in St. Cyrus, Kincardine, Scotland.

They probably had the following children:

34 F i. **Janet GRAHAM** was christened on 3 Sep 1769 in St. Cyrus, Kincardineshire, Scotland to 'Alexander Grame in Pitbeadlie.'

35 F ii. **Mary GRAHAM** was christened on 11 Mar 1771 in St. Cyrus, Kincardineshire, Scotland to 'Alexander Graham in Pitbeadlie.'

36 F iii. **Anne GRAHAM** was christened on 4 Oct 1772 in St. Cyrus, Kincardineshire, Scotland to 'Alexander GRAME in Pitbeadlie.'

+ 37 M iv. **Alexander GRAHAM** was christened on 26 Sep 1773. He died on 8 Apr 1840.

38 F v. **Margaret GRAHAM** was christened on 18 Jun 1777 in St. Cyrus, Kincardineshire, Scotland. The OPR stated that "Alexander Graham in Pitbeadley had a daughter Margaret baptized in face of the Congregation." She must have died before 1780 as evidenced by another Margaret born to her parents in 1781 (see below). She died before 1780.

+ 39 Mvi. **Robert GRAHAM** was christened on 11 Jun 1778 to Alexr Graham in Hill of Morphy. We can be very confident that this Robert GRAHAM is our direct ancestor and that he was born to Alexander Graham, cotterman in Pitbeadlie now Hill of Morphy.

40 Mvii. **William GRAHAM** was christened on 15 Dec 1779 in St. Cyrus, Kincardine, Scotland. "Alexander GRAME in Hill of Morphy had a son baptized named William. Witness Alexr Greig, Kirk Officer."

41 Fviii. **Margaret GRAHAM** was christened on 25 Aug 1781 in St. Cyrus, Kincardine, Scotland.

+ 42 Fix. **Helen GRAHAM** was christened on 26 Jun 1783. "Alexander Graham and Jane Mitchel in Hill of Morphy had a daughter baptized before the congregation named Helen." [Source: notes taken by D. Graham of LDS microfiche records.]

29. **Alexander GRAHAM** (Alexander GRAHAM, James) was christened on 14 Jul 1754 in St. Cyrus, Kincardine, Scotland. He probably died sometime after 1841 but before the census of 1851. We know this because he was listed in the 1841 census but cannot be located in the 1851 census. In the 1841 census, this Alexander Graham was living in Lochside Village of St. Cyrus and listed as 85 years of age meaning he could have been born anytime between 1751 and 1756. His occupation was listed as Navy – retired and wife Isobel (age 75) was still living as well. Also in the household was Charlotte Graham, age 14, female servant. This Charlotte (#77) is the daughter of James Graham (#45) and Mary Jack, and a granddaughter to Alexander (#29) and Isobel.

> Listed in 1841 Census for St. Cyrus, he was retired Navy, which correlates well with fact that witnesses to the christening of his son Aikman were Capt Joseph Aikman and Alex Martin. There was a Joseph Aikman christened 7 Jul 1733 in Marykirk to a James Aikman and Mary Austin. Perhaps he joined the Navy and brought Alexander Graham under his command.

Alexander married **Isobel YOUNG** daughter of James YOUNG and Jane WALKER on 11 Nov 1787 in St. Cyrus, Kincardine, Scotland. Isobel was christened[1] on 14 Apr 1766 in Kinneff & Catterline, Kincardineshire, Scotland. She likely also died after 1841 in St. Cyrus, Kincardineshire, Scotland.

They had the following children all of whom were born and baptized in St. Cyrus, Kincardineshire:

+ 43 F i. Janet GRAHAM was christened on 29 Sep 1788. She died on 29 Dec 1839.
+ 44 Mii. Aikman GRAHAM was born on 20 Jul 1790. He died on 2 Apr 1878.
+ 45 Miii. James GRAHAM was christened on 26 Jul 1792. He died on 6 May 1881.
  46 Miv. William GRAHAM was christened on 12 Jul 1795 in St. Cyrus, Kincardine, Scotland.
+ 47 Fv. Susan GRAHAM was christened on 28 May 1797.
  48 Fvi. Anne GRAHAM was christened on 4 Mar 1804 in St. Cyrus, Kincardine, Scotland.

Two Generations of Descendants of Alexander Graham b. 1743

1. **Alexander Graham (c.28 May 1743-St. Cyrus,Kincardine,Scotland)**
   - sp: Jean or Jane Mitchel (m.24 Jul 1768)
     - 2. Janet Graham (c.3 Sep 1769-St. Cyrus,Kincardineshire,Scotland)
     - 2. Mary Graham (c.11 Mar 1771-St. Cyrus,Kincardineshire,Scotland)
     - 2. Anne Graham (c.4 Oct 1772-St. Cyrus,Kincardineshire,Scotland)
     - 2. Alexander Graham (c.26 Sep 1773-St. Cyrus,Kincardine,Scotland;d.8 Apr 1840-St. Cyrus,Kincardine,Scotland)
       - sp: Jean Black (m.7 Apr 1799;d.22 Oct 1837-St. Cyrus,Kincardine,Scotland)
         - 3. Betty Graham (b.11 Nov 1799-Montrose,Angus,Scotland;d.17 Oct 1866-Montrose,Angus,Scotland)
         - 3. Ann Graham (b.21 Sep 1801-Montrose,Angus,Scotland;d.7 Jan 1824-St. Cyrus,Kincardine,Scotland)
         - 3. William Graham (b.11 Aug 1803-Montrose,Angus,Scotland;d.14 Apr 1881-St. Cyrus,Kincardineshire,Scotland)
           - sp: Jean Donald (b.Abt 1801-Monymusk,Aberdeenshire,Scotland;d.Aft 1881-St. Cyrus,Kincardineshire,Scotland)
         - 3. Isobelle Graham (b.9 Jun 1805-Montrose,Angus,Scotland;d.11 Jan 1822-St. Cyrus,Kincardine,Scotland)
         - 3. Jean Graham (b.15 Oct 1807-Montrose,Angus,Scotland;d.24 Oct 1867-St. Cyrus,Kincardineshire,Scotland)
         - 3. Janet Graham (b.4 Feb 1813-St. Cyrus,Kincardine,Scotland;d.3 Nov 1824-St. Cyrus,Kincardine,Scotland)
     - 2. Margaret Graham (c.18 Jun 1777-St. Cyrus,Kincardineshire,Scotland;d.Bef 1780)
     - 2. **Robert Graham (c.11 Jun 1778-St. Cyrus,Kincardine,Scotland)**
       - sp: Mary Nicol (m.Not married)
         - 3. **Alexander Graham (b.Feb/Mar 1797-Marykirk,Kincardine,Scotland;d.17 Jun 1871-Dundee,Angus,Scotland)**
           - sp: Elisabeth Sharp (m.Not married)
           - sp: Christian Doig (c.10 Jan 1784-Glamis,Angus,Scotland;m.Not married;d.27 Dec 1847-Glamis,Angus,Scotland)
           - sp: Ann Lindsay (b.btw 1791-1796-Angus,Scotland;m.22 Sep 1821;d.btw 1841-1848)
           - sp: Barbara Fettes (b.1828-Prob St. Vigeans,Angus Scotland;m.31 Dec 1848;d.21 Jun 1869-Dundee,Angus,Scotland)
       - sp: Henrietta Law (m.14 Jul 1798)
         - 3. Archibald Douglas Graham (b.10 Apr 1799-Kilmarnock,Ayr,Scotland)
       - sp: Elizabeth Gove (c.20 Jul 1795-Craig,Angus,Scotland;m.13 Dec 1829)
         - 3. Elizabeth Graham or MacKenzie (b.1826-Craig,Angus,Scotland;d.1 Jan 1906-Craig,Angus,Scotland)
           - sp: Michael Whyte (b.30 Aug 1818-Dun,Angus,Scotland;m.21 Dec 1845;d.7 Oct 1888-Craig,Angus,Scotland)
         - 3. Robert Graham (b.10 Nov 1833-Craig,Angus,Scotland)
     - 2. William Graham (c.15 Dec 1779-St. Cyrus,Kincardine,Scotland)
     - 2. Margaret Graham (c.25 Aug 1781-St. Cyrus,Kincardine,Scotland)
     - 2. Helen Graham (c.26 Jun 1783-St. Cyrus,Kincardine,Scotland)
       - sp: David Mouat or Mowat (c.3 Aug 1783-Kinneff & Catterline,Kincardine,Scoltand;m.20 Apr 1805)
         - 3. Anne Mouat (b.28 Oct 1805-St. Cyrus,Kincardine,Scotland)
         - 3. David Mowat (b.17 Sep 1807-Kinneff & Catterline,Kincardineshire,Scotland)
         - 3. Margaret Mowat (b.27 Aug 1809-Kinneff & Catterline,Kincardineshire,Scotland)
         - 3. John Mowat (b.4 Jun 1811-Kinneff & Catterline,Kincardineshire,Scotland)
         - 3. Robert Mowat (b.11 Aug 1813-Kinneff & Catterline,Kincardineshire,Scotland)
         - 3. Elizabeth Mowat (c.11 Mar 1819-Kinneff & Catterline,Kincardineshire,Scotland)
         - 3. Alexander Mowat (b.3 Sep 1821-Kinneff & Catterline,Kincardineshire,Scotland)
         - 3. David Mowat (b.7 Nov 1823-Kinneff & Catterline,Kincardine,Scoltand)

Fourth Generation

37. Alexander GRAHAM (Alexander GRAHAM, Robert GRAHAM, James) was christened on 26 Sep 1773 in St. Cyrus, Kincardine, Scotland. He died on 8 Apr 1840 in St. Cyrus, Kincardine, Scotland and was buried in Nether Kirk. Alexander married **Jean BLACK** [1] on 7 Apr 1799 in Montrose, Angus, Scotland. Jean died 22 Oct 1837 in St. Cyrus, Kincardine, Scotland. The gravestone pictured below lists much of this family and is located in the St. Cyrus Netherkirk cemetery located at the base of the heughs facing the North Sea.

They had the following children:

    49 F i. **Betty GRAHAM** was born on 11 Nov 1799 in Montrose, Angus, Scotland. She died on 17 Oct 1866.

Listed in 1851 Montrose census in household of Catherine Lyall, widow age 72 which shows Betsy Graham, servant, unmarried, age 48 (birth year of 1803 but close enough), born St. Cyrus. But could be that her parents had their children in Montrose but lived mainly in St. Cyrus.

    50 Fii. **Ann GRAHAM** was born on 21 Sep 1801 in Montrose, Angus, Scotland. She died on 7 Jan 1824 in St. Cyrus, Kincardine, Scotland. She was buried in Nether Kirk.

+ 51 Miii. **William GRAHAME** was born on 11 Aug 1803. He died on 14 Apr 1881.

    52 Fiv. **Isobelle GRAHAM** was born on 9 Jun 1805 in Montrose, Angus, Scotland. She died on 11 Jan 1822 in St. Cyrus, Kincardine, Scotland. She was buried in Nether Kirk.

    53 Fv. **Jean GRAHAM** was born on 15 Oct 1807 in Montrose, Angus, Scotland. She died on 24 Oct 1867 in St. Cyrus, Kincardineshire, Scotland. She was buried in Nether Kirk. I obtained a copy of her Last Will & Testament entered in Stonehaven 18 January 1868. She was listed as tenant at Broomhill of Morphie. Executor of estate was William Graham, farmer at Hill of Morphie, Qua nearest of kin, her brother.

    54 Fvi. **Janet GRAHAM** was born on 4 Feb 1813 in St. Cyrus, Kincardine, Scotland. She was christened on 14 Feb 1813 in St. Cyrus, Kincardine, Scotland. She died on 3 Nov 1824 in St. Cyrus, Kincardine, Scotland. She was buried in Nether Kirk. The youngest child born to Alexander Graham and Jean Black, her OPR entry indicates that she was born at Brownhill in St. Cyrus while her older sibs were born in Montrose.

+ 39 Mvi. **Robert GRAHAM** (Alexander GRAHAM, Robert GRAHAM, James) was christened on 11 Jun 1778 in St. Cyrus, Kincardine, Scotland. Father was Alexr. GRAHAM, no listing for mother but strongly suspect mother was Jean/Jane Mitchell. IGI lists a marriage between a Robert GRAHAM and Henrietta LAW m 15 Jul 1798 Fordoun. He was listed as from St. Cyrus parish. This couple had one child Archibald Douglas b. 10 Apr 1799 Kilmarnock where Robert was with the Angusshire militia. Later studies showed that Robert GRAHAM of St. Cyrus joined the Royal Regiment of Artillery in 1803 and served for 21 years, finishing in Ireland. We are left to speculate as to what happened to Henrietta, Archibald Graham and any other potential offspring.

Information from his military discharge obtained from PRO.

"Robert GRAHAM, Gunner, Driver served in the Second Battalion of the Royal Regt of Artillery Whereof Field Marshal the Duke of Wellington KG is Colonel, from 25 Nov 1803 to 31 May 1824, discharged at age 45, 'being judged unfit for service by a medical Board held at Islandbridge on the 8th of May 1824 thro' Very infirm and weak constitution and ordered to be placed upon the pension list at One Shilling per diem. to commence on the 1st June 1824, per Boards Order of 17th May, 1824." Was Private for 12 years 151 days and Corporal for 8 years 93 days for total service of 20 years 244 days. Description: "He is about 45 years of age, is, Five Feet Ten Inches in height, Light hair, Grey eyes, Fresh complexion; and by Trade or Occupation a Laborer.

Was given sum of One pound Two shillings being thirty three days Marching Money at /8 (18?)d per diem (the difference between his Pension and 1/8d per diem) allowed by His Majesty's Regulations to carry him from Dublin to Aberdeen the place of his original Enlistment, and that he has received Five Shillings Passage Money from Donaghadee to Port Patrick."

Robert returned to the Montrose area ultimately marrying Elizabeth Gove. Together they had at least one child and perhaps two. There is evidence for Elizabeth MacKenzie Whyte whose mother was Elizabeth GRAHAM m.s Gove. The death registration for Elizabeth MacKenzie Whyte lists her mother but no father. I now speculate that she was born illegitimately and was adopted by Robert GRAHAM. Robert and Elizabeth Gove had a son Robert b. 1833 but no further records of this son have yet been located.

Robert was not married to **Mary NICOL** when they conceived a child in early 1796 when Robert was only eighteen years old. Robert and Mary had the following child, the original 'brickwall' Alexander Graham. I learned about an Alexander Graham, tailor and father of James Campbell Graham in my very first foray into family history research during that fateful 2001 day in Edinburgh. Some months later, as I got more and more engrossed in the research, I obtained a copy of his death certificate which provided clues that helped establish this Alexander as our direct descendent.

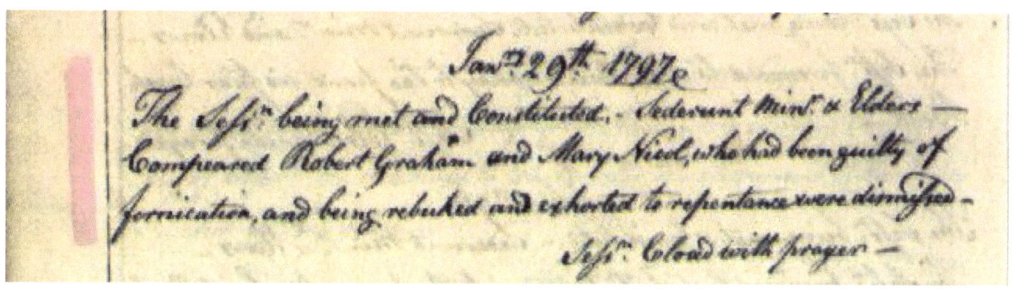

Earlier kirk session records for Aberluthnot (Marykirk) read " *January 29th 1797 The session being met and constituted, sederunt minister and elders, compeared Robert Graham and Mary Nicol, who had been guilty of fornication, and being rebuked and exhorted to repentence were dismissed.*"

However, the death registration for Alexander GRAHAM indicated parents names as Robert GRAHAM and Mary NICHOLSON. Alexander named his first (illegitimate) daughter Margaret Nicholson GRAHAM but certainly there is some confusion. We have not located any birth information for a Mary Nicol though the Nicol name is prevalent in Kincardineshire in the 1700s.

As for his mother, despite extensive research, I have been unable to locate birth or baptism information for Mary Nicol or Nicholson or any information about her subsequent to the birth of Alexander GRAHAM. She must have played some role in bringing up her son as we note that his first child was named in part for her (see Margaret Nicholson Graham #98). We can only speculate that Alexander was brought up by Mary Nicol once his father went off to the Angusshire Militia and then the Royal Regiment of Artillery in the British Army.

+ 55 Mi. **Alexander GRAHAM** was born in Feb 1797 and was christened 3 Jun 1798 in Marykirk. He died on 17 Jun 1871 in Dundee.

Robert did marry **Henrietta LAW** on 14 Jul 1798 in Fourdoun, Kincardine, Scotland. Robert and Henrietta had the following child:

56 Mii. **Archibald Douglas GRAHAM** was born on 10 Apr 1799 in Kilmarnock, Ayr, Scotland. He was christened in Kilmarnock, Ayr, Scotland. [NFR]

> *Register of Births. April 1799.* 217
>
> Graham | Archibald Douglass Graham, 1st child of Robert Graham, Soldier in the Angus Shire Militia, and Henrietta Law his wife, was born April 10th 1799

No further births to Robert Graham and Henrietta Law. I surmise that she and son Archibald were 'camp followers' and perhaps died abroad during any one of Robert's campaigns. I cannot confirm that he fought under Wellington's command at Waterloo but he was discharged in Ireland in 1824. He returned to the Montrose area where he married Elizabeth Gove and had one son, Robert in 1833.

Robert married **Elizabeth GOVE** daughter of Alexander GOVE and Christian WILLIAMSON on 13 Dec 1829 in Montrose, Angus, Scotland. Elizabeth was born to Alexander GOVE and Christian Williamson and christened on 20 Jul 1795 in Craig, Angus, Scotland. She was the third of five children born to this couple.

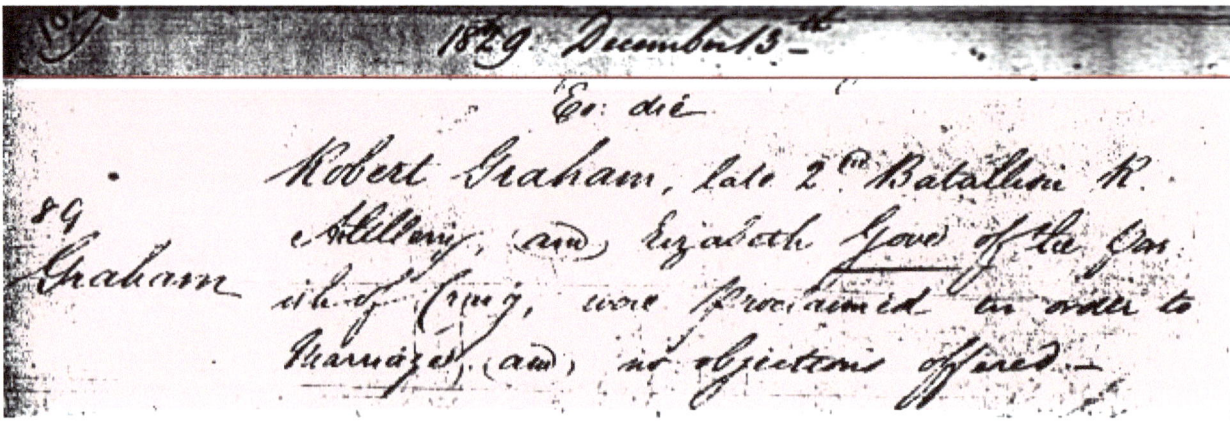

Robert and Elizabeth may have had the following children:

+ 57 Fiii. **Elizabeth Graham or MACKENZIE** was born in 1826. She died on 1 Jan 1906. [In all likelihood, this Elizabeth was probably born out-of-wedlock to Elizabeth GOVE and a MacKenzie who was not recorded.]

58 Miv. **Robert GRAHAM** was born on 10 Nov 1833 in Craig, Angus, Scotland and christened on 22 Nov 1833 in the same parish. No other records for him have been located suggesting an early death although it is possible that they immigrated somewhere else. NFR

42. **Helen GRAHAM** (Alexander GRAHAM, Robert GRAHAM, James) was christened on 26 Jun 1783 in St. Cyrus, Kincardine, Scotland. Helen married **David MOUAT OR MOWAT** son of David MOWAT and Jane COWIE on 20 Apr 1805 in St. Cyrus, Kincardine, Scotland. David was christened on 3 Aug 1783 in Kinneff & Catterline, Kincardineshire, Scotland.

They had the following children:

59   F i.   **Anne MOUAT** as born on 28 Oct 1805 in St. Cyrus, Kincardine, Scotland. She was christened on 3 Nov 1805 in St. Cyrus, Kincardine, Scotland.

60   Mii. **David MOWAT** was born on 17 Sep 1807 in Kinneff & Catterline, Kincardineshire, Scotland. He was christened on 25 Sep 1807 in Kinneff & Catterline, Kincardineshire, Scotland.

61   Fiii. **Margaret MOWAT** was born on 27 Aug 1809 in Kinneff & Catterline, Kincardineshire, Scotland. She was christened on 31 Aug 1809 in Kinneff & Catterline, Kincardineshire, Scotland.

62   Miv. **John MOWAT** was born on 4 Jun 1811 in Kinneff & Catterline, Kincardineshire, Scotland. He was christened on 17 Jun 1811 in Kinneff & Catterline, Kincardineshire, Scotland.

63   Mv. **Robert MOWAT** as born on 11 Aug 1813 in Kinneff & Catterline, Kincardineshire, Scotland. He was christened on 19 Aug 1813 in Kinneff & Catterline, Kincardineshire, Scotland.

64   Fvi. **Elizabeth MOWAT** was christened on 11 Mar 1819 in Kinneff & Catterline, Kincardineshire, Scotland.

65   Mvii. **Alexander MOWAT** was born on 3 Sep 1821 in Kinneff & Catterline, Kincardineshire, Scotland. He was christened on 15 Oct 1821 in Kinneff & Catterline, Kincardineshire, Scotland.

66   Mviii. **David MOWAT** was born on 7 Nov 1823 in Kinneff & Catterline, Kincardine, Scotland. He was christened on 22 Nov 1823 in Kinneff & Catterline, Kincardine, Scotland.

43. **Janet GRAHAM** (Alexander GRAHAM, Alexander GRAHAM, James) was christened on 29 Sep 1788 in St. Cyrus, Kincardine, Scotland. She died on 29 Dec 1839 in Guthrie, Angus, Scotland. She was buried in Guthrie, Angus, Scotland. Janet married **Alexander STRACHAN** on 25 Nov 1815 in St. Cyrus, Kincardine, Scotland. Alexander was born in 1781. He died on 14 Feb 1864 in Guthrie, Angus, Scotland.

They had the following children:

67   Mi.   **James STRACHAN** was born on 14 Jul 1817 in St. Cyrus, Kincardine, Scotland.

68   Mii. **Alexander STRACHAN** was born on 12 Jan 1821 in St. Cyrus, Kincardine, Scotland.

69   Fiii. **Jean STRACHAN** was born on 17 Jan 1823 in St. Cyrus, Kincardine, Scotland.

44. **Aikman GRAHAM** (Alexander GRAHAM, Alexander GRAHAM, James) was born on 20 Jul 1790 in St. Cyrus, Kincardine, Scotland. He was christened on 8 Aug 1790 in St. Cyrus, Kincardine, Scotland. He died[2] on 2 Apr 1878 in Inverallan, Grantown, Aberdeen, Scotland. Aikman married **Susan GOW** on 23 Dec 1821 in Kettins, Angus, Scotland. Susan must have died before 1878 because he was listed as widower on his death registration. His death registration indicated the he was 'formerly grieve (farm overseer) to the Earl of Seaforth. Aikman and Susan had the following children:

+ 70   F i.   **May GRAHAM** was born on 1 Oct 1822.

71   Mii. **Aikman GRAHAM** was christened on 27 Oct 1824 in Kettins, Angus, Scotland.

72   Fiii. **Phanuel GRAHAM** was christened on 29 Sep 1826 in Kettins, Angus, Scotland.

+ 73   Fiv. **Isabella GRAHAM** was born on 17 Jun 1828.

45. **James GRAHAM** (Alexander GRAHAM, Alexander GRAHAM, James) was christened on 26 Jul 1792 in St. Cyrus, Kincardine, Scotland. He died on 6 May 1881 in St. Cyrus, Kincardine, Scotland. Listed in 1851

census as Ag Lab. Son John listed as salmon fisherman. At death, occupation listed as salmon fisher. Witness to death was neighbor James Lyall leaving us to wonder where his sons & daughters were. James married **Mary JACK** daughter of John JACK and Ann NICOL on 21 May 1820 in St. Cyrus, Kincardine, Scotland. Mary was christened on 5 Aug 1795 in Logie-Pert, Angus, Scotland. She died[3] on 17 Jan 1862 in St. Cyrus, Kincardine, Scotland.

They had the following children:

    74 M i. **William GRAHAM** was christened on 25 Mar 1821 in St. Cyrus, Kincardine, Scotland.

+ 75 M ii. **John GRAHAM** was christened on 6 Jul 1823. He died on 20 Dec 1889.

    76 Fiii. **Mary GRAHAM** was christened on 4 Sep 1825 in St. Cyrus, Kincardine, Scotland.

+ 77 Fiv. **Charlotte GRAHAM** was christened on 4 Feb 1827.

+ 78 Fv. **Ann GRAHAM** was born on 11 Mar 1829.

    79 Fvi. **Julia GRAHAM** was born in 1831 in St. Cyrus, Kincardine, Scotland.

        1841 census shows the James Graham/Mary Jack household with 4 children - John 15 (salmon fisher), Julia 10, Isobel 1, and Janet 1, these latter two presumably were twins. There is no birth listing for Julia Graham in 1831, however.

    80 Fvii. **Janet GRAHAM** was born on 12 Aug 1839 in St. Cyrus, Kincardine, Scotland.

    81 Fviii. **Isabella GRAHAM** was born on 12 Aug 1839 in St. Cyrus, Kincardine, Scotland.

47. Susan GRAHAM (Alexander GRAHAM, Alexander GRAHAM, James) was christened on 28 May 1797 in St. Cyrus, Kincardine, Scotland. Susan married **Phanuel DUNCAN** son of John DUNCAN and Jean MURRAY on 11 Jun 1820 in St. Cyrus, Kincardine, Scotland. Phanuel was christened on 15 Oct 1792 in Benholm, Kincardine, Scotland.

They had the following children:

  82 Mi. **Alexander DUNCAN** was born on 11 Apr 1821 in St. Cyrus, Kincardine, Scotland. He was christened on 6 May 1821 in St. Cyrus, Kincardine, Scotland.

  83 Mii. **Phanuel DUNCAN** was born on 10 Nov 1822 in St. Cyrus, Kincardine, Scotland. He was christened on 24 Nov 1822 in St. Cyrus, Kincardine, Scotland.

  84 Fiii. **Isobel DUNCAN** was born on 14 Jul 1824 in St. Cyrus, Kincardine, Scotland. She was christened on 25 Jul 1824 in St. Cyrus, Kincardine, Scotland.

  85 Miv. **Aikman DUNCAN** was born on 23 Mar 1826 in St. Cyrus, Kincardine, Scotland. He was christened on 9 Apr 1826 in St. Cyrus, Kincardine, Scotland.

  86 Fv. **Anna DUNCAN** was born on 24 Jan 1828 in St. Cyrus, Kincardine, Scotland. She was christened on 9 Feb 1828 in St. Cyrus, Kincardine, Scotland.

  87 Mvi. **William DUNCAN** was born on 14 Mar 1830 in St. Cyrus, Kincardine, Scotland. He was christened on 5 Apr 1830 in St. Cyrus, Kincardine, Scotland.

  88 Mvii. **John DUNCAN** was born on 23 Nov 1831 in St. Cyrus, Kincardine, Scotland. He was christened on 25 Dec 1831 in St. Cyrus, Kincardine, Scotland.

  89 Fviii. **Anne DUNCAN** was born on 19 Dec 1833 in St. Cyrus, Kincardine, Scotland. She was christened on 19 Dec 1833 in St. Cyrus, Kincardine, Scotland.

  90 Mix. **George DUNCAN** was born on 20 Mar 1836 in Montrose, Angus, Scotland.

  91 Fx. **Susan DUNCAN** was born on 13 May 1838 in Montrose, Angus, Scotland. She was christened on 11 Jun 1838 in Montrose, Angus, Scotland.

  92 Mxi. **David Foote DUNCAN** was born on 13 May 1838 in Montrose, Angus, Scotland. He was christened on 11 Jun 1838 in Montrose, Angus, Scotland.

93 Fxii.**Christina DUNCAN** was born on 18 Oct 1841 in Montrose, Angus, Scotland.

Map of St. Cyrus & Morphy, ca 1775

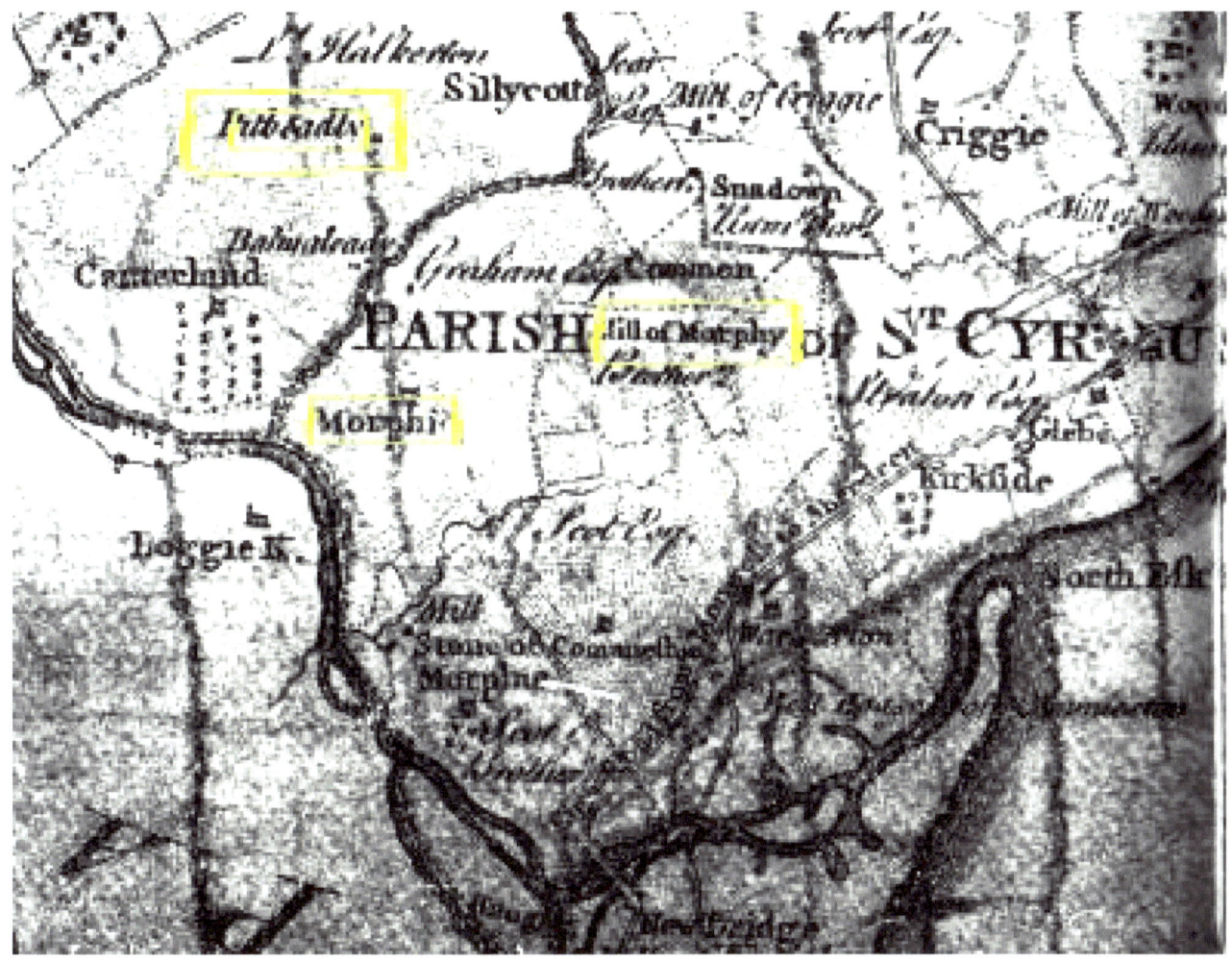

1871 Census Entry Jas Watson & Family

Fifth Generation

51. **William GRAHAME** (Alexander GRAHAM, Alexander GRAHAM, Robert GRAHAM, James) was born on 11 Aug 1803 in Montrose, Angus, Scotland. He was christened on 11 Aug 1803 in Montrose, Angus, Scotland and died on 14 Apr 1881 in St. Cyrus, Kincardineshire, Scotland. William married **Jean DONALD** who, according to census records only, was born about 1801 in Monymusk, Aberdeenshire, Scotland. She died after 1881 in St. Cyrus, Kincardineshire, Scotland. They had the following children:

+ 94 F i. **Jean GRAHAME** was born on 30 Nov 1833. She died on 1 Mar 1914.

95 M ii. **Alexander GRAHAME** was born on 28 Jul 1835 in Arbuthnott, Kincardineshire, Scotland. He was christened on 3 Aug 1835 in Arbuthnott, Kincardineshire, Scotland.

> Per father William's will probated in Stonehaven 16 Jul 1881, Alexander was listed to receive a portion of the estate but was then living in New Zealand. The will suggests that two other siblings Jean (Graham) Suttie and William Graham were to receive a one-third share as well. We speculate therefore that John Thomson Graham died at a young age.

96 M iii. **William GRAHAME** was born on 15 Aug 1837 in Arbuthnott, Kincardineshire, Scotland. He was christened on 12 Sep 1837 in Arbuthnott, Kincardineshire, Scotland. He died 6 Oct 1907 in the Sunnyside Asylum in Montrose and was listed as a Lunatic Pauper though his usual residence was listed as Arbuthnott. One wonders why his sister living in the area was not a witness to his death.

> 1881 census shows Wm Graham and Margaret Graham living in household headed by Margaret Lawrence (widowed) age 76 with granddaughters Helen E. Laurence age 11, and Fanny H. Laurence age 2. 1891 census shows Wm Graham, Farm Laborer (retired), age 54, widowed, living at Dryplaid Cottage, Fettercairn. Also states he was 'imbecile'.

William married **Margaret LAWRENCE** daughter of Benjamin LAWRENCE and Margaret ROBERTSON on 25 Nov 1880 in Laurencekirk, Kincardineshire, Scotland. Margaret was born on 26 Jan 1845 in Laurencekirk, Kincardineshire, Scotland. She was christened on 15 Feb 1845 in Laurencekirk, Kincardineshire, Scotland. She died of uterine cancer on 7 May 1887 in Brechin, Angus, Scotland. At time of her death, the couple lived at Drumachlie Cottar Houses, Brechin.

97 M iv. **John Thomson GRAHAME** was born on 7 Aug 1841 in Arbuthnott, Kincardineshire, Scotland. He was christened on 7 Sep 1841 in Arbuthnott, Kincardineshire, Scotland. Because he was not listed in his father's will, I surmise that he died young.

55. **Alexander GRAHAM** (Robert GRAHAM, Alexander GRAHAM, Robert GRAHAM, James) was born in Feb 1797 in Marykirk, Kincardine, Scotland and was christened[1] there on 3 Jun 1798. He died[2] on 17 Jun 1871 in Dundee, Angus, Scotland and was listed as a Tailor, journeyman. The cause of death was hemiplegia (stroke). While I cannot absolutely confirm that this Alexander GRAHAM is the father of James Campbell GRAHAM, the evidence overwhelmingly supports this claim. First, James Campbell GRAHAM's death certificate in 1865 lists father as Alexander Graham, Tailor and suggests that Alexander was still alive at this time while Christina Graham (m.s DOIG), mother, was listed as deceased. This fact fits with our discovery of the Christian DOIG (b. 1784) of Glamis who died 1847. Second, the marriage entry for Alexander GRAHAM and Ann LINDSAY states that he was from the "parish of Glammis" which fits with the knowledge that Christian DOIG was from that parish and that the Glamis Kirk Session minutes reprimand her for "a relapse in fornication.

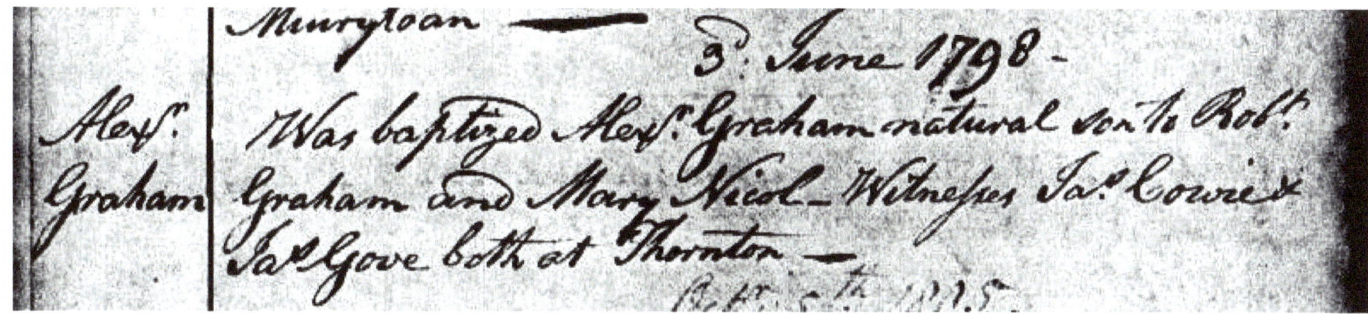

After extensive research, I identified several Alexander GRAHAMs born in Angus or Kincardineshire in the 1770-1820 time period. My leading candidate is this particular Alexander GRAHAM, illegitimately born to Robert GRAHAM, ploughman and Mary NICOL or NICHOLSON, farm servant (according to his death certificate). He was christened 3 Jun 1798 Marykirk Kincardine. His death certificate indicates that he died 17 Jun 1871 St Peter District Dundee, was a Tailor, journeyman and had two marriages, the first to Ann LINDSAY (m. 22 Sep 1821 Marykirk, Kincardineshire) and the second to Barbara FETTES (m. 31 Dec 1848 Blairgowrie Perth). On Alexander GRAHAM's death certificate his daughter Margaret WATTS was a family witness. I located marriage info for Margaret GRAHAM and Charles WATT 27 Dec 1846 Montrose Angus. My first thought that his legitimate daughter with Ann Lindsay, Mary Ann GRAHAM, preferred or changed her name to Margaret but subsequent investigations revealed that Margaret Nicholson Graham was born to Alexander GRAHAM and Elisabeth SHARP as an illegitimate daughter. Who raised him if father Robert was in the military from 1803-1824? Where was he raised? Who taught him the tailoring trade?

Alexander was not married to **Elisabeth SHARP** but they had the following child:

+ 98   F i. **Margaret Nicholson GRAHAM** was born on 8 May 1821. She died on 28 Jan 1897.

Alexander was also not married to **Christian DOIG** daughter of Robert DOIG and Isabell NEAVE. Christian was christened[3] on 10 Jan 1784 in Glamis, Angus, Scotland. She died[4] on 27 Dec 1847 in Glamis, Angus, Scotland.

Cristain, or Christian, was the twin of George and one of nine children born to Robert DOIG, shoemaker and Isabell NEAVE. Christian had illegitimate sons by William Donaldson and Alexander Graham. The first son, named William Donaldson was ch 26 Apr 1812, Glamis, Angus and confirmed via IGI. James Campbell Graham was probably born in early 1822 based upon the session minutes and 1861 census data. His name may have arisen due to Christian's youngest sister Janet DOIG who married a James CAMPBELL on 21 Mar 1822. It's conceivable though impossible to prove that Janet and James CAMPBELL may have raised him, at least for a while. Christian Doig (age not specified) died on 27 Dec 1847 in the house of Robert Doig in Glamis. [Source: Kenneth Frank Doig, ken@doig.net, www.doig.net.] In 1841 census for Glamis, there is listing for Wm MUIR, 45, shoemaker, born in cty and Christina DOIG, 55 born in cty and James GRAHAM, 15 born in cty. An 1861 census for James Graham indicates that he was 39, stone mason and born in Glamis.

Alexander and Christian had the following child:

+ 99   M ii. **James Campbell GRAHAM** was born in early 1822 and died on 18 Dec 1865.

Alexander married **Ann LINDSAY** on 22 Sep 1821 in Marykirk, Kincardine, Scotland. Ann was born sometime between 1791 and 1796 in Angus according to the 1841 census. There are several candidates born in Angus during the 1791-1796 time period but it is difficult to pinpoint the exact one. She probably died after the 1841 census but before 1848 when Alexander remarried Barbara Fettes.

Jul 2007 - New Data!!! 1841 census entry shows Ann Graham with several children (including step daughter Margaret Nicolson Graham) working as flax spinner in Logie Pert. In addition to son Alexander (age 19), other sons include John (16), Andrew (13), Renwick (11) and daughter Elizabeth (9) and a Rachel Low/Law age 3. Ann listed as being born in county (Angus) but all children not born in county and therefore likely to have been born in Marykirk, KCD. This helps confirm the Elizabeth Graham, Good Sister, in the Watt 1851 census entry. Good Sister meant that Margaret was the illegitimate half-sister to Elizabeth,

Alexander and Ann had the following children:

100 M iii. **Alexander GRAHAM** was born[5] on 3 Nov 1821 in Marykirk, Kincardine, Scotland. He may have died on 4 Jun 1843 in Marykirk, Kincardineshire, Scotland. Nothing known about this child after

his christening record. The lack of other records suggests an early death, perhaps along with his mother Ann Lindsay. A summary of Old Parish Records for Marykirk show a birth but no christening - perhaps he died shortly after birth!!??!! CONFIRMATION NEEDED. 16 Feb 2006. Reviewed Marykirk OPR and found the following entry [typed transcription of OPR entry]"4 Jun 1843 to M.C. for Alexander Graham, 3s" This entry suggests that this Alexander Graham died at or around the age of 21 in the parish of Marykirk and that a mort cloth donation of 3 shillings was made on his behalf. However, there can be no definitive claim here as there was no other information about this person. I was unable to locate any mort cloth entries for Ann (Lindsay) Graham. July 2007. With the finding of an 1841 census entry for Ann (Lindsay) Graham and children, it showed that Alexander Graham was alive and working as a flax dresser in Logie Pert along with several other heretofore unknown siblings. It is still possible that he died in 1843.

+ 101 Fiv.**Mary Ann GRAHAM** was born on 20 Dec 1822. She died on 26 May 1902.

+ 102 Mv.**John GRAHAM** was born about 1824. No birth or baptism record exists so his age is estimated from census entries. It appears that he died in Toowoomba Australia in 1905 and that his ashes were conveyed to his daughter Amelia's gravesite in Wanganui New Zealand.

Photo of grave marker for John Graham in Toowoomba, Queensland, Australia. Kindly provided by Toowoomba Cemetery Administrator.

+ 103 Mvi.**Andrew GRAHAM** was born about 1828. Again, no formal birth or baptism record exists. He died on 1 Jan 1902.

104 Mvii.**Renwick GRAHAM** was born in 1830 in Marykirk, Kincardine, Scotland. He died on 28 Jun 1904 in Dundee, Angus, Scotland. Renwick married first a **Mary PETRIE** daughter of David PETRIE and Margaret DUNCAN on 28 Jun 1858 in Dundee, Angus, Scotland. The wedding registration does indicate that his mother Ann Lindsay was deceased. Mary was born on 31 Oct 1819 in Forfar, Angus, Scotland. She was christened on 7 Nov 1819 in Forfar, Angus, Scotland. She died on 6 Feb 1886 in Dundee, Angus, Scotland.

Renwick then remarried, this time to **Barbara TAYLOR** daughter of John TAYLOR and Elizbeth CATHRO on 19 Nov 1886 in Dundee, Angus, Scotland. Barbara, widowed herself by George Coupar, was born in 1833 in Dundee, Angus, Scotland. She died on 29 Mar 1904 in Dundee, Angus, Scotland and her death was witnessed by her son George Coupar living at 1 Bonnybank Road. Unfortunately, Renwick did not appear to have any offspring with either wife. Census data showed that Renwick was a tailor like his father but spent most of his working life in Dundee.

+ 105 Fviii.**Elizabeth GRAHAM** was born in 1832 to Alexander and Ann, probably in Marykirk or Logie Pert.

Presumably widowed sometime in the mid-1840's, Alexander Graham (#55) then married **Barbara FETTES** daughter of John FETTES and Agnes STEVEN on 31 Dec 1848 in Blairgowrie, Perth, Scotland. Barbara was born in 1828 in St. Vigeans, Angus Scotland. She died on 21 Jun 1869 in Dundee, Angus, Scotland. How or why Alexander landed in Blairgowrie remains a mystery, especially since his last two decades of life were spent in Dundee.

Using birth and census data, we can create an interesting and detailed though not complete picture of Alexander Graham's life. After his birth in Marykirk in 1797 we know nothing of his upbringing other than his father was married and off in the military – clearly not a major influence in his life. We have no indication of who raised him or taught him the tailoring trade although we can infer that his mother Mary Nicol (or Nicholson) must have been significant to him or he would not have named his first daughter Margaret Nicholson Graham. His next appearances cluster around 1821 with two illegitimate children sandwiching a marriage and birth of a first child (Alexander Graham #100). It is puzzling to think that he sired four children with three different women in the space of less than two years. And while we don't know who or how the children were raised, Margaret Nicholson Graham was in the household of Ann Lindsay in 1841 as were his most of his other 'lawful' children by her, the exception being James Campbell and Mary Ann. James Campbell Graham by all appearances was brought up by Christina Doig in the Glamis area. We are also left to ponder how Alexander made his way to Blairgowrie and married Barbara Fettes. Finally, he migrated to Dundee and lived quite near to his son Renwick and his first wife Mary Petrie on Park Entry near Temple Lane. Perhaps the two of them shared a shop or provided work to one another.

57. **Elizabeth Graham or MACKENZIE** (Robert GRAHAM, Alexander GRAHAM, Robert GRAHAM, James) was born in 1826 in Craig, Angus, Scotland. She died on 1 Jan 1906 in Craig, Angus, Scotland. The death certificate for this Elizabeth lists her as widow of Michael WHYTE. For parents, there was no listing of a father, but the mother was listed as Elizabeth GRAHAM, m.s. GOVE. On Michael WHYTE's death certificate, his widow is listed as Elizabeth McKenzie GOVE. Therefore, it may be that this Elizabeth was born illegitimately to Elizabeth GOVE fathered by a MacKenzie. No birth record exists for her in the IGI.

Elizabeth married **Michael WHYTE** son of David WHYTE and Mary Ann WATT on 21 Dec 1845 in Montrose, Angus, Scotland. Michael was born on 30 Aug 1818 and was christened on 13 Sep 1818 in Dun, Angus, Scotland. He died on 7 Oct 1888 in Craig, Angus, Scotland and was a journeyman mason by trade. Michael and Elizabeth had the following child:

106 F i. **Elizabeth Nicol WHYTE** was born on 12 Apr 1849 in Montrose, Angus, Scotland. She died on 25 Jun 1892 in Craig, Angus, Scotland. The cause of death was Pulmonary phthisis (i.e. tuberculosis). Death registration indicates that Elizabeth was single, a dressmaker and living at 10 West Terrace Ferryden Craig, probably with her mother. Once again, I find her middle name NICOL to be intriguing and perhaps related to her grandfather Robert's early relation with Mary NICOL.

70. **May GRAHAM** (Aikman GRAHAM, Alexander GRAHAM, Alexander GRAHAM, James) was born on 1 Oct 1822 in Kettins, Angus, Scotland. She was christened on 6 Oct 1822 in Kettins, Angus, Scotland. May married **Burnet GORDON** on 28 May 1841 in Ruthven, Angus, Scotland.

They had the following children:

107 M i. **David Graham GORDON** was born on 5 Sep 1857 in Banchory Devenick, Kincardine, Scotland.

108 M ii. **Lewis GORDON** was born on 13 Dec 1861 in Fetteresso, Kincardineshire, Scotland.

73. **Isabella GRAHAM** (Aikman GRAHAM, Alexander GRAHAM, Alexander GRAHAM, James) was born on 17 Jun 1828 in Kettins, Angus, Scotland. She was christened on 28 Jun 1828 in Kettins, Angus, Scotland. Isabella married[6] **William GIBSON** on 1 Jun 1852 in Edinburgh, Midlothian, Scotland. She died 1917.

They had the following children:

109 Mi. **William GIBSON** was born on 29 Jun 1855 in Edinburgh, Midlothian, Scotland.

110 Mii. **Aikman Graham GIBSON** was born on 14 Jun 1857 in Edinburgh, Midlothian, Scotland. Died 1889.

111 Miii. **Grant Bowie GIBSON** was born on 17 Dec 1859 in Edinburgh, Midlothian, Scotland.

112 Fiv. **Agnes Henry GIBSON** was born on 27 Apr 1862 in Edinburgh, Midlothian, Scotland.

113 Fv. **Isabella Graham GIBSON** was born on 22 Jun 1866 in Edinburgh, Midlothian, Scotland.

114 Mvi. **Alexander GIBSON** was born on 28 Apr 1864 in Edinburgh, Midlothian, Scotland.

115 Mvii. **Thomas Finlayson GIBSON** was born on 28 Aug 1868 in Edinburgh, Midlothian, Scotland.

116 Fviii. **Mary Lang GIBSON** was born on 31 Oct 1871 in Edinburgh, Midlothian, Scotland.

75. **John GRAHAM** (James GRAHAM, Alexander GRAHAM, Alexander GRAHAM, James) was christened on 6 Jul 1823 in St. Cyrus, Kincardine, Scotland. He died on 20 Dec 1889 in Edinburgh, Midlothian, Scotland. The cause of death was stomach cancer. John married **Jean or Jane OFFICER** on 15 Jun 1851 in St. Cyrus, Kincardineshire, Scotland. Jean was born on 4 May 1823 in Dundee, Angus, Scotland. She was christened on 1 Jun 1823 in Dundee, Angus, Scotland. She died in 1896 in Edinburgh, Midlothian, Scotland.

They had the following children:

117 F i. **Julia Ann GRAHAM** was born on 28 Jun 1857 in Edinburgh, Midlothian, Scotland.

118 Mii. **William Officer GRAHAM** was born on 1 Jun 1860 in Edinburgh, Midlothian, Scotland. He died before 1881 in Edinburgh, Midlothian, Scotland.

119 Fiii. **Helen GRAHAM** was born on 1 Sep 1862 in Edinburgh, Midlothian, Scotland.

120 Miv. **James GRAHAM** was born about 1865 in Edinburgh, Midlothian, Scotland.

121 Fv. **Mary Jane GRAHAM** was born on 4 Nov 1867 in Edinburgh, Midlothian, Scotland. She died before 1881 in Edinburgh, Midlothian, Scotland.

77. **Charlotte GRAHAM** (James GRAHAM, Alexander GRAHAM, Alexander GRAHAM, James) was christened on 4 Feb 1827 in St. Cyrus, Kincardine, Scotland. Charlotte married **Robert JOHNSTON** on 9 Oct 1861 in St. Cyrus, Kincardine, Scotland. They had the following children:

122 Mi. **Hugh JOHNSTON** was born on 2 Jul 1862 in Longside, Aberdeen, Scotland.

123 Mii. **Graeme JOHNSTON** was born on 16 Mar 1864 in Oyne, Aberdeen, Scotland.

124 Miii. **William JOHNSTON** was born on 18 Jul 1867 in Oyne, Aberdeen, Scotland.

125 Fiv. **Mary Jane JOHNSTON** was born on 29 Apr 1870 in Oyne, Aberdeen, Scotland.

78. **Ann GRAHAM** (James GRAHAM, Alexander GRAHAM, Alexander GRAHAM, James) was born on 11 Mar 1829 in St. Cyrus, Kincardine, Scotland. Ann married **George WYNESS** on 23 Dec 1855 in St. Cyrus, Kincardine, Scotland. George was born on 17 Feb 1823 in Aboyne, Aberdeen, Scotland. They had the following children:

126 Mi. **Alexander WYNESS** was born on 23 Oct 1856 in Craig by Montrose, Angus, Scotland.

127 Fii. **Ann WYNESS** was born on 18 May 1858 in Craig by Montrose, Angus, Scotland.

128 Fiii. **Jane WYNESS** was born on 12 Jan 1861 in Craig by Montrose, Angus, Scotland.

129 Miv. **George WYNESS** was born on 5 Aug 1863 in Craig by Montrose, Angus, Scotland.

130 Fv. **Julia WYNESS** was born on 21 Jan 1872 in Craig by Montrose, Angus, Scotland.

Two Generations of Descendants of Alexander GRAHAM, Tailor

1. **Alexander GRAHAM** (b.Feb/Mar 1797-Marykirk,Kincardine,Scotland;d.17 Jun 1871-Dundee,Angus,Scotland)
    sp: Elisabeth SHARP (m.Not married)
    - 2. Margaret Nicholson GRAHAM (b.8 May 1821-Marykirk,Kincardine,Scotland;d.28 Jan 1897-Ceres,Fife,Scotland)
        sp: Charles WATT (b.1822-Montrose,Angus,Scotland;m.27 Dec 1846)
        - 3. John WATT (b.1847-Montrose,Angus,Scotland;d.26 Dec 1925-Cupar,Fife,Scotland)
            sp: Mary Ann ANDERSON (b.29 Jan 1850-Marykirk,Kincardine,Scotland)
    sp: Christian DOIG (c.10 Jan 1784-Glamis,Angus,Scotland;m.Not married;d.27 Dec 1847-Glamis,Angus,Scotland)
    - 2. James Campbell GRAHAM (b.1822-Glamis,Angus,Scotland;d.18 Dec 1865-Dundee,Angus,Scotland)
        sp: Catherine WILKIE (c.1 Feb 1826-Forfar,Angus,Scotland;m.9 Jul 1848;d.21 Feb 1898-Dundee,Angus,Scotland)
        - 3. David Alma GRAHAM (b.1 May 1854-Stirling,Stirlingshire Scotland;d.21 Oct 1933-Hollis,Queens,NY,USA)
            sp: Agnes Robb CUTHBERT (b.6 May 1857-Dundee,Angus,Scotland;m.20 Aug 1885;d.14 Nov 1922-Brooklyn,NY,USA)
        - 3. James Talford GRAHAM (b.28 Mar 1856-Govan,Lanark Scotland)
        - 3. Charles Iconaclast Bradlauch GRAHAM (b.10 Aug 1861-New Monkland,Lanark Scotland;d.15 Dec 1945-D,Angus Scotland)
            sp: Agnes Small CANDOW (b.17 Feb 1863-Longforgan,Perth Scotland;m.28 Dec 1886;d.7 Jul 1891-Dundee,A,Scotland)
            sp: Agnes Dickson SOUTAR (b.19 Aug 1859-Errol,Perth,Scotland;m.27 Apr 1892;d,14 Dec 1943-Dundee,Angus Scotland)
        - 3. George Heron GRAHAM (b.6 Sep 1864-Dundee,Angus Scotland)
    sp: Ann LINDSAY (b.btw 1791-1796-Angus,Scotland;m.22 Sep 1821;d.btw 1841-1848)
    - 2. Alexander GRAHAM (b.3 Nov 1821-Marykirk,Kincardine,Scotland;d.4 Jun 1843-Marykirk,Kincardineshire,SCT)
    - 2. Mary Ann GRAHAM (b.20 Dec 1822-Marykirk,Kincardine,Scotland;d.26 May 1902-Fetteresso,Kincardine,Scotland)
        sp: John DOIG (b.1828-Montrose,Angus,Scotland;m.Not married;d.1897-Montrose,Angus,Scotland)
        - 3. Elizabeth DOIG (b.~May 1850-Montrose,Angus,Scotland;d.23 Apr 1893-Cupar,Fife,Scotland)
            sp: UNKNOWN
        sp: James Sime SMITH (m.Not married)
        - 3. Renwick GRAHAM (b.3 Aug 1856-Dundee,Angus,Scotland;d.6 May 1858-Dundee,Angus,Scotland)
        sp: Thomas FALCONER (b.1823-Dundee,Angus,Scotland;m.16 Jan 1864;d.18 Feb 1895-Logie Pert,Angus,Scotland)
    - 2. John GRAHAM (b.Abt 1824-Marykirk,Kincardineshire,Scotland;d.5 Jun 1905-Brisbane,Queensland,Australia)
        sp: Mary MILNE (b.8 Sep 1824-Logie-Pert,Angus,Scotland;m.Not married;d.25 Mar 1910-Logie-Pert,Angus,Scotland)
        - 3. Mary Ann GRAHAM (b.1 Dec 1844-Logie-Pert,Angus,Scotland;d.13 Aug 1938-Wellington,New Zealand)
            sp: Joseph Blyth GRAHAM (b.1852-Dunblane,Perth,Scotland;m.27 Jun 1871;d.24 Dec 1915-Wellington,New Zealand)
        - 3. Amelia GRAHAM (b.2 Aug 1848-Logie-Pert,Angus,Scotland;d.4 Aug 1917-Wanganui,New Zealand)
            sp: Robert William Oswald STEWART (b.Abt 1845-Dumfries,D,Scotland;m.7 Jun 1872;d.30 Jun 1927-Kogarah,N,Australia)
    - 2. Andrew GRAHAM (b.1828-Marykirk,Kincardine,Scotland;d.1 Jan 1902-Little Dunkeld,Perth,Scotland)
        sp: Ann BLYTHE (b.~1830-Dugary,Tyrone,Ireland;m.4 Jan 1851;d.27 Feb 1886-Dunblane,Perth,Scotland)
        - 3. Joseph Blyth GRAHAM (b.1852-Dunblane,Perth,Scotland;d.24 Dec 1915-Wellington,New Zealand)
            sp: Mary Ann GRAHAM (b.1 Dec 1844-Logie-Pert,Angus,Scotland;m.27 Jun 1871;d.13 Aug 1938-Wellington,New Zealand)
        - 3. John Blyth GRAHAM (b.1854-Dunblane,Perth,Scotland;d.27 Dec 1942-Auchterarder,Perth,Scotland)
            sp: Janet MCINTYRE (b.9 May 1857-Dunblane,Perth,Scotland;m.26 Jul 1878;d.23 Nov 1937-Auchterarder,Perth,Scotland)
        - 3. James GRAHAM (b.25 Feb 1855-Dunblane,Perth,Scotland;d.20 Mar 1856-Dunblane,Perth,Scotland)

Descendants of Alexander GRAHAM

- 3. Jessie GRAHAM (b.6 Dec 1856-Dunblane,Perth,Scotland;d.24 Jun 1898-Saline,Fife,Scotland)
  - sp: William ROBERTSON (b.14 Nov 1848-Keith,Banffshire,Scotland;m.25 Jan 1878)
- 3. Andrew GRAHAM (b.13 May 1859-Dunblane,Perth,Scotland;d.16 Apr 1860-Dunblane,Perth,Scotland)
- 3. Mary Anne GRAHAM (b.22 Feb 1861-Dunblane,Perth,Scotland;d.15 Aug 1862-Dunblane,Perth,Scotland)
- 2. Renwick GRAHAM (b.1830-Marykirk,Kincardine,Scotland;d.28 Jun 1904-Dundee,Angus,Scotland)
  - sp: Mary PETRIE (b.31 Oct 1819-Forfar,Angus,Scotland;m.28 Jun 1858;d.6 Feb 1886-Dundee,Angus,Scotland)
  - sp: Barbara TAYLOR (b.1833-Dundee,Angus,Scotland;m.19 Nov 1886;d.29 Mar 1904-Dundee,Angus,Scotland)
- 2. Elizabeth GRAHAM (b.1832-Marykirk,Kincardine,Scotland)
  - sp: John Barrie WHITTON (b.31 Mar 1832-Montrose,Angus,Scotland;m.28 Sep 1853)
    - 3. Mary Ann WHITTON (b.Abt 1855-Perth,Perth,Scotland)
    - 3. William WHITTON (b.11 Oct 1858-Montrose,Angus,Scotland;d.18 Apr 1901-Bay of Bengal)
    - 3. Susan WHITTON (b.17 Feb 1861-Montrose,Angus,Scotland;d.16 Sep 1861-Montrose,Angus,Scotland)
    - 3. John Barry WHITTON (b.15 Oct 1866-Dundee,Angus,Scotland)

sp: Barbara FETTES (b.1828-Prob St. Vigeans,Angus Scotland;m.31 Dec 1848;d.21 Jun 1869-Dundee,Angus,Scotland)

Ronald & Sheila Rattray, Maureen Graham and John Whitehead at wedding of Claire Graham and Steve Simon, 2004.

Sixth Generation

94. **Jean GRAHAME** (William GRAHAME, Alexander GRAHAM, Alexander GRAHAM, Robert GRAHAM, James) was born on 30 Nov 1833 in Laurencekirk, Kincardineshire, Scotland. She was christened on 14 Dec 1833 in Laurencekirk, Kincardineshire, Scotland. She died on 1 Mar 1914 in Garvock, Kincardineshire, Scotland.

Jean married **David SUTTIE** about 1860 in St. Cyrus, Kincardineshire, Scotland.

They had the following children:

131 F i. **Elisabeth SUTTIE** was born on 24 Jun 1861 in Brechin, Angus, Scotland.

132 F ii. **Jane SUTTIE** was born on 18 Feb 1863 in St. Cyrus, Kincardine, Scotland.

133 M iii. **David SUTTIE** was born on 11 Apr 1871 in St. Cyrus, Kincardine, Scotland. David married **Jeanie McGREGOR** daughter of John MCGREGOR and Mary ANDERSON on 3 Apr 1896 in Garvock, Kincardineshire, Scotland.

98. **Margaret Nicholson GRAHAM** (Alexander GRAHAM, Robert GRAHAM, Alexander GRAHAM, Robert GRAHAM, James) was born on 8 May 1821 in Marykirk, Kincardine, Scotland. She was christened[1] 2 Jun 1821 in Marykirk, Kincardine, Scotland. She died[2] 28 Jan 1897 in Ceres, Fife, Scotland. The cause of death was "cardiac disease, 2 years".

Illegitmate daughter of Alexander GRAHAM and Elisabeth SHARP. IGI lists her name as Margaret Nicholson GRAHAM (without the H). Who raised her? If she married in Montrose, presumably she stayed in the St. Cyrus/Marykirk/Montrose area from birth to marriage. She knew of her father and was witness to his death in Dundee 17 Jun 1871. There must have been some contact as she was living in Rattray, Perth at the time. From www.Doig.net, Dave1750.htm file --"in 1851 Mary's daughter Elizabeth Doig lived with her sister, Elisabeth Graham (born 1833/4 in Mary Kirk, Montrose) at 8 Upper Hall Street, Montrose; they lived with Charles Wall (born 1821/2 in Montrose) wife Margaret Graham (born 1823/4 in Mary Kirk, Kincardine) and son John Wall (born 1844/5 in Montrose). In 1861 Mary and daughter Elizabeth lived at 12 William Street, Dundee; she was an unmarried mill worker. There was also a lodger and son in the house." [Note: Ken Doig had trouble reading the penmanship and thought Watt was Wall].

1851 Census, Montrose, ED 14 pp1&2
8 Upper Hill Street, Montrose
Watt, Charles 29 flax dresser Montrose
Watt, Margaret wife 27 Marykirk, Kincardine
Watt, John son 6 Montrose
Graham, Elisabeth "good sister" 17 flax spinner Marykirk, Kincardine
Doig, Elisabeth niece 10mo Montrose

Margaret married[3] **Charles WATT** on 27 Dec 1846 in Montrose, Angus, Scotland. Charles was probably born[4] in 1822 in Montrose, Angus, Scotland, this according to the 1851 census because no birth or death record has been located. He was listed as Flax dresser on death registration of Margaret WATT. Charles and Margaret had the following child:

+ 134 Mi. **John WATT** was born in 1847, probably in Montrose, Angus but no birth record was found. He died on 26 Dec 1925 in Cupar, Fife, Scotland and was variously described as a mill manager.

99. James Campbell GRAHAM (Alexander GRAHAM, Robert GRAHAM, Alexander GRAHAM, Robert GRAHAM, James) was born in 1822 in Glamis, Angus, Scotland. He died on 18 Dec 1865 in Dundee, Angus, Scotland. The cause of death was typhus.

Derivation of his name may arise from Christina/Christian DOIG's sister Janet DOIG who married James Campbell Mar 1822, Dundee Angus. Marriage record says he was of Forfar parish when married to Catherine WILKIE in 1848. However, the 1861 census for New Monkland (below) gives us our first evidence of his birth place and year. Probably born early 1822.

1861 Census	New Monkland 651/1		ED6	17			
110 Clark St, New Monkland							
Thomas Torrance	Head	Wid	73	Cotton Weaver		Cambusnethan	
James Graham	Visitor	M	39	Stone Mason		Forf	Glamis
Catherine Graham	Visitor	M	33	Stone Mason's wife		Forf	Forfar
David A Graham	Visitor	U	6	Stone Mason's Son		Stir	Stirling
James T Graham	Visitor	U	5	Stone Mason's Son		Lk	Govan

Listed as Mason on his death certificate. All four (recorded) children were born in different towns around Scotland suggesting that he moved the family as part of his employment. They gave their four sons very intriguing middle names, Alma, Talford, Iconaclast Bradlaugh, and Heron.

James married **Catherine WILKIE** daughter of David WILKIE and Margaret MCLEAN on 9 Jul 1848 in Forfar, Angus Scotland. Catherine was born in Forfar, Angus, Scotland. She was christened on 1 Feb 1826 in Forfar, Angus, Scotland. She died of burns to the head and neck on 21 Feb 1898 in Dundee, Angus, Scotland. She was buried[5] 23 Feb 1898 in Western Cemetery, Dundee, Scotland. Catherine's must have been a hard life – widowed twice before she reached age 52 and bore seven children one of whom did not survive infancy.

In 1871, Catherine was wife to James WATSON (age 71, House Proprietor) residing at 238 Hawkhill aong with daughters Catherine WATSON age 3 and Willamina WATSON age 1 and stepsons David GRAHAM (17) tinsmith, James GRAHAM (15) tinsmith and George GRAHAM (6) scholar. In 1881 Catherine was a widow residing at 224 Blackness Road, Liff & Benvie, Angus (page 13) with her children David Graham (tinsmith), George Graham (factory worker), Catherine Watson, and Minnie Watson. In 1891 census, Catherine WATSON (63) was still living at 224 Blackness Rd with daughters Catherine (23) and William (Wilhelmina) (21). The daughters were listed as jute weavers while Catherine was a "housekeeper." Probably buried in Section III Lair 98 of Western Cemetery Dundee (see Summons to CIB Graham from half sisters Catherine (Watson) Marshall and Minnie (Watson) MacDonald, 14 Jun 1898).

James and Catherine had the following children:

+ 135 Mi. **David Alma GRAHAM** was born on 1 May 1854. He died on 21 Oct 1933.

  136 Mii. **James Talford GRAHAM** was born on 28 Mar 1856 in Govan, Lanark Scotland.

  > Listed in 1861 census in New Monkland. In 1871, Catherine is wife to James WATSON (age 71, House Proprietor) residing at 238 Hawkhill along with daughters Catherine WATSON age 3 and Willamina WATSON age 1 and stepsons David GRAHAM (17) tinsmith, James GRAHAM (15) tinsmith and George GRAHAM (6) scholar. There is an 1881 census entry in Aberdeen for a James GRAHAM, age 26, unmarried, born Govan, Renfrew (should have been listed as Lanarkshire), occupation tinsmith. Because of the age and occupation similar to his older brother David's and now confirmed with 1871 census, this could be a viable candidate for James T. GRAHAM. However, further searches for marriages or deaths in the Aberdeen area have been unsuccessful. No Further Records (NFR) have been found.

+ 137 Miii. **Charles Iconaclast Bradlauch GRAHAM** was born on 10 Aug 1861. He died on 15 Dec 1945.

  138 Miv. **George Heron GRAHAM** was born[6] on 6 Sep 1864 in Dundee, Angus Scotland.

  > Possibly named after George Wilkie HERON, an uncle on his mother's side. Listed as 'Factory Worker' age 16 in the 1881 Census living with Catherine WATSON 'W' age 53, David GRAHAM age 26, tinsmith; Catherine WATSON age 13, scholar; and Minnie WATSON age 11, scholar. Family lived at 224 Blackness Rd. Like his older brother James, we can find no record of him after this 1881 census. There are no family documents that relate to him. What happened? Where did he go? NFR

101. **Mary Ann GRAHAM** (Alexander GRAHAM, Robert GRAHAM, Alexander GRAHAM, Robert GRAHAM, James) was born on 20 Dec 1822 in Marykirk, Kincardine, Scotland. She was christened on 15 Jan 1823 in Marykirk, Kincardine, Scotland. She died on 26 May 1902 in Fetteresso, Kincardine, Scotland.

An 1841 census entry in Montrose (ED16, p.24) shows
Elizabeth CLARK, 70, N=not born in cty
Jean do, 25, flax spinner, N
Elisabeth McDonald, 12, flax spinner, N
Ann Gordan, 20, flax spinner, Y
Mary Ann GRAHAM, 15, flax spinner, N

Given the rounding done in the 1841 census, this Mary Ann GRAHAM could have been born anytime between 1822 and 1826, hence I believe this is the Mary Ann Graham born to Alexander GRAHAM and Ann LINDSAY.

1881 census

Census Place: Logie Pert, Forfar, Scotland_Source: FHL Film 0203495 GRO Ref Volume 304 EnumDist 4 Page 3

8 The Square (Logie)_

Thomas FALCONER M 60 M Dundee, Forfar, Scotland Rel: Head Occ: Flax Dresser
Mary Ann FALCONER M 56 F Marykirk, Kincardine, Scotland Rel: Wife Occ: Millworker Flax Spinner
Elizth. Doig FALCONER U 30 F Montrose, Forfar, Scotland Rel: Daur Occ: Millworker Flax Spinner

In 1891 census

Census Place: Logie Pert, Forfar, Scotland
Source: Scotland'sPeople.gov.uk, ED??, p.8

Thomas FALCONER, head, M, 68, Flax Dresser, Forfarshire Dundee
Mary Ann FALCONER, wife, M, 68, Flax Spinner, Kincardineshire Marykirk
Catherine CHRISTISOW, boarder, U, 16, flax spinner, Forfarshire Lochee
Mary A. OREAND, boarder, U, 22, jute preparer, England

Mary Ann died a pauper in the Fetteresso Combination Poorhouse in 1902. The cause of death was listed as Rheumatism (chronic) and Softening of the Brain. The evidence suggests that hers was a hard life requiring millwork until well into the mid-1890's. She had only two children that can be established - both out of wedlock: Elizabeth Doig with John Doig in 1850 (Montrose) and Renwick Graham with James Sime Smith in 1856 (Dundee). Her daughter Elizabeth Doig appears part of the family in the 1881 census and this after she, too, had one child born illegitimately, a daughter that lived only a few months. Mary Ann must have had a relationship with her half-sister Margaret, at least during the 1850's since it was Margaret (Graham) Watt that had her niece Elizabeth Doig in her household in 1851.

Mary was not married to **John DOIG** son of Thomas DOIG and Agnes MCDONALD. John was born in 1828 in Montrose, Angus, Scotland. He died in 1897 in Montrose, Angus, Scotland.

The link of the illegitimate daughter by Mary Ann Graham is not certain. John was a private in the 93rd Regiment of Foot, British Army. In 1881 John was a general laborer in Montrose. In 1884 to 1888 he was a carter living at 12 Ferry Street, Montrose. In 1891 he and Helen lived in Montrose. [Prepared by Kenneth Frank Doig, ken@doig.net, www.doig.net.]

John and Mary had the following child:

+ 139 F i. **Elizabeth DOIG** was born in May 1850. She died on 23 Apr 1893.

In a second unfortunate experience, Mary was also not married to **James Sime SMITH** but had the following child by him:

140 M ii. **Renwick GRAHAM** was born on 3 Aug 1856 in Dundee, Angus, Scotland. He died on 6 May 1858 in Dundee and was buried on 7 May 1858 in New Howff Cemetery. It seems noteworthy that Mary Ann would name her second child Renwick after her younger brother of the same name, and a unique one at that.

1856 GRAHAM, RENWICK (Statutory Births 282/01 1066)

© Crown Copyright. Image was generated at 27 November 2008 05:56

[Birth register image for Renwick Grahame, born August 1856, 1 PM, Foundry Lane, Dundee; father James Sime Smith; mother Mary Ann Grahame, millworker; informant John Whitton, iron moulder, uncle; registered 23 August 1856 at Dundee.]

This Renwick Graham was born illegitimately to James Sime Smith and Mary Ann Graham. Birth location was Foundry Lane where Mary Ann was a millworker. The birth entry contains a note from Dec 1857 that recognizes James Sime Smith as the father according to the Sheriff Court of Forfarshire. The birth entry lists a John Whitton, iron moulder, as informant and indicates him as an 'uncle.' (This became a clue that led to the confirmation of Elizabeth Graham, youngest daughter to Alexander and Ann Lindsay, which I had been unable to positively identify in other records other than the 1851 census entry for the WATT family.) Young Renwick died less than two years later of 'jaundice' and the father was not listed. Interestingly, on his death cert, the witness was Margaret Graham, aunt. His death information was the result of a search of the TVFHS site's Howff database. Another intriguing point is that this bastard son was given the Graham name whereas Mary Ann's first illegitimate child Elizabeth Doig was given her father's name. Perhaps the simplest explanation is that young Renwick's father was in dispute so the default was to use his mother's maiden name.

Mary Ann, despite two illegitimate children by two different men, did finally marry **Thomas FALCONER** son of John FALCONER and Amelia DUNCAN on 16 Jan 1864 in Montrose, Angus, Scotland. Thomas was born[7] in 1823 in Dundee, Angus, Scotland. He died[8] on 18 Feb 1895 at Logie Square in Logie Pert, Angus, Scotland. The clue to this marriage was an 1881 census entry for Margaret (Nicholson Graham) Watt who was living in the home of her son John Watt at 21 Watson Street in Dundee but there was also in the household a 'visitor' John Falconer born in Blairgowrie, Perth. This fellow was the oldest son of Thomas Falconer by his first wife Christina BLACK. Here again, we have evidence that at least some of the children of Alexander Graham, both legitimate and not, were in contact with one another some fifty or sixty years after their births in the 1820's.

102. **John GRAHAM** (Alexander GRAHAM, Robert GRAHAM, Alexander GRAHAM, Robert GRAHAM, James) was born about 1824 in Marykirk, Kincardine, Scotland. He probably died in 1905 in Brisbane, Queensland, Australia, though this needs confirmation. Only record is 1841 census in which he is listed as age 16, flaxdresser. [28 Dec 2008] New research suggests that this John Graham may have been named John Peter Graham and might have become a journeyman plumber. He did not marry Mary Milne of Logie Pert but had two daughters by her. Mary Milne did marry an Alexander Towns in 1848 just before the birth of Amelia, daughter #2. Amelia's wedding registration lists her father as John Peter Graham, Plumber (journeyman) and DOES NOT list him as deceased so he should have been alive in 1872. [2 Nov 2009] Email from Margaret O'Conner states that Amelia's grave in Wanganui, NZ has a statement that on her grave at the Wanganui cenetery there is a note that says, "from Brisbane Australia the ashes of John Graham"

John never married **Mary MILNE** daughter of David MILNE and Elizabeth TRAIL but had two illegitimate daughters with her. Mary was born on 8 Sep 1824 in Logie-Pert, Angus, Scotland. She was christened on 5 Oct 1824 in Logie-Pert, Angus, Scotland. She died on 25 Mar 1910 in Logie-Pert, Angus, Scotland.

Interestingly, Mary Milne married Alexander Towns in May 1948, three months before the birth of Amelia Graham (#142)! Despite the lack of marriage, this pair had the following children:

+ 141 F i. **Mary Ann GRAHAM** was born on 1 Dec 1844, Logie-Pert, Angus, Scotland.

+ 142 Fii. **Amelia GRAHAM** was born on 2 Aug 1848, Logie-Pert, Angus, Scotland.

Mary Ann (l) and Amelia Graham (r) taken in NZ ca 1915. Photo courtesy of Margaret O'Connor, Dunedin, NZ and sent Nov 2009.

103. **Andrew GRAHAM** (Alexander GRAHAM, Robert GRAHAM, Alexander GRAHAM, Robert GRAHAM, James) was born in 1828 in Marykirk, Kincardine, Scotland. He died on 1 Jan 1902 in Little Dunkeld, Perth, Scotland. The cause of death was Senile Decay. Andrew married **Ann BLYTHE** daughter of Thomas BLYTHE on 4 Jan 1851 in Dunblane, Perth, Scotland. Ann was born[9] in 1830 in Dugary, Tyrone, Ireland. She died on 27 Feb 1886 in Dunblane, Perth, Scotland.

They had the following children:

+ 143 Mi. **Joseph Blyth(e) GRAHAM** was born in 1852. No birth record has been found as yet. He died in New Zealand in 1915.

+ 144 Mii. **John Blyth GRAHAM** was born in 1854. He died on 27 Dec 1942.

145 Miii. **James GRAHAM** was born on 25 Feb 1855 in Dunblane, Perth, Scotland. NFR

+ 146 F iv. **Jessie GRAHAM** was born[10] on 6 Dec 1856 in Dunblane, Perth, Scotland. She married **William Robertson** 25 Jan 1878 in Stirling, Stirlingshire Scotland. Together, they had five children born in Dunblane or Saline, Fife, Scotland. Sadly, Jessie died 24 Jun 1898 in Saline, Fife due to pulmonary phthisis (tuberculosis).

147 Mv. **Andrew GRAHAM** was born on 13 May 1859 in Dunblane, Perth, Scotland. He died[11] on 16 Apr 1860 at High Street in Dunblane, Perth, Scotland. The cause of death was febricula - fortnight. He was buried on 18 Apr 1860 in Episcopal Churchyard, Dunblane.

148 Fvi. **Mary Anne GRAHAM** was born on 22 Feb 1861 in Dunblane, Perth, Scotland. She died on 15 Aug 1862 at Sinclair's Wynd in Dunblane, Perth, Scotland.

105. **Elizabeth GRAHAM** (Alexander GRAHAM, Robert GRAHAM, Alexander GRAHAM, Robert GRAHAM, James) was born in 1832 in Marykirk, Kincardine, Scotland. Elizabeth married **John Barrie**

WHITTON son of Thomas WHITTON and Susan GLEN on 28 Sep 1853 in Dundee, Angus, Scotland. John was born on 31 Mar 1832 in Montrose, Angus, Scotland. They had the following children:

149 F i. **Mary Ann WHITTON** was born about 1855 in Perth, Perth, Scotland. There is no birth record for this person but the 1861 census entry for John Whitton and wife Elizabeth (Graham) Whitton lists a daughter Mary Ann, age 6 born Perth, Perthshire.

150 Mii. **William WHITTON** was born on 11 Oct 1858 in Montrose, Angus, Scotland. He died on 18 Apr 1901 in Bay of Bengal. The cause of death was heat apoplexy. He was buried in at sea. Death information presumed correct and sourced from Rootsweb database of Les Williamson (lesliew) although this record is now missing.

151 Fiii. **Susan WHITTON** was born on 17 Feb 1861 in Montrose, Angus, Scotland. She died seven months later on 16 Sep 1861 in Montrose, Angus, Scotland. Died at home 91 Castle St. Montrose; father listed as iron moulder (journeyman)

152 Miv. **John Barry WHITTON** was born on 15 Oct 1866 in Dundee, Angus, Scotland.

Sources

1. The Church of Jesus Christ of Latter-day Saints, International Genealogical Index (R) v5.0, 12 Jan 2004.

2. General Registry Office for Scotland; www.scotlandspeople.gov.uk, Statutory Register Index Deaths (1855-1951), 13 Jan 2004, 415/00 0002."Margaret (Graham) Watt, cardiac disease two years, witness by John Watt, son, present."widow of Charles Watt, flaxdresser (deceased).see www.scotlandspeople.gov.uk.

3. The Church of Jesus Christ of Latter-day Saints, International Genealogical Index (R) v5.0, Copyright (c) 1980, 2000, data as of January 2002, 12 Jan 2004, Family History Library, 35 N West Temple Street, Salt Lake City, Utah 84150 USA, 0993498.Batch M113124.

4. 1851 Scottish Census, 2 May 2005, Family History Library, 35 N West Temple Street, Salt Lake City, Utah 84150 USA."entry for Wilkie family at 23 Castle Street, Forfar.". Upon review of 1851 census entry in Montrose, Charles Watt was listed as age 29 and from Forfarshire, Montrose.

5. Irene Brady, Burial Administration
Leisure & Arts Department
Floor 13 Tayside House
Dundee, DD1 3RA
(01382 433089, 16 Sep 2004.

"Dear Dave, In reply to your e-mail I have searched our burial records and have found the following information. Western Cemetery, Perth Road, Dundee Lair No. 98aFebruary 23 1898   Catherine Wilkie or Graham, relict. of James Watson age 70yrs 224 Blackness Road   Dundee   Died in Royal Infirmary. cause of death – Burning Lair No. 98bApril 26 1866   Christina Christie wife of James Watson age 65   Mid Wynd   Dundee   cause of Death – Paralysis April 6 1873   Georgina Nicoll Watson Daughter of James, Wright age 1 year   238 Hawkhill   Dundee   cause of death – Teething October 22 1875   James Watson (Pawnbroker) age 61 years   238 Hawkhill   Dundee   cause of death - Liver Complaint.

I hope this information is helpful to you, I cannot give you copies of our records but if you wish to get copies of death certificates you can go to www.dundeecity.gove.uk and under D for Death you can apply to get copies from the registrars, they will also give you costs involved." [email received 9/16/2004.]

6. General Registry Office of Scotland, ScotlandsPeople.gov.uk , 24 Sep 1864.2nd District Dundee, page 448.

7. 1891 Scottish Census, 304/00_004/000_008; _011/000_033, 6 May 2004.

8. General Registry Office of Scotland, ScotlandsPeople.gov.uk , 282/01/0397, 7 May 2004."Death Registration."

9. Caroline Makein, Fife Rootsearch, Caroline Makein, Report May 2008, 8 May 2008.

10. The Church of Jesus Christ of Latter-day Saints, International Genealogical Index (R), Copyright (c) 1980, 2002, data as of March 26, 2004, C113481, 9 Oct 2007, Family History Library, 35 N West Temple Street, Salt Lake City, Utah 84150 USA.

11. Caroline Makein, Fife Rootsearch, Caroline Makein, 8 May 2008.

Seventh Generation

134. **John WATT** (Margaret Nicholson GRAHAM, Alexander GRAHAM, Robert GRAHAM, Alexander GRAHAM, Robert GRAHAM, James) was born in 1847 in Montrose, Angus, Scotland. He died on 26 Dec 1925 in Cupar, Fife, Scotland.

> His death certificate indicates his marriage to Mary Anderson but states that his parents were John WATT and Mary (Davidson) WATT. It also states that he was a flax mill manager. Most of the information is consistent with earlier census information about age and occupation but the parentage info is probably erroneous.

John married **Mary Ann ANDERSON** daughter of David ANDERSON and Margaret LINDSAY. Mary was born on 29 Jan 1850 in Marykirk, Kincardine, Scotland. They had the following children:

153 Mi. **David Faulkner WATT** was born on 18 Apr 1875 in Ceres, Fife, Scotland.

> Birth registration lists David F. Watt as Illegitimate; mother as Mary Anderson, flax mill worker and father as John Watt, flax mill

154 Fii. **Mary WATT** was born in 1877 in Dundee, Angus, Scotland.

155 Miii. **John WATT** was born in 1880 in Dundee, Angus, Scotland. He died in Cupar, Fife in 1958 from stomach cancer and was listed as a retired forester.

> Just below the 1901 census entry for his father, John WATT head of household at 73 Tarvit Spinning Mill Cott(age), there is an entry for a John WATT at 74 Tarvit Spinning Mill Cott(age). John WATT, head, married, age 20, Cattleman on farm, born Forfarshire, Dundee Jane WATT, wife, married, age 28, Cattleman's wife, born Perthshire, Alyth Annie STEWART, sister in law, age 12, scholar, born Forfarshire, Dundee Joseph STEWART, brother in law, age 9, scholar, born Forfarshire, Dundee

John married **Jane Malcolm STEWART**. Jane was born circa 1872 in Alyth, Perth, Scotland. They had at least one child, a son named John who was witness to his father's death in 1958. This son, John Watt was listed as living at 10 St. Georges Drive, Victoria, London.

156 Miv. **Fred WATT** was born in 1885 in Dundee, Angus, Scotland.

157 Fv. **Isabella WATT** was born in 1886 in Cupar, Fife, Scotland.

135. **David Alma GRAHAM** (James Campbell GRAHAM, Alexander GRAHAM, Robert GRAHAM, Alexander GRAHAM, Robert GRAHAM, James) was born on 1 May 1854 in Stirling, Stirlingshire Scotland. He was christened on 6 May 1855 in Stirling, Stirlingshire, Scotland. He died on 21 Oct 1933 in Hollis, Queens, NY, USA. The cause of death was gastric hemorrhage, chronic myocarditis. He was buried[1] 24 Oct 1933 in Cypress Hills Cemetery, Brooklyn, NY, USA. The middle name Alma may stem from the Battle of Alma 20 Sep 1854, the first battle of the Crimean War which resulted in a victory of the Franco-English forces over the Russians. Several Scottish regiments were instrumental in the fight including the Black Watch and the Coldstream Guards and there were several poems and ballards written to glorify the struggle. The first recorded entry was the baptism of David in May 1855, nearly a year after his birth.

> In 1881 Census:
> Catherine WATSON, W 53 Forfar Housekeeper
> David GRAHAM, U 26, Stirling tinsmith
> George GRAHAM U 16, factory worker
> Catherine WATSON, Dau, 13 F Scholar
> Minnie WATSON, Dau 11 F Scholar

Immigrated to US along with wife Agnes Cuthbert GRAHAM via SS Furnessia (Anchor Line) arriving New York via Greenock (SCT) and Moville (IRE) on 28 Sep 1885. Port of Embarkation Greenock and Moville, Master - John Hedderwick (Glasgow). Entry reads:

> D. Graham age 30 male plumber Scotland, 3 pieces luggage, second cabin, PS (protracted sojourn)

> Mrs. Graham, 29 female, wife, Scotland

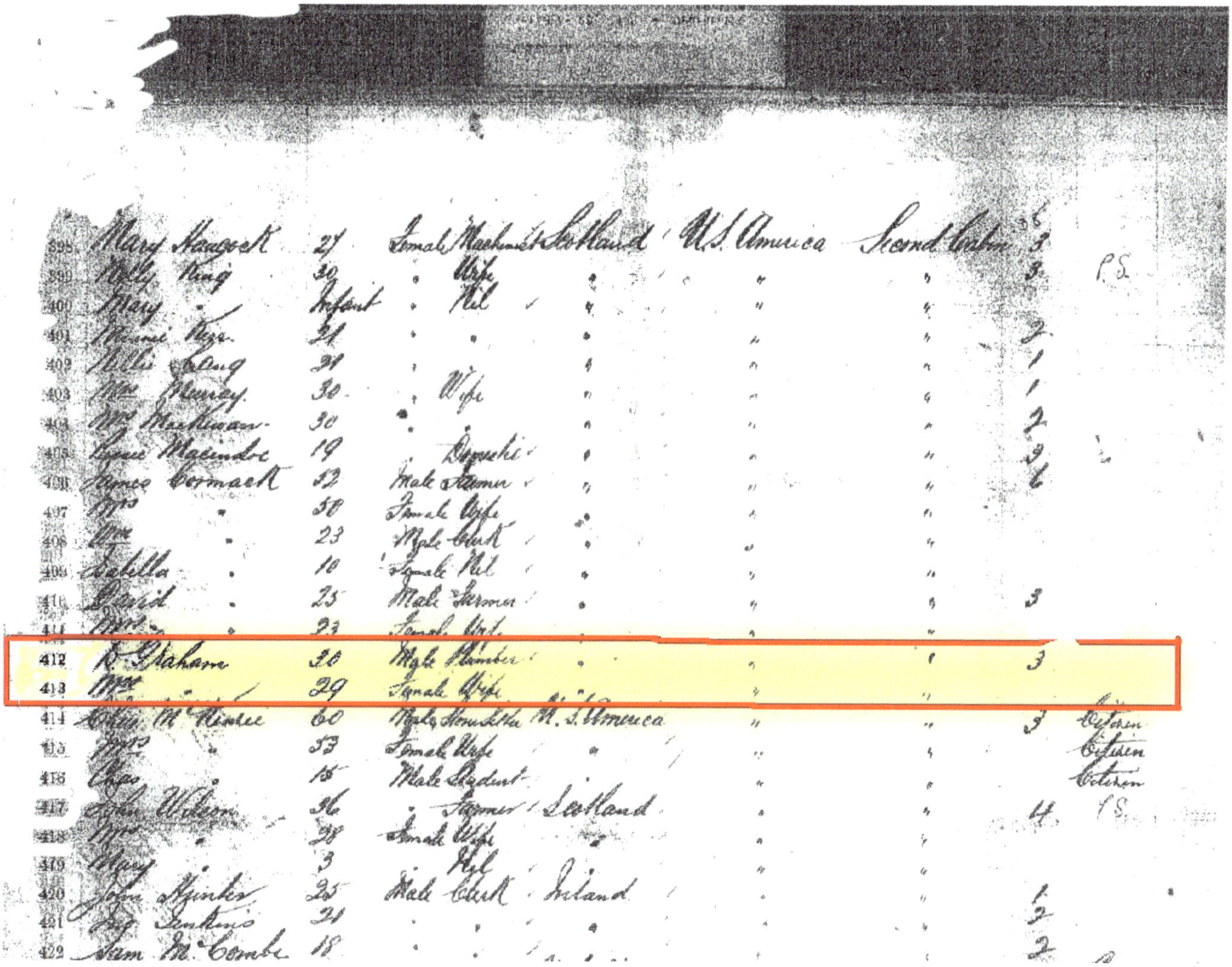

[source: NARA, Passenger Lists of Vessels Arriving NYC 1820-1897, roll #490, entry 1204]

SS. Furnessia manifest and picture of ship.

Occupation listed on his son David Alma Graham's US birth certificate is plumber. Listed as steamfitter on 1900 census which also indicated that he emigrated to US from Scotland in 1881, NOT YET CONFIRMED.

In 1900 he was a steam fitter at 53 Hope Street, Brooklyn, Kings Co., NY (page 84) with his wife Agnes and 5 children (including 1 yr old Charles who later died in infancy). He lived at 1270 Madison Street, Brooklyn, NY from at least 1914 until 1930 before moving in with his youngest son, George. His will dated 29 Sep 1929 removed his eldest three children from any inheritance "since the death of their beloved mother (they) have not shown the proper love and respect due me."

Purportedly was an elder at the Cypress Hills Presbyterian Church which was founded in 1902. Efforts to locate any confirming records have not yet been successful.

DAG's Cetificate of Naturalization - the certificate number seems to be 2238050 (preprinted in red), but the number is given as Petition Volume 180, Number 45556- he is described as 71 years old, 5'4", white, fair, blue eyes, gray hair and residing at 1270 Madison, Brooklyn dated 8 Sept 1925; and a Certificate of Literacy for David Graham at 1270 Madison St dated Oct 7th 1926 (a note at bottom says to show it to all election inspectors, so perhaps he decided to start voting).

Moved to Hollis LI in 1930 to live with George & Ora Graham family. According to granddaughter Ruth, David "was a very nice man, but couldn't get around well. Had quite a Scottish accent. Liked to play with the kids. Had hardening of arteries and walked with a cane. Did not get along well with his other children and this is why he moved in with George & Ora in his last years. May not have been easy to get along with." This opinion from Ruth reinforces what we uncovered with his will.

David married **Agnes Robb CUTHBERT** daughter of George CUTHBERT and Agnes KIDD on 20 Aug 1885 in Dundee, Angus Scotland. Interestingly, the witnesses were Charles Graham and Agnes Candow demonstrating that these brothers were in close contact. Agnes was born[2] 6 May 1857 in Dundee, Angus, Scotland. She died[3] 4 Nov 1922 in Brooklyn, NY, USA. She was buried[4] on 17 Nov 1922 in Cypress Hills Cemetery, Glendale, NY.

In 1871 Dundee census, Agnes CUTHBERT (16) power loom weaver, is living with her widowed mother Agnes K CUTHBERT (40) Housekeeper and brother George (16)coachbuilder at 11 Park Street, Lochee. This entry suggests that she had a twin brother or one born close in age though no birth record has been located for him that directly links him to George CUTHBERT and Agnes Kidd CUTHBERT.

According to the 1900 US Census, Agnes immigrated to Brooklyn, NY in 1884. This is not confirmed. By contrast, her death certificate lists her birthdate as 6 May 1858 rather than 1857 per Scottish records. It also states that she was in the USA for 37 years which places her arrival at 1885 - in keeping with other known records. She died of acute cholecystitis that she had for 25 days, though a contributing factor was chronic colitis duration of 5 years.

David and Agnes had the following children:

158 F i. **Jennie Francis GRAHAM** was born on 11 Jun 1886 in Brooklyn, NY. She died on 30 Dec 1969 in Brooklyn, NY. She was buried[5] 2 Jan 1970 in Cypress Hills Cemetery, Brooklyn NY.

Jennie as a young woman and on the right with her sister Agnes (left) from a photo probably taken 1 Jan 1942.

Never married, worked as secretary for executives at the Borden Company in NYC. According to her niece, Ruth Graham Fuller, Jennie was outgoing and personable, would take a drink, or smoke, and loved to dance. Took Ruth on Labor Day trips to Lake George when Ruth was a teenager. Why did she never marry?

+ 159 Mii. **David Alma GRAHAM** was born on 26 Jan 1888. He died on 18 Aug 1955.

160 Miii. **Alexander J GRAHAM** was born on 1 Jan 1889 in Brooklyn, Kings, NY. He died on 2 Apr 1889 at 107 Havermayer St in Brooklyn, Kings, NY, and was buried on 3 Apr 1889 in Lutheran Cemetery, Middle Village NY.

161 Fiv. **Agnes Cuthbert GRAHAM** was born on 25 Jan 1890 in Brooklyn, NY. She died on 15 Nov 1955 in Forest Hills, NY. She was buried[6] 19 Nov 1955 in Cypress Hills Cemetery, Glendale, NY.

Left NY for Los Angeles to open an infant clothing store for about 4-5 years though exact dates and times are not known. [Some believe that it was a notions store.] May not have been successful. Then moved back to NY and lived with Jennie in an apartment. A 1930 US Census entry indicated that Jennie and Agnes were living together at 57 Hancock St., Brooklyn. Agnes was listed as an accountant for a hospital. This may have been before or after Agnes' California sojourn. Ultimately bought a 2 BR home in Forest Hills, NY. Worked for a bank. Upon her death she left her house to Jenny. Her handwritten will left the rest of her estate to her nieces and nephews for the education of their children. According to Bob her financial assets were modest but well invested in a variety of blue chip stocks. Divided the estate four ways - Bob, Chuck, George and Ruth. Jenny sold the house. According to Ruth (Graham) Fuller, Agnes was prudish and straitlaced and she did not get along well with her sister Jennie. Why, like her older sister, did she never marry?

+ 162 Mv. **George Forbes GRAHAM** was born on 7 Aug 1892. He died on 17 Jun 1972.

163 Mvi. **Charles James GRAHAM** was born[7] in Apr 1899 in Brooklyn NY. He died on 18 Jun 1904 in Brooklyn, Kings NY. He was buried on 18 Jun 1904 in Lutheran Cemetery, Middle Village NY. Died in infancy; may have been source of Charles James GRAHAM's (#180) name according to his brother Robert. DLG and GCG visited Lutheran Cemetery and the gravesite on 20 Aug 2004. We were amazed at the quality of the gravestone - it appeared almost new, however there was no way of determining when the stone was made and placed. Cemetery records indicated that Agnes Cuthbert Graham must have taken some responsibility for the grave & maintenance until her death in 1955 after which Jennie took over until her death in 1969 and finally George F. Graham from 1969 to his death in 1972. Grave maintenance then lapsed.

137. **Charles Iconaclast Bradlauch GRAHAM** (James Campbell GRAHAM, Alexander GRAHAM, Robert GRAHAM, Alexander GRAHAM, Robert GRAHAM, James) was born[8] on 10 Aug 1861 in New Monkland, Lanark Scotland. He died[9] at the age of 84 on 15 Dec 1945 in Dundee, Angus Scotland. The cause of death was Myocardial degeneration. He was buried on 18 Dec 1945.

Original birth registration entry shows the name as Charles Iconaclast Bradlauch Graham in all likelihood he was named after the "Iconoclast" Charles Bradlaugh (1833-1890) famous as an atheist and founder of the National Secular Society.

1871 census shows an entry for a Charles Graham living in household of William Melville and Margaret (Watson) Melville at 238 Hawkhill. Charles was listed as 'wife's brother' suggesting that Margaret was probably daughter of James Watson. This is likely to be the reason CIB Graham named one son William Melville Graham. 1891 Census Liff & Benvie, St. Marks, Dundee shows Charles GRAHAM (age 29) head of household living at 9 St. Peter Street. Wife is Agnes S.C. GRAHAM (age 27). Children are Charles G. GRAHAM (age 3), William M. GRAHAM (age 2) and Agnes M. GRAHAM (age 2 weeks). Charles was listed as Joiner and birth place Airdrie Perth (though IGI lists him born in New Monkland, Lanark). Agnes' birth location given as Kingoodie, Perth though IGI records suggest Longforgan Perth.

Both first and second marriages were done "according to the forms of the Free Church of Scotland."

1901 Census Liff & Benvie, St. Marks, Dundee lists Charles GRAHAM age 39, head of household at 39 Step Row. Profession is joiner. His birthplace in this census is listed as Airdrie Lanarkshire suggesting that previous census was recorded in error. Wife is Agnes age 40. William age 11, David age 8, Charles age 5, Agnes age 3. These data confirm that Agnes Small Candow died in 1892 as did Agnes M. The first Charles must also have died between 1891 and 1896.

Grahams o' the Mearns

"Have just been talking to cousin Charlie's widow, Ethel, a delightful person who will be ninety on 10th October - still very alert and capable. Her maiden name was Elizabeth Ethel Eccleston, daughter of Arthur Eccleston, a customs officer from London who came to work in Glasgow where Ethel was born. She remembers Grandpa Charles I.B. as a "bit of a card" and was very pleased when he asked if she would give him a run in the car she was learning to drive as a teenager." [source: email from Sheila (Graham) Rattray 4/7/2004]

"Charles I.B. was apprenticed at the age of eleven (presumably 1872) to a joiner at Abernyte in the Carse of Gowrie hills. His first pay was two shillings and sixpence a week - the equivalent of twelve and a half pence or one eighth of a pound, and the little lad ran all the way home and put it in his widowed mother's lap. His boss was a heavy drinker and Grandpa (a lifelong teetotaller) didn't like that and once ran off home mid-week, but he was re-installed the following day. When he lived in Peddie Street, Dundee, he laid the foundations of his "fortune" (Grace's term). He made a bed, table, and two fireside chairs and sold them for £5:- With his first £100:- he bought property, and continued to buy houses which explains the varying descriptions of his career as Master Joiner and Property Owner. He hired a horse and trap to visit his various houses, and the property vote gave him several votes at election time which he used. The hired horse stopped at every inn, but young Charles just indulged in ginger beer. Grace went on to say that she ran an "Aid To Russia" shop during the Second World War. Grandpa handed in his mother's gold chains, but Grace retained a bracelet of Catherine Wilkie's. Let's hope that Donald in Canada has it now. I remember him as a member of the Brethren sect, who would never go to a theatre or cinema. Grandma and Auntie Nan were members of the Church of Scotland and less inhibited in their outlook. Nevertheless Grandpa was the one who visited David and Grace and took Donald to the park. Grace said that he loved to play Santa Claus at the Mission Hall. He was always on the move and scared Auntie Nan by climbing a tree in his eighties and sawing off a troublesome branch. Grandma used to say he was either "up a lummy (chimney) or doon a drain!" As a child, I used to love visiting "Ashcliffe" their home in Newport, Fife, with its own private pebbly beach on the River Tay opposite Dundee. I much regret that none of us has one item made by our grandfather." [Source: Sheila (Graham) Rattray email dated 4/19/2004]

Western Cemetrey   Section - XIII   Lairs 191B & 191C   Proprietor - Charles Graham
Lair 191B
16/12/1943   Agnes Dickson Soutar or Graham   84 Years
15/12/1945   Charles Graham   84 Years
Lair 191C
10/07/1891   Agnes Candow Wife of Charles   28 Years
06/08/1891   Agnes Minnie Graham (daughter of Charles)   4 Month
01/12/1892   Charles George Grahan (son of Charles)   5 Years
07/10/1896   George Albert Graham (son of Charles)   2 Years 7 Month
02/09/1932   Gordon Richard Bradlaw Graham   2 Years
[source: email from Sheila Rattray 24 Jul 2006]

The Charles Graham/Mary Fox sibs – Sheila, Donald and Maureen

Charles first married[10] **Agnes Small CANDOW** daughter of Robert William CANDOW and Ann ROSS on 28 Dec 1886 in Dundee, Angus Scotland. Agnes was born on 17 Feb 1863 in Longforgan, Perth Scotland. She died on 7 Jul 1891 in Dundee and was buried on 10 Jul 1891 in Western Cemetery, Dundee. Death certificate dated 7 Jul 1891 age 28 years, father Robert Candow, farmer; mother Ann Candow, m.s. Ross (deceased). Died of "Phthisis 3 Months'; witnessed by Charles Graham, Widower, present.

Charles and Agnes had the following children:

 164 M i. **Charles George GRAHAM** was born on 5 Oct 1887 in Dundee, Angus Scotland. He died[11] on 29 Nov 1892 in Dundee and was buried on 1 Dec 1892 in Western Cemetery, Dundee, Angus, Scotland. At time of birth, family was living at 23 St. Peter St. Dundee.

Agnes Small Candow and Charles IB Graham, ca 1885

+ 165 Mii.**William Melville GRAHAM** was born on 14 Apr 1889. He died on 30 Jan 1961.

166 Fiii. **Agnes Minnie GRAHAM** was born[12] 18 Mar 1891 in Dundee, Angus Scotland. She died[13] 4 Aug 1891 in Dundee, Angus, Scotland. The cause of death was meningitis, 7 days. She was buried on 6 Aug 1891 in Western Cemetery, Dundee. Presumably named after her father's half-sister Wilhelmina Watson.

Charles remarried **Agnes Dickson SOUTAR** daughter of David SOUTAR and Elizabeth LONGMUIR on 27 Apr 1892 in St. Andrew Dundee, Angus Scotland. Agnes was born on 19 Aug 1859 in Errol, Perth, Scotland. She died on 14 Dec 1943 in Dundee, Angus Scotland. She was buried on 16 Dec 1943 in Western Cemetery, Dundee. May have had twin sister, Isabel Miller SOUTAR. Died 14 Dec 1943 of "Cardiovascular Degeneration" age 84. Residence listed as 2 Stewart Street, Lochee. Father was David Soutar, Crofter (deceased) and Elizabeth Soutar, m.s. Longmuir (deceased).

Charles and Agnes had the following children:

+ 167 Miv.**David Soutar GRAHAM** was born on 24 Jan 1893. He died on 19 May 1965.

 168 Mv.**George Albert GRAHAM** was born in Feb 1894 in Dundee, Angus, Scotland. He died on 7 Oct 1896

in Dundee and was buried on 7 Oct 1896 in Western Cemetery, Dundee.

+ 169 Mvi. **Charles GRAHAM** was born on 10 Nov 1895. He died on 20 Sep 1979.

170 Fvii. **Agnes GRAHAM** "Nan; Auntie Nan" was born[14] on 24 May 1897 in Dundee, Angus Scotland. She died in Sep 1960.

Listed as 3 yr old daughter of Charles GRAHAM and Agnes (Dickson Soutar) GRAHAM in 1901 Dundee census.

Married widower Frank Fairweather in Nov 1949. According to Sheila (Graham) Rattray, she has a letter sent from Nan describing a trip to NY, USA and Alberta, Canada in 1957. I suspect that Nan and Frank accompanied Aunt Jennie to my christening (David L. Graham) at First Congregational Church, Pittsfield MA in May 1957.

During a June 2006 trip to Scotland, Maureen and Dave went to visit the daughter of Frank Fairweather by his first wife. This woman, Marguerite Fairweather, was quite gracious but told the story of how she was hurt when her father decided to remarry (Agnes Graham) in 1949. She had been taking care of her dad and thought she was 'indispensable' but on a visit to her brother in Canada, was sent a telegram informing her of the new arrangement. She subsequently lived in Toronto for 30 years before returning to Scotland in 1978. She continues to live in Newport in the same house her father owned until his death in 1971.

Agnes married[15] **Frank Howard FAIRWEATHER** son of William Gilchrest FAIRWEATHER and Eliza Jane DICKSON on 5 Nov 1949 in Glasgow, Lanark, Scotland. Frank was born in 1891 in Forgan, Fife, Scotland. He died in 1971. [From Rootsweb's WorldConnect database, birthdate and parents provided by Pam Fairweather Thomson]

139. **Elizabeth DOIG** (Mary Ann GRAHAM, Alexander GRAHAM, Robert GRAHAM, Alexander GRAHAM, Robert GRAHAM, James) was born in May 1850 in Montrose, Angus, Scotland. She died[16] at age 42 on 23 Apr 1893 in Cupar, Fife, Scotland. She was listed as a Flax Mill Worker but no cause of death was listed and her address was listed as 'County Buildings' and the witness was George White, Cupar Sanitary Inspector.

In 1861 Mary Ann and daughter Elizabeth lived at 12 William Street, Dundee; she was an unmarried mill worker. There was also a lodger and son in the house." Elizabeth was a flax mill worker. Was illiterate as on death cert for her 5 mo old dau Mary Ann DOIG, she signed her name "X". Have found no record of her past the 1881 census when she was living in the same household as her mother and stepfather, Thomas Falconer. In 1861 Mary Ann and daughter Elizabeth lived at 12 William Street, Dundee; she was an unmarried mill worker. There was also a lodger and son in the house." Prepared by Kenneth Frank Doig, ken@doig.net, www.doig.net.

Elizabeth had the following child:

171 F i. **Mary Ann DOIG** was born on 7 Feb 1874 in Dundee, Angus, Scotland. She died on 2 Jul 1874 in Kinnaber Mills, Montrose, Angus, Scotland. The cause of death was marasmus (severe protein deficiency). We are left to speculate – were they too poor for meat? Did her mother not care and starve her?

141. **Mary Ann GRAHAM** (John GRAHAM, Alexander GRAHAM, Robert GRAHAM, Alexander GRAHAM, Robert GRAHAM, James) was born on 1 Dec 1844 in Logie-Pert, Angus, Scotland. She was christened on 3 Mar 1845 in Logie-Pert, Angus, Scotland. She died mid-August 1938 in New Zealand.

The marriage between Mary Ann Graham and Joseph Graham states that they were "cousins german" or first cousins. Mary Ann must have been the daughter of John Graham born 1824-25 whose brother Andrew was father to Joseph. Mary Ann and Joseph were married at St. Mary's Episcopal Church in Montrose although the usual addresses for both were in Dundee.

1871 GRAHAM, JOSEPH - GRAHAM, MARY ANN (Statutory Marriages 312/00 0051)

Mary married **Joseph GRAHAM** son of Andrew GRAHAM and Ann BLYTHE on 27 Jun 1871 in Montrose, Angus, Scotland. Joseph was born in 1852 in Dunblane, Perth, Scotland. This discovery occurred in December 2008 when looking for information on the whereabouts of Joseph GRAHAM. Needless to say, it was quite a surprise to find additional blood relations of Alexander the Tailor and to find that there was a marriage between these first cousins. One wonders how they met and why they were living in Dundee and went to Montrose to be married. They stayed there as evidenced by the birth of their daughter below. Interestingly, they married in the Episcopal Church of Scotland although Joseph's mother Ann Blythe was from Ireland and presumably Roman Catholic.

Joseph and Mary Ann had the following children, first in Scotland and then in New Zealand:

172 F i. **Mary Ann GRAHAM** was born on 27 Nov 1873 in Montrose, Angus, Scotland. She died in 1955 purportedly in Christchurch, NZ but no cemetery records have been located as yet. In NZ she was known as Molly.

1873 GRAHAM, MARY ANN (Statutory Births 312/00 0425)

173 Mii. **Charles Riper GRAHAM** was born on 31 Jan 1876 in Ripa Island Lyttleton, New Zealand. He died in May 1931 in Wellington, New Zealand. He was buried on 20 May 1931 in Karori, Wellington, New Zealand. Middle Name in NZ records variously recorded as Riper, Ripa and Rippon. Was tailor just like his father Joseph. Charles married Edith Emma Margaret SPENCER in 1914 in New Zealand.

174 Miii. **John Harland GRAHAM** was born in 1881 in New Zealand. He died on 17 Jul 1952 in Palmerston North, New Zealand. He was buried on 18 Jul 1952 in Kelvin Grove, Palmerston North, New Zealand. John married Annie Elizabeth? Annie was born about 1888. She died on 21 Jun 1984 in Palmerston North, New Zealand. She was buried on 23 Jun 1984 in Kelvin Grove, Palmerston North, New Zealand.

175 Miv. **Ernest GRAHAM** was born in 1885 in New Zealand. He died in Apr 1917 in Wellington, New Zealand. He was buried 20 on 12 Apr 1917 in Karori, Wellington, New Zealand. Was listed as a Clerk in Karori Wellington burial record.

176 Mv. **Edwin Allen GRAHAM** was born on 27 Oct 1886 in New Zealand. He died on 17 Apr 1975 in Dannevirke, New Zealand. He was buried on 21 Apr 1975 in Takapau Cemetery, New Zealand. 11/9/2009-cemetery search yields burial record in Takapau cemetery. Edwin Allen Graham listed as retired sheepfarmer, 50 yrs in area, photo of headstone included. His death certificate listed him as 'not married' so presumably he was a life-long bachelor. Intriguing to see his headstone listing him as 2nd son when he was actually 4th born to Joseph & Mary Ann. And who would have erected or paid for his headstone?

177 Mvi. **Joseph Ivon GRAHAM** was born after Apr 1888 in New Zealand. He died on 5 Apr 1908 in Palmerston North, New Zealand. He was buried on 7 Apr 1908 in Palmerston North, New Zealand and burial registry lists him as driver, age 19 at death.

178 Mvii. **Herbert Rowell GRAHAM** was born in 1890 in New Zealand. He died in 1947 in New Zealand. Herbert married Clarice Mary Claire McALINDON in 1925 in New Zealand.

179 Fviii. **Alice Elizabeth GRAHAM** was born on 14 Aug 1892 in New Zealand. She died in 1988 in New Zealand. Alice married Reginald Lewis HULSTON in 1914 in New Zealand.

142. **Amelia GRAHAM** (John GRAHAM, Alexander GRAHAM, Robert GRAHAM, Alexander GRAHAM, Robert GRAHAM, James) was born on 2 Aug 1848 in Logie-Pert, Angus, Scotland. She was christened on 11 Dec 1848 in Logie-Pert, Angus, Scotland. She died on 4 Aug 1917 in Wanganui, New Zealand and was buried on 6 Aug 1917 in Aramaho Cemetery blk A row 6 plot 305. Amelia had one daughter out-of-wedlock, **Wilhelmina Graham** born 23 Apr 1869, Dundee, Angus with no father listed. Amelia was listed as 'winder' living at 1 Rose St.. She ultimately married **Robert William Oswald STEWART** son of **Duncan STEWART** and **Helena RICHARDSON** on 7 Jun 1872 in Montrose, Angus, Scotland. Robert was born about 1845 in Dumfries, Dumfriesshire, Scotland. He died on 30 Jun 1927 in Kogarah, NSW, Australia. Robert and Amelia, with Mina but not ROW Stewart listed below, sailed to Port Chalmers, NZ on the Invercargill arriving Oct 1874. Together, they had the children listed below with the exception of Mina:

180A F **Wilhelmina GRAHAM** was born 23 Apr 1869 in Dundee, Angus, Scotland to Amelia with no father listed. She was listed on the Ivercargill ship register as Mina, age 5. NFR

180 Mi. **Robert Oswald William STEWART** was born on 30 Jun 1873 in Govan, Lanark, Scotland. Probably died young or during the sea voyage to NZ. NFR

181 Mii. **George STEWART** was born in 1876 in New Zealand.

182 Fiii. **Amelia Gillespie STEWART** was born in 1878 in New Zealand.

183 Miv. **John Taylor STEWART** was born in 1879 in New Zealand. He died in 1941 in New Zealand. John married Florence Jane THOMSON in 1918 in New Zealand.

184 Fv. **Mary Eleanor STEWART** was born on 22 Jul 1880 in Hampden, Otago, New Zealand. Mary married Charles Arthur BOWEN on 24 Apr 1900 in Wanganui, New Zealand. Charles was born in 1878 in Kaipoi, New Zealand. *[Editorial Note: It was this woman's granddaughter Margaret (Wright) O'Connor that contacted me in Oct. 2009 and opened up the entire New Zealand Graham and Stewart family members, and I will be forever grateful for the connection.]*

185 Fvi. **Jessie Anna STEWART** was born in 1882 in New Zealand. She died by drowning in 1885 in New Zealand.

186 Mvii. **Andrew Duncan STEWART** was born in 1883 in New Zealand. He died in 1911 in New Zealand.

187 Mviii. **James Sinclair STEWART** was born in 1885 in New Zealand.

+ 188 Fix. **Louisa Carter STEWART** was born in 1887. She died in 1945.

189 Fx. **Elizabeth Florence Maude STEWART** was born in 1890 in New Zealand.

190 Fxi. **Ruby Valerie Castlemaine Ballance STEWART** was born in 1895 in New Zealand. She died in 1973 in New Zealand. Ruby married **Norman Herbert MCEWEN** in 1918 in New Zealand.

143. **Joseph (Blythe) GRAHAM** (Andrew GRAHAM, Alexander GRAHAM, Robert GRAHAM, Alexander GRAHAM, Robert GRAHAM, James) was born in 1852 in Dunblane, Perth, Scotland. Joseph married **Mary Ann GRAHAM** daughter of John GRAHAM and Mary MILNE on 27 Jun 1871 in Montrose, Angus, Scotland. Mary was born on 1 Dec 1844 in Logie-Pert, Angus, Scotland. She was christened on 3 Mar 1845 in Logie-Pert, Angus, Scotland. As stated earlier, Joseph and Mary had at least one child – Mary Ann Graham born in Montrose. Joseph was living with his Uncle Renwick in Dundee in the 1871 census and listed as an apprentice tailor. The census occurred in April so he must have known of his cousin Mary Ann as they married less than three months later. What brought these two together? In Scotland, he was listed in the censuses as Joseph but in NZ his burial name is listed at Joseph Blythe Graham.

144. **John Blyth GRAHAM** (Andrew GRAHAM, Alexander GRAHAM, Robert GRAHAM, Alexander GRAHAM, Robert GRAHAM, James) was born in 1854 in Dunblane, Perth, Scotland. He died on 27 Dec 1942 in Auchterarder, Perth, Scotland. John married **Janet MCINTYRE** daughter of Duncan MCINTYRE and Mary GILCHRIST on 26 Jul 1878 in Dunblane, Perth, Scotland. Janet was born on 9 May 1857 in Dunblane, Perth, Scotland. She died on 23 Nov 1937 in Auchterarder, Perth, Scotland. They had the following children:

199 Mi. **Andrew Herbert Francis GRAHAM** was born on 19 May 1879 in Dunblane, Perth, Scotland. He died on 26 Dec 1896 in Dunblane, Perth, Scotland the apparent cause being fearlatina angina and hyperprexies (high fever).

200 Mii. **Duncan Henry Malcolm GRAHAM** was born in 1883 in Dunblane, Perth, Scotland. He died on 15 May 1942 in Renfrew, Renfrew, Scotland. The cause of death was severe crushing right thigh; internal injuries probably due to his occupation as a dynamite worker. Duncan married **Edith HOLLYER** daughter of **Walter HOLLYER** and **Rose Ann RILEY** Reilly on 1 Aug 1915 in New Ardrossan, Ayr, Scotland. Edith was born[17] in 1878 in Colaba, Bombay, India. She died after 1942 but no death record located yet.

201 Fiii. **Mary Anne GRAHAM** was born on 24 Mar 1887 in Dunblane, Perth, Scotland. NFR

See 1901 census entry for John Graham and Janet McIntyre showing children Victoria age 14 and John age 9, all living at 155 High Street, Dunblane. No records of Mary Anne or Victoria have been found as yet.

202 Miv. **John Alexander GRAHAM** was born on 24 Jan 1891 in Dunblane, Perth, Scotland but died just two months later on 22 Mar 1891 of 'congestion of the lungs, 14 days.'

203 Miv. **John (Alexander) GRAHAM** was born on 5 Apr 1892 in Dunblane, Perth, Scotland. This John was witness to the death of his brother Duncan Henry Malcolm Graham in May 1942 and was listed as living 8 Airthrey Cottages, Bridge of Allan, Stirling. No death was recorded by 1956. His marriage entry in 1921 lists him as age 29, Pvt 2nd Battalion of Black Watch living at Hillrow, Dunblane. John married **Ann HENDERSON** daughter of **Archibald HENDERSON** and **Ann Melville Matthews BAXTER** on 7 Jan 1921 in Stirling, Stirlingshire, Scotland. Ann was born on 27 Apr 1884 in Stirling, Stirlingshire, Scotland. In a somewhat intriguing finding, Ann (Henderson) Graham died on 28 Jun 1948 in Logie, Stirling, Scotland with the cause listed as coal gas poisoning (suicide) due to melancholia. Because Ann was 37 when married, it may be that the couple did not have any children or perhaps that children born did not survive WWII. No records of children have yet been

located and searches for burials of either John or Ann have turned up nothing as yet. However, I did locate a death registration for a John Alexander Graham stating that he died 16 Jul 1983 at Bellsdyke near Larbert. The cause of death was acute myocardial infarction and secondarily ischaemic heart disease. His birth was listed as 24 Jan 1890 which leads me to believe that the coroner or county officials looked up and found the birth info for his older but deceased brother. He was listed as widowed and I am confident that this death registration represents John Alexander Graham (born 1892). Alas, no children or survivors appear on his death registration though it is still a possibility.

Sources

1. Cypress Hills Burial Deed."Plot Northeast 1/4 Lot No. 792, Section 14." Deed executed by David A Graham on 17 Nov 1922.Notation on Register of Internments.
2. The Church of Jesus Christ of Latter-day Saints, International Genealogical Index (R) v5.0, Copyright (c) 1980, 2000, data as of January 2002, 21 Jun 2004, Family History Library, 35 N West Temple Street, Salt Lake City, Utah 84150 USA, 6035516.Batch C112821.
3. State of New York/Dept. of Health/NYC, Death Certificate-Agnes Robb Cuthbert Graham, 14 Apr 2005, 20440.Age was given as 6 May 1858 instead of 1857.
4. State of New York/Dept. of Health/NYC, Death Certificate-Agnes Robb Cuthbert Graham.
5. Cypress Hills Burial Deed.handwritten notes by Robert D. Graham 1/2/1970.
6. Cypress Hills Burial Deed.David A. Graham, residing at 1270 Madison Street, Brooklyn NY.
7. 1900 US Census.rec'd from Ken Doig 5/28/02.
8. General Registry Office Scotland.
9. General Registry Office Scotland.
10. General Registry Office Scotland.
11. General Registry Office of Scotland, *ScotlandsPeople.gov.uk* , 14 Jan 2005.Internet search 1/14/2005.
12. General Registry Office of Scotland, *ScotlandsPeople.gov.uk* , 282/01 0240, 26 Jun 2006."Birth Registration, 2nd District Dundee, page 448.".
13. General Registry Office for Scotlandwww.scotlandspeople.gov.uk, Statutory Register Index Deaths (1855-1951), 14 Jan 2005, 282/10149."Georgina Nicoll WATSON Death Year 1873, sex F, Age 1, District St. Peter Dundee.".
14. General Registry Office for Scotland; www.scotlandspeople.gov.uk, Statutory Register Index Births (1855-1902), 28 Jan 2004, 282/010399.
15. Sheila (Graham) Rattray, Personal Communication, 30 Mar 2004."I won't attempt to answer your queries until I have had time to study it more thoroughly, but must tell you something quite exciting - to me at least! I am somewhat of a hoarder, and I have found a letter from my Auntie Nan, i.e. Agnes Graham, my father's sister. She married a widower, Frank Fairweather, on 5th November, 1949, in Glasgow, and they lived in Newport, Fife. They had no family, although he had children from his first marriage."email dated 3/30/2004.
16. Doig website http:doig.net, 11 May 2006.found on doig.net website.
17. Peter Walker, Hollyer One Name Study.http://www.hollyer.info/tng/getperson.php?personID=I00581&tree=hol.

Death Registration for Duncan Henry Malcolm Graham. His younger brother John lived in Bridge of Allan and may have offspring though none located as yet.

Headstone for John Harland and Annie Elizabeth Graham

Eighth Generation

159. **David Alma GRAHAM** (David Alma GRAHAM, James Campbell GRAHAM, Alexander GRAHAM, Robert GRAHAM, Alexander GRAHAM, Robert GRAHAM, James) was born on 26 Jan 1888 in Brooklyn, Kings County, NY, USA. He died on 18 Aug 1955 in Ridgewood, Queens, NY, USA. The cause of death was Acute myocardial infarction (heart attack). He was buried[1] 20 Aug 1955 in Cypress Hills Cemetery, Glendale, NY.

Went to Pratt Institute (1908-1909, major - Science Technology) and then went to work for NYC public school system in 1914. Was industrial arts (shop teacher) schoolteacher in NY City Public Schools PS 93, Houston Street. In 1920 US census, David and Emma were living on 1723 Putnam Avenue, Brooklyn. David was close to the principal of his school. He retired at age 60 (1948). For 12 years he taught day school (8-3 pm) returned home at 4 pm, napped, had dinner at 5:30 then went back into the city again from 7-10 pm to teach night school. Did this to earn extra money. Wrote a manual (six or seven books) on industrial arts that were used in the public school system. During WW2 worked at Laguardia Airport on some job that son Bob cannot remember.

In 1920 US census, David and Emma were living on 1723 Putnam Avenue, Brooklyn. His first (and self-published) manual on sheet metal working (1924) listed his address as 1724 George Street, Brooklyn, NY. This house was owned until his wife Emma's death in 1978, a tenure of at least 54 years! He was a quiet, intelligent man, though when he spoke, people listened. His brother in law Robert Schwarz worked for Chemical Bank and learned about investments. David used his advice and invested in numerous 'blue-chip' companies which was part of his estate when he died. Emma held on to these stocks until she passed away in 1978.

Had heart attack at age 62 (1950) and a subsequent attack at 67 at which time he died.

David & Emma, ca 1915.

David married **Emma Frances SCHWARZ** daughter of **Heinrich SCHWARZ** and **Barbara FAAS** on 25 Nov 1914 in Brooklyn, NY. Emma was born on 3 Aug 1893 in Brooklyn, NY, USA. She died on 21 Apr 1978 in Ridgewood, NY and was buried[2] on 26 Apr 1978 in Cypress Hills Cemetery, Glendale, NY, USA. From a booklet "Our Family History", Emma Frances Schwarz was born at 1457 DeKalb Avenue, Brooklyn, NY. Oldest of three siblings. She was proud of her German heritage and used to make potato pancakes with applesauce. Loved sweets.

David and Emma had the following children:

+ 204 M i. **Robert David GRAHAM** was born on 6 Jan 1921. He died on 16 Oct 2004.
+ 205 M ii. **Charles James GRAHAM** was born on 12 May 1929. He died on 12 Nov 1990.

162. **George Forbes GRAHAM** (David Alma GRAHAM, James Campbell GRAHAM, Alexander GRAHAM, Robert GRAHAM, Alexander GRAHAM, Robert GRAHAM, James) was born on 7 Aug 1892 in Brooklyn, NY. He died on 17 Jun 1972 in Hempstead, Nassau, NY. He was buried in Long Island National Cemetery, Farmingdale NY.

Was a veteran of WWI (Army Infantry), received the Purple Heart due to shrapnel taken in the shoulder. The shrapnel could not be removed, purportedly because it was too close to an artery. Insurance underwriter with Metropolitan Insurance for 45 years.

George married **Lenora WIRTH** on 5 Jun 1920 in Brooklyn NY. Lenora, or Ora, was born on 31 Jan 1896 in Liberty PA. She died on 15 Aug 1971 in Centereach, Suffolk, NY and was buried in Long Island National Cemetery, Farmingdale NY.

They had the following children:

+ 206 Mi. **George Charles GRAHAM MD** was born on 9 May 1921. He died on 8 Oct 1996.

+ 207 Fii. **Ruth Lenora GRAHAM** was born on 27 Jul 1925.

L to R. unknown woman, David Graham, wife Emma, George Graham and wife Ora, ca 1942

165. **William Melville GRAHAM** (Charles Iconaclast Bradlauch GRAHAM, James Campbell GRAHAM, Alexander GRAHAM, Robert GRAHAM, Alexander GRAHAM, Robert GRAHAM, James) was born on 14 Apr 1889 in Dundee, Angus Scotland. He died on 30 Jan 1961 in Thornhill, Dumfries & Galloway, Scotland. He was buried in Lanark, Lanark, Scotland.

Was probably named after William Melville, grocer of Hawkhill who was married to Margaret Watson daughter of James Watson. Worked for Prudential Insurance Company although his marriage certificate stated that he was a laundry van driver at that early age. Died in the home of son Charles & wife Ethel, Thornhill, Dumfries in Jan. 1961. Death was due to 'a huge growth removed from his abdomen which resulted in a colostomy.' Charlie and Ethel agreed to take care of him with Ethel providing most of the care.

William married[3] **Helen Kilpatrick LYON** daughter of William LYON and Christina Cameron KILPATRICK on 4 Nov 1910 in Lanark, Lanark, Scotland. Helen was born in 1882. She died on 25 Mar 1976 in Lanark, Lanark, Scotland.

Marriage entry in Lanark states Helen's age as 28 (while William was 21), suggesting her birth in 1882. "Was carrying twin boys but one died before Charlie was born" [source: email from Sheila (Graham) Rattray 4/7/2004]

William and Helen had the following child:

+ 208 Mi. **Charles Lord GRAHAM** was born on 6 Sep 1911. He died on 5 May 2000.

167. **David Soutar GRAHAM** (Charles Iconaclast Bradlauch GRAHAM, James Campbell GRAHAM, Alexander GRAHAM, Robert GRAHAM, Alexander GRAHAM, Robert GRAHAM, James) was born[4] on 24 Jan 1893 in Dundee, Angus Scotland. He died on 19 May 1965 in Arrochar, Argyll, Scotland. He was buried in Arrochar, Argyll, Scotland.

"...David as I've suggested was an unusual man, and also an iconoclast of sorts! He was fiercely nationalistic, desperate for Scottish Independence, separate from the rest of the United Kingdom, and greatly irritated my mother, a southern Irish Protestant, loyal to the Royal Family, when he wrote regularly to the local newspaper signing off - Yours for Scotland, Sandy McIntosh." [Source: email of 3/8/2004 from Sheila (Graham) Rattray]

"Grace, David's partner, is no longer alive. She was known as Mrs Grace Graham, although Meg, David's wife, would never agree to a divorce. Uncle David owned an advertising agency in Dundee, and was both astute and politically active. One wonders if he inherited those traits from his grandfather James. I have just lent Donald a booklet written by David entitled "100 Home Rule Questions Answered by Sandy McIntosh". It says in the preface that it was republished in 1966 after his death with the permission of Mrs. Graham (Grace) . He wrote a second book "England's Vassal State." You know which poor downtrodden country that is! The last time I saw him was at Auntie Nan's funeral, resplendent in kilt and sandals, his dark curly hair turning grey, but he departed immediately after the service - rather sad; I would have liked to talk to this "outcast." Neither Maureen nor Donald ever knew him. My Dad (Chas.) used to meet him for coffee in Dundee and attended his funeral in Arrochar. Dad came home bowled over by the charms of Grace whom he had never met before. Wonder if their son Donald has M.B.Ch.B. after his name?" [Source: email of 4/7/2004 from Sheila (Graham) Rattray]

David married **Margaret Gardiner BRAND** daughter of Andrew Wishart BRAND and Ann Sturrock WALKER on 15 Apr 1916 in Dundee, Angus Scotland. Margaret was born on 29 May 1890 in Arbroath, Angus, Scotland. She died 15 Jan 1965 living at 4 Garland Place in Dundee. Witness to her death was her son Ken Graham who's address was listed as 19 Penrith Avenue, Sale, Cheshire. Family lore suggests that "Meg" would not grant David a divorce so that he could never marry his ultimate companion – Grace Winter.

David and Margaret had the following child:

209 Mi. **Kenneth GRAHAM** was born in 1920 in Arbroath, Angus, Scotland. According to Don Graham (#210), he visited his half-brother Kenneth around 1956-57 when Kenneth lived in Salford near Manchester where he was a manager in a chemical company. A very recent inquiry initiated by Ros Barclay and followed up by me was with Audrey Graham, Ken's second wife. She informed us that Ken died 3 Jan 2007. Unfortunately, Audrey was neither pleased nor interested in the Graham family history and was unwilling to disclose information about herself, Ken or his children other than to write "Ken was an intensely private and contained man and I doubt very much that he would have welcomed your contact." Purportedly he had a son Stewart Richard Graham and a daughter (who may have been adopted but this is unconfirmed.)

David was not married to **Grace Coupar WINTER** "Sissy" daughter of Thomas Neilson WINTER and Margaret Jane KIRK. Grace was born on 12 Jan 1912 in Coupar Angus, Angus, Scotland. She died[5] on 25 Feb 2002 in Newport-on-Tay, Fife, Scotland. She was buried in Arrochar, Argyll, Scotland.

"Grace Coupar Winter (Graham) was born January 24, 1912 in, I believe, Coupar Angus (in what was then the county of Angus, and is now in Tayside Region). She died February 25, 2002 at Seymour Nursing Home, 111 Tay Street, Newport-on-Tay, Fife DD6 8AR. Until she was 84, she looked and acted much younger than her age, but became seriously ill, requiring surgery. As sometimes happens with elderly patients, the anesthetic did permanent brain damage, and she suffered thereafter from severe dementia, which became progressively worse. When she died at age 90, she looked 110, and there was essentially no mind left. It was difficult to see her like that, since I knew her as a strong, intelligent, energetic woman, astute in business, with a quirky sense of humour, which seems to have been passed on to Nicole through me." [Source: son Don Graham, 2007]

Mary and Charles Graham

David and Grace had the following child:

+ 210 M ii. **Donald Malcolm GRAHAM** was born on 6 Apr 1938.

169. **Charles GRAHAM** (Charles Iconaclast Bradlauch GRAHAM, James Campbell GRAHAM, Alexander GRAHAM, Robert GRAHAM, Alexander GRAHAM, Robert GRAHAM, James) was born[6] on 10 Nov 1895 in Dundee, Angus Scotland. He died[7] on 20 Sep 1979 in Dumfries, Dumfries, Scotland.

Second Charles born to Charles IB GRAHAM and his second wife Agnes Dickson Soutar. At birth, family was living at 306 Perth Road, Dundee. Was witness to his father's death certificate of 18 Dec 1945 and listed as living on Hillcrest, Hill Street, Monifieth. Was church organist, town councilor, and insurance agent.

Charles married **Mary Constance FOX** on 7 Jul 1924 in, County Wicklow, Ireland.

They had the following children:

+ 211 F i. **Sheila GRAHAM** was born on 19 Jul 1926.

212 M ii. **Gordon Richard Bradlaw GRAHAM** was born in 1930. He died on 31 Aug 1932 in Dundee, Angus, Scotland. The cause of death was brain tumor. He was buried on 2 Sep 1932 in Western Cemetery, Dundee, Angus, Scotland.

213 F iii. **Maureen GRAHAM** was born on 30 Dec 1933 in Dundee, Angus, Scotland.

+ 214 M iv. **Donald Charles GRAHAM** was born on 15 Jul 1938.

172. **Mary Ann GRAHAM** (Mary Ann GRAHAM, John GRAHAM, Alexander GRAHAM, Robert GRAHAM, Alexander GRAHAM, Robert GRAHAM, James) was born on 27 Nov 1873 in Montrose, Angus, Scotland. She died[8] in 1955 in Christchurch, New Zealand. Mary married **Decimus ROWE** son of Samuel Henry ROWE and Mary Anne JONES on 23 Mar 1899 in Wellington, New Zealand. Decimus was born on 27 Aug 1875 in Christchurch, New Zealand. He died on 21 Sep 1946 in Wellington and was buried[9] 24 Sep 1946 in Karori Cemetery, Wellington, New Zealand. Source: Birthdate and death date from Lyn

Winkel's tree on GenesReunited, 27 Oct 2009. NZ BMD site suggests his death was registered in 1946. Decimus was convicted of embezzling from his employer in 1905 and sentenced to 12 months hard labor.

Decimus and Mary had five children:

+ 215 F i. **Ethel Inez ROWE** was born in 1900. She died on 27 Jul 1980.

216 Mii. **Charles Francis ROWE** was born on 10 Mar 1901 in New Zealand. He died on 25 Oct 1994 in New Zealand. He was buried on 4 Nov 1994 in Akatawara Cemetery, Upper Hutt, New Zealand. Charles married **Marjorie Rowsell WAINWRIGHT** in 1926 in Wellington, New Zealand. Marjorie was born about 1901. She died on 3 Oct 1995 in Upper Hutt, New Zealand. She was buried on 20 Oct 1995 in Akatawara Cemetery, Upper Hutt, New Zealand.

217 Miii. **Henry Graham ROWE** was born on 7 Nov 1904 in New Zealand. He died[10] on 1 Sep 1977 in New Zealand. The cause of death was myocardial infarction. Henry married **Greta Mary HOPPER**.

218 Miv. **Sidney Eric ROWE** was born on 21 Dec 1911 in Wellington, New Zealand. He died on 3 Jul 1997 in Dunedin, Otago, New Zealand. He was buried on 7 Jul 1997 in Green Park, Waldronville, Otago, New Zealand. Retired drainage inspector. Sidney married **Ethel Friday MCKAY** in Dunedin, Otago, New Zealand. Ethel was born about 1916 in Dunedin, Otago, New Zealand. She died on 29 Nov 1994 in Dunedin, Otago, New Zealand. She was buried on 2 Dec 1994 in Green Park, Waldronville, Otago, New Zealand.

219 Fv. **Lottie Joan (aka Paddy) ROWE** was born in 1921 in New Zealand.

> Death cert for Decimus Rowe indicates five children; two daughters and three sons. The youngest daughter's age is listed as 25 at time of death suggesting a birthdate in 1921.

188. **Louisa Carter STEWART** (Amelia GRAHAM, John GRAHAM, Alexander GRAHAM, Robert GRAHAM, Alexander GRAHAM, Robert GRAHAM, James) was born in 1887 in New Zealand. She died in 1945 in New Zealand. Louisa married **John DALZELL** in 1906 in New Zealand. They had at least one child:

220 Mi. **Howard DALZELL** was born in 4 Aug 1906 in Wanganui, New Zealand.

Sources

1. Cypress Hills Burial Deed.

2. Cypress Hills Burial Deed.

3. General Registry Office of Scotland, *ScotlandsPeople.gov.uk* , 11 Jan 2004. District of Lanark, County of Lanark, p 32.

4. General Registry Office for Scotland - www.scotlandspeople.gov.uk, Statutory Register Index Births, 30 Jan 2004, 282/01 0768.

5. Donald M. Graham, Email dated 23 Jul 2006. "I was born April 6, 1938, at 166 Perth Road, Dundee, the home of my grandparents, Thomas and Margaret Winter.".

6. General Registry Office for Scotland - www.scotlandspeople.gov.uk.birth registration for Charles Graham recorded 29 Nov 1895. Birth listed as 10 Nov 1895.

7. Maureen Graham, Personal Communication, "Dear David, I had a phone call this evening from Barrie Jack wondering if I could help you find relatives - yes, of course I can! You've found one! I am a daughter of Charles Graham,(born 10 November,1895, not April) insurance manager, town councillor, church organist etc. Dad died on 20 September, 1979. Charles Iconoclast Bradlaugh Graham was my grandfather. I am single and retired." [Email 4 Feb 2004 from Maureen Graham to David Graham.]

Headstone for David A. Graham and wife Emma F. (Schwarz) Graham, Cypress Hills Cemetery, Brooklyn NY

Ninth Generation

204.**Robert David GRAHAM** (David Alma GRAHAM, David Alma GRAHAM, James Campbell GRAHAM, Alexander GRAHAM, Robert GRAHAM, Alexander GRAHAM, Robert GRAHAM, James) was born[1] on 6 Jan 1921 in Ridgewood, Queens, NY, USA. He died on 16 Oct 2004 in Chesapeake, Norfolk, Virginia. The cause of death was Kidney & heart failure.

Aug 1944

According to his own recollection Bob Graham was named after his mother Emma's brother, Robert, and his father, David. The reason that he was not named David Robert Graham had something to do with his father's discomfort with the Hebrew origins of the name DAVID (which is unfortunate as there are several David's in early Scottish royalty!). Was born by mid-wife at 1723 Putnam Avenue, Ridgewood, NY.

Education

Richmond Hill HS (played football, basketball and baseball, the latter with Phil Rizzuto of NY Yankee fame)

Pratt Institute May 1942, Mechanical Engineering (four years of varsity basketball and baseball)

Career

General Electric 1942-1944

U. S. Navy, 1944-1946, reported aboard LCI 480

General Electric, 1946-1980, Engineering, Marketing & General Mgmt positions in many business units living in

Bridgeport, CT (1953-1956), Providence, RI (1956-1959), Louisville, KY (1959-1962), Providence, RI (1962-1964),

Wayne, NJ (1964-1973), Frankfurt, IL (1973-1980)

Died of kidney failure & congestive heart failure 16 Oct 2004, the 61st anniversary of his wedding to Dorothy Bachman, the love of his life.

Memorial statement by David L. Graham on 16 Oct 2004.

"I knew him as Uncle Bob, and it was he that helped start me on my Graham family history quest back in 2001. He was a tall man, athletic in his youth and an avid golfer until late in life. He was a successful engineer and executive with General Electric over a 36 year career that was interrupted by service in the US Navy during WWII.

Perhaps the most important aspect of his life was his deep and abiding love for his wife Dorothy who died before him in 1994. In an act of grace or strange coincidence (I think it is the former), Bob died on what would have been the 61st anniversary of his wedding to Dorothy (16 Oct 1943, Bridgeport Connecticut). The strength of this love was palpable and matched only by his love of his two daughters Linda and Barbara. He was also devoted to his family – his parents and his younger brother Chuck (my dad) who also preceded him in death in 1990.

From my perspective, Bob was the patriarch of my branch of the Graham family, a mantle he wore proudly and well. One of my great pleasures over the past few years was sharing all my findings about our Graham ancestry, quizzing him about any remembrances and getting him to share his own stories. Most recently, Barbara had printed out the DAGers Digest Vol. 6 that covered my trip to Brooklyn and shared it with Bob who then called me to thank me for the effort to revisit the place of his youth. Our conversation was cut short when he ran out of breath but I will always know that he enjoyed reading about my family history studies."

Robert married **Dorothy E. BACHMAN** daughter of Julius BACHMAN and Esther WINBERG on 16 Oct 1943 in Bridgeport, CT. Dorothy was born on 4 Mar 1922 in Bridgeport, CT. She died of heart failure on 21 May 1994 in Virginia Beach, VA. They had the following children:

+ 221 F i. **Linda Carol GRAHAM** was born on 13 May 1948.

222 Fii. **Barbara Lee GRAHAM** was born on 7 Apr 1952 in Bridgeport, CT.

Barbara married **William Terry PATE** on 28 May 1993 in Chesapeake, VA. Terry was born on 20 Oct 1957 in Conway, SC.

Barb & Terry, 2007

205.**Charles James GRAHAM** "Chuck" (David Alma GRAHAM, David Alma GRAHAM, James Campbell GRAHAM, Alexander GRAHAM, Robert GRAHAM, Alexander GRAHAM, Robert GRAHAM, James) was born on 12 May 1929 in Brooklyn, NY. He died on 12 Nov 1990 in Marietta, GA. The cause of death was Acute myocardial infarction/ruptured hemorrhagic plaque. He was buried[2] on 16 Nov 1990 in Arlington Cemetery Sandy Springs, GA.

Probably named after a son of his grandparents that died in infancy. The 1900 census lists Charles (age 1) living in the Graham household on Hope St. in Brooklyn NY. He was calm, thoughtful, friendly, intelligent and upbeat. Caddies at Pittsfield Country Club jokingly referred to him as "Smilin' Chuck" a testament to his good humor and positive demeanor on the golf course. He was a man of strong but quiet faith and had many volunteer activites in addition to a successful career as a business executive in the electrical equipment and telecommunications industries.

Education & Career

Mechanical Engineer, BSE, Pratt Institute 1949
General Electric, Technical Marketing Program, Transformers, Lightening Arresters, Protective Equipment Products 1953-1974
Northeast Electronics (unit of Northern Telecom USA) 1975-1978
Northern Telecom, Group Vice President 1978-1981
Orion Group, consulting 1981
Contel, Group VP 1982-1985
Audichron, President 1985-1989

Charles married **Marilyn Louise LAFRANCE** daughter of Leon Henry LAFRANCE and Alice Mae MCWITHEY on 9 Jun 1951 in Scotia, NY. Marilyn was born on 8 Aug 1928 in Schenectady, NY.

They had the following children:

+ 223 Mi. **David Lee GRAHAM** was born on 4 Oct 1956.

+ 224 Fii. **Nancy Lynn GRAHAM** was born on 14 Mar 1961.

206.**George Charles GRAHAM MD** (George Forbes GRAHAM, David Alma GRAHAM, James Campbell GRAHAM, Alexander GRAHAM, Robert GRAHAM, Alexander GRAHAM, Robert GRAHAM, James) was born on 9 May 1921 in Brooklyn NY. He died[3] 8 Oct 1996 in Hempstead, Nassau NY. He was buried on 11 Oct 1996 in Cutchogue Cemetery, Cutchogue NY.

Head of Polio at Meadowbrook

George married **Muriel Elsie HUENE MD** on 23 Jun 1945 in Bellrose Village, NY. Muriel was born on 19 Sep 1921 in Lakeview, Nassau, NY. She died on 22 Oct 2005 in Cutchogue, NY. She was buried in Cutchogue, NY.

They had the following children:

    225 F i. **Heather GRAHAM** was born on 19 Apr 1950 in Mineola, NY. She died on 5 Aug 1982 in West Hempstead, NY, USA. The cause of death was complications from diabetes.

  + 226 Fii. **Lorna Nancy GRAHAM** was born on 18 Apr 1954.

    227 Miii. **George Charles GRAHAM** was born on 1 Jul 1957 in Mineola, NY.

207. **Ruth Lenora GRAHAM** (George Forbes GRAHAM, David Alma GRAHAM, James Campbell GRAHAM, Alexander GRAHAM, Robert GRAHAM, Alexander GRAHAM, Robert GRAHAM, James) was born on 27 Jul 1925 in Woodhaven, Queens, NY. She died 12 Sep 2010 in Leesburg, FL.

> According to Ruth, she was born on Elderts Lane, near the Cypress Hills Cemetery. She was christened in a United Presbyterian Church (8815 86th Street, Woodhaven, NY) but, because her mother was Lutheran, she was confirmed in a Lutheran Church.

Ruth married **Edmund FULLER** on 11 Nov 1944 in Queens Village, Queens, New York, USA. Edmund was born on 6 Jun 1923 in Brooklyn NY. He died on 27 May 1997 in Tampa, FL.

They had the following children:

+ 228 F i. **Diane FULLER** was born on 11 Oct 1945.

+ 229 Fii. **Jean FULLER** was born on 29 Aug 1947.

208. **Charles Lord GRAHAM** "Charlie" (William Melville GRAHAM, Charles Iconaclast Bradlauch GRAHAM, James Campbell GRAHAM, Alexander GRAHAM, Robert GRAHAM, Alexander GRAHAM, Robert GRAHAM, James) was born on 6 Sep 1911 in Lanark, Lanark, Scotland. He died[4] on 5 May 2000 in Lanark, Lanark, Scotland.

> According to Sheila Graham, Charlie did not like his middle name Lord and changed it to Lyon, the surname of his mother. "Her (Ethel) husband Charlie built and drove his own racing cars as a hobby. He and his father Uncle Willie both worked for the Prudential Insurance Company. Ronald (before he met me) remembers his father, also in the Prudential, commenting every month "Those Grahams again!" They always topped the list for finding new business. You may be interested to know that Helen, Charlie's mother, was carrying twin boys but one died before Charlie was born." [SOURCE: email from Sheila (Graham) Rattray 4/7/2004]

Charles married **Elizabeth Ethel ECCLESTON** daughter of Arthur ECCLESTON on 29 Apr 1938 in Lanark, Lanark, Scotland. Elizabeth was born[5] on 10 Oct 1914 in Glasgow, Lanark, Scotland. She died on 17 May 2006 in Lanark, Lanark, Scotland.

> Have just been talking to cousin Charlie's widow, Ethel, a delightful person who will be ninety on 10th October - still very alert and capable. Her maiden name was Elizabeth Ethel Eccleston, daughter of Arthur Eccleston, a customs officer from London who came to work in Glasgow where Ethel was born. She remembers Grandpa Charles I.B. as a "bit of a card" and was very pleased when he asked if she would give him a run in the car she was learning to drive as a teenager.

Charles and Ethel had the following children:

+ 230 F i. **Agnes Helen GRAHAM** was born on 24 Jul 1940.

231 F ii. **Jean Arthur GRAHAM, "Jeanine"** was born on 27 Aug 1946. She changed her name to Jeanine shortly after college while living on the Isle of Jersey. Jeanine married **Nicos TOMBRAS** on 27 Jul 1984 in Greece.

185. **Donald Malcolm GRAHAM** (David Soutar GRAHAM, Charles Iconaclast Bradlauch GRAHAM, James Campbell GRAHAM, Alexander GRAHAM, Robert GRAHAM, Alexander GRAHAM, Robert GRAHAM, James) was born[6] on 6 Apr 1938 in Dundee, Angus, Scotland. Donald married **Melinda LEE** on 3 May 1974 in Vancouver, BC, Canada. The marriage ended in divorce.

They had the following child:

233 F i. **Nicole Choei-Lin GRAHAM** was born on 23 Feb 1984 in Vancouver, BC, Canada.

Donald then married[7] **Mary Louise WILSON** on 11 May 1992 in Vancouver, BC, Canada but this union also did not last.

Nicole & Don Graham, March 2007, Seattle WA

Nicole was a willing model in Apr 2007 for my armrest business which sold adjustable armrests to medical clinics and tattoo artists. We searched high and low for women with interesting tattoos and overall style, yet Nicole proved to be the most intriguing model of all. Thank you Nicole for your grace and beauty. I still chuckle that my third cousin proved to be my 'best' model!

Grahams o' the Mearns

211. **Sheila GRAHAM** (Charles GRAHAM, Charles Iconaclast Bradlauch GRAHAM, James Campbell GRAHAM, Alexander GRAHAM, Robert GRAHAM, Alexander GRAHAM, Robert GRAHAM, James) was born on 19 Jul 1926 in Maidstone, Kent, England. Sheila married **Ronald RATTRAY** on 11 Oct 1951 in Monifieth, Angus Scotland. Ronald was born on 8 Apr 1927 in Carnoustie, Angus, Scotland.

Ronald and Sheila on their wedding day 1951

They had the following children:

+ 234 F i. **Rosalyn Mary RATTRAY** was born on 16 Jul 1953.

+ 235 Fii. **Joy Alexandra RATTRAY** was born on 20 Apr 1956.

+ 236 Miii. **Howard John Charles RATTRAY** was born on 10 Nov 1961.

214. **Donald Charles GRAHAM** (Charles GRAHAM, Charles Iconaclast Bradlauch GRAHAM, James Campbell GRAHAM, Alexander GRAHAM, Robert GRAHAM, Alexander GRAHAM, Robert GRAHAM, James) was born on 15 Jul 1938. Donald married **Wilma Breathwood GIBB** on 19 Dec 1964 in Dundee, Angus, Scotland. Wilma was born on 25 Aug 1943 in Dundee, Angus, Scotland. They had the following children:

+ 237 F i. **Laura GRAHAM** was born on 27 Oct 1965.

+ 238 Fii. **Jane GRAHAM** was born[8] on 5 Jan 1967 in Dundee, Angus, Scotland. Jane married Anthony CARACCIOLO on 22 Jun 2008 in Reading, Surrey, UK.

239 Fiii. **Kirstin GRAHAM** was born[9] on 25 Jul 1970 in Perth, Perthshire, Scotland and currently resides in Sydney, NSW, Australia

+ 240 Fiv. **Claire GRAHAM** was born on 29 Mar 1977.

215. **Ethel Inez ROWE** (Mary Ann GRAHAM, Mary Ann GRAHAM, John GRAHAM, Alexander GRAHAM, Robert GRAHAM, Alexander GRAHAM, Robert GRAHAM, James) was born in 1900 in New Zealand. She died on 27 Jul 1980 in Masterton, New Zealand. Ethel married **Albert John SIDEY** on 26 Dec 1923 in Wellington, New Zealand. Albert was born in 1884. He died in 1935. They had the following children:

241 F i. **Denzel Molly SIDEY** was born in 1924 in New Zealand. Denzel married (1) **Percy MILLAR**. Denzel then married (2) **Frank PAYNE**.

242 Mii. **Rodney Graham SIDEY** was born in 1926 in New Zealand. He died in 2000 in New Zealand. Rodney married **Angela**.

+ 243 Fiii. **Yvonne Ngaire SIDEY** was born in 1930. She died of acute myeloid leukemia in Wellington New Zealand in 1986.

Sources

1. City of New York, Dept. of Health, Bureau of Records."Certificate of Birth.".born at 1723 Putnam Ave. Ridgewood, Borough of Queens.
2. David Graham, Personal knowledge.
3. Soc Sec Death Index.
4. Sheila (Graham) Rattray, Personal Communication, 7 Apr 2004.email dated 4/7/2004.
5. Sheila (Graham) Rattray, Personal Communication, 7 Apr 2004.
6. Donald M. Graham, Email dated 23 Jul 2006.
7. Donald M. Graham, Email dated 23 Jul 2006.
8. Sheila (Graham) Rattray, Personal Communication.
9. Sheila (Graham) Rattray, Personal Communication.

The Donald Graham family, summer 2008. Jane, Kirstin, Tony Caracciolo, Alice, Donald, Grace, Wilma, Laura, Molly, Scott Witchalls, Lily, Claire and Steve Simon.

Chuck & Dave Graham teeing off at #1 Country Club of Pittsfield, ca 1965.

Tenth Generation

235.   **Linda Carol GRAHAM** (Robert David Graham, David Alma Graham, David Alma Graham, James Campbell Graham, Alexander Graham, Robert Graham, Alexander Graham, Robert Graham, James) was born on 13 May 1948 in Bridgeport, CT.

Linda married Thomas Bradley on 14 Jun 1969 in Wayne, NJ. They had the following child:

+ 270   M i.   **Kenneth Bradley** was born on 25 Feb 1973.

Taylor with grandparents Linda and Tom Bradley

237.   **David Lee GRAHAM** (Charles James Graham, David Alma Graham, David Alma Graham, James Campbell Graham, Alexander Graham, Robert Graham, Alexander Graham, Robert Graham, James) was born on 4 Oct 1956 in Pittsfield, MA. He was christened on 12 May 1957 in First Congregational Church, Pittsfield, MA. David married **Jane Ellen Harbaugh** daughter of Elbert Kermit Harbaugh and Catherine Ryall Winters on 10 Sep 1983 in Mountainside, NY. Jane was born on 12 Nov 1957 in New York, NY.   They had the following children:

271   M i.   **Connor David GRAHAM** was born on 7 Aug 1989 in Seattle, WA. He was christened in May 1995 in Mt. Baker Park Pres Ch, Seattle WA.

272   M ii.   **Charles James GRAHAM** was born on 23 Jul 1991 in Seattle, WA. He was christened in May 1995 in Mt. Baker Park Pres Ch, Seattle WA. Named after his grandfather Charles James GRAHAM who died in November 1990 at the time CJ was conceived.

CJ, Jane, Connor & Dave Graham, Aug 2010

238.   **Nancy Lynn GRAHAM** (Charles James Graham, David Alma Graham, David Alma Graham, James Campbell Graham, Alexander Graham, Robert Graham, Alexander Graham, Robert Graham, James) was born on 14 Mar 1961 in Pittsfield, MA. She was christened in First Congregational Church, Pittsfield, MA.

Nancy first married **Richard Brian Barker** son of Richard L. Barker and Margaret Mary Danic on 24 Sep 1994 in Atlanta, GA. The marriage ended in divorce. Richard was born on 14 Feb 1954 in Detroit, MI. They had the following children:

273   M   i.   **Chase Riley BARKER** was born on 10 Sep 1998 in Atlanta, GA. He was christened on 29 Nov 1998 in Atlanta, GA.

274   M   ii.   **Kyle Danic BARKER** was born on 10 Sep 1998 in Atlanta, GA. He was christened on 29 Nov 1998 in Atlanta, GA

Kyle, Nancy, Bob and Chase Sep 2011

Nancy remarried, this time to **Dr. Robert Hamilton** on 16 Oct 2008 in Atlanta, Fulton, Georgia.

240.   **Lorna Nancy Graham** (George Charles Graham, George Forbes Graham, David Alma Graham, James Campbell Graham, Alexander Graham, Robert Graham, Alexander Graham, Robert Graham, James) was born on 18 Apr 1954 in Mineola, NY.

Lorna is partnered with Kenneth Jonathon Brophy. Kenneth was born on 30 May 1951 in Rahway, NJ, USA.

They had the following child:

   275   M i.   **Connor George GRAHAM** was born on 25 Oct 1997 in Scranton, PA, USA.

   242.   **Diane FULLER** (Ruth Lenora Graham, George Forbes Graham, David Alma Graham, James Campbell Graham, Alexander Graham, Robert Graham, Alexander Graham, Robert Graham, James) was born on 11 Oct 1945 in Jamaica Queens, Queens NY. Diane married **Neil Lamparter** on 25 Jul 1965 in Mineola, NY. The marriage ended in divorce.

They had the following child:

   276   M i.   **Neil Roger Lamparter** was born on 5 May 1966 in Bethpage, NY.

   243.   **Jean FULLER** (Ruth Lenora Graham, George Forbes Graham, David Alma Graham, James Campbell Graham, Alexander Graham, Robert Graham, Alexander Graham, Robert Graham, James) was born on 29 Aug 1947 in Queens Village, Queens NY. Jean married **William Lamparter** on 30 May 1971 in Huntington, NY. They had the following children:

   277   M i.   **Sean Lamparter** was born on 29 Dec 1975 in Syosset, NY.

+ 278   F ii.   **Dana Lamparter** was born on 18 Jun 1979.

   244.   **Agnes Helen GRAHAM** "Nan" (Charles Lord Graham, William Melville Graham, Charles Iconaclast Bradlauch Graham, James Campbell Graham, Alexander Graham, Robert Graham, Alexander Graham, Robert Graham, James) was born on 24 Jul 1940 in Thornhill, Dumfries & Galloway, Scotland. Born at home in Thornhill according to Ethel Graham (letter January 2005)

Nan first married **Frederick Harvey SMAIL** on 2 Oct 1964. The marriage ended in divorce. They had the following children:

+ 279 M i. **Michael Charles SMAIL** was born on 2 Nov 1966.

+ 280 M ii. **Jonathan William SMAIL** was born on 7 May 1968.

281 M iii. **Peter Graham SMAIL** was born on 28 Nov 1975.

Nan remarried, this time to **John HOLROYD** on 6 Oct 1991.

248. **Rosalyn Mary RATTRAY** (Sheila Graham, Charles Graham, Charles Iconaclast Bradlauch Graham, James Campbell Graham, Alexander Graham, Robert Graham, Alexander Graham, Robert Graham, James) was born on 16 Jul 1953 in Horsforth, Yorkshire, England. Rosalyn married **Kenneth Stewart Barclay** on 14 Feb 1975. Kenneth was born on 14 Jan 1952 in Glasgow, Lanark Scotland. They had the following child:

+ 282 F i. **Rona Margaret BARCLAY** was born on 10 Jan 1980.

Ros and Rona Barclay, Nov 2009

249.   **Joy Alexandra RATTRAY** (Sheila Graham, Charles Graham, Charles Iconaclast Bradlauch Graham, James Campbell Graham, Alexander Graham, Robert Graham, Alexander Graham, Robert Graham, James) was born on 20 Apr 1956 in Dumfries, Scotland. Joy married[1] **William Wishart Campbell** on 5 Aug 1978 in Uddingston, Lanark Scotland. William was born on 24 May 1954 in Helensburgh, Dunbartonshire, Scotland.

They had the following children:

283   F   i.   **Rachel Mary CAMPBELL** was born on 26 Aug 1983 in Glasgow, Lanark Scotland.

284   F   ii.   **Sonia Helen CAMPBELL** was born[2] on 2 May 1986 in Glasgow, Lanark Scotland.

Joy, Willie, Sonia and Rachel

250.   **Howard John Charles RATTRAY** (Sheila Graham, Charles Graham, Charles Iconaclast Bradlauch Graham, James Campbell Graham, Alexander Graham, Robert Graham, Alexander Graham, Robert Graham, James) was born on 10 Nov 1961 in Dumfries, Dumfriesshire, Scotland. Howard married **Angela Masterson** on 16 Aug 1990. Angela was born[3] in Glasgow, Lanark, Scotland. They had the following children:

285   F   i.   **Georgia Amy RATTRAY** was born[4] on 25 Sep 1997 in Falkirk, Stirlingshire, Scotland.

286   M   ii.   **Gavin Alexander RATTRAY** was born[5] on 19 May 2000 in Falkirk, Stirlingshire, Scotland.

Alice, Grace and Molly Witchalls, 2009

251. **Laura GRAHAM** (Donald Charles Graham, Charles Graham, Charles Iconaclast Bradlauch Graham, James Campbell Graham, Alexander Graham, Robert Graham, Alexander Graham, Robert Graham, James) was born[6] on 27 Oct 1965 in Dundee, Angus, Scotland. Laura married **Scott Witchalls** 1 Jun 1990. They had the following children:

287	F	i.	**Molly Hannah WITCHALLS** was born on 9 Jan 1995 in Reading, England.
288	F	ii.	**Alice Rose WITCHALLS** was born on 28 Dec 1996 in Reading, England.
289	F	iii.	**Grace Mary WITCHALLS** was born on 11 Jan 2003 in Reading, England.

252. **Jane GRAHAM** (Donald Charles Graham, Charles Graham, Charles Iconaclast Bradlauch Graham, James Campbell Graham, Alexander Graham, Robert Graham, Alexander Graham, Robert Graham, James) was born[7] on 5 Jan 1967 in Dundee, Angus, Scotland. Jane married **Anthony CARACCIOLO** on 22 Jun 2008 in Reading, Surrey, UK.

Jane and Tony with twins Lola and Cruz

They had the following children:

    290   M i.   **Cruz CARACCIOLO** was born on 20 Dec 2009 in Reading, Berkshire, England.

    291   F ii.   **Lola CARACCIOLO** was born on 20 Dec 2009 in Reading, Berkshire, England.

    254.   **Claire GRAHAM** (Donald Charles Graham, Charles Graham, Charles Iconaclast Bradlauch Graham, James Campbell Graham, Alexander Graham, Robert Graham, Alexander Graham, Robert Graham, James) was born[8] on 29 Mar 1977 in Bellshill, Lanark, Scotland. Claire married Steven Simon 14 Aug 2004 in Berwick-upon-Tweed, Northumberland, England.

The Simon Family - Lily, Steve, Brodie & Claire, January 2011

They had the following children:

    292   F   i.   **Lily Eve SIMON** was born on 26 Apr 2007 in Edinburgh, Midlothian, Scotland.

    293   M ii.   **Brodie Donald SIMON** was born on 1 Jan 2011 in Edinburgh, Midlothian, Scotland.

255.   **Denzel Molly SIDEY** (Ethel Inez Rowe, Mary Ann Graham, Mary Ann Graham, John Graham, Alexander Graham, Robert Graham, Alexander Graham, Robert Graham, James) was born in 1924 in New Zealand. Denzel married (1) Percy Millar. They had the following children:

    294   M i.   **Kenneth Albert MILLAR** was born in May 1945.

Denzel married (2) Frank Payne. Frank was born about 1915 in Lower Hutt, New Zealand. He died[9] in 2000 in Lower Hutt, New Zealand.

256.   **Rodney Graham SIDEY** (Ethel Inez Rowe, Mary Ann Graham, Mary Ann Graham, John Graham, Alexander Graham, Robert Graham, Alexander Graham, Robert Graham, James) was born on 18 Feb 1926 in Wellington, New Zealand. He died in 2000 in Papamoa, Bay of Plenty, New Zealand. Rodney married **Mary Angela Byron-Wood**. The marriage ended in divorce. Mary was born on 9 Jun 1921. She died on 19 Feb 1983 in Waihake Island, Auckland, NZ. They had the following children:

295	F	i.	**Sharon Gail SIDEY** was born on 21 Jan 1945.
296	M	ii.	**Kevin Graham SIDEY** was born on 25 Oct 1947 in Lower Hutt, New Zealand. He died in 1979.
297	M	iii.	**Rodney Desmond SIDEY** was born on 11 Dec 1950 in Lower Hutt, New Zealand.
298	M	iv.	**Michael Dennis SIDEY** was born on 1 Jul 1951 in Lower Hutt, New Zealand.
299	M	v.	**Geoffrey Colin SIDEY** was born on 28 Jan 1954 in Lower Hutt, New Zealand.
300	M	vi.	**Keith Robert SIDEY** was born on 25 Aug 1961 in Lower Hutt, New Zealand.

257. **Yvonne Ngaire SIDEY** (Ethel Inez Rowe, Mary Ann Graham, Mary Ann Graham, John Graham, Alexander Graham, Robert Graham, Alexander Graham, Robert Graham, James) was born on 31 Oct 1930 in Wellington, New Zealand. She died on 1 Jun 1987 in Greytown, New Zealand. Yvonne married **Gordon Alister PAYNE**. Gordon was born on 28 Aug 1924 in Lower Hutt, New Zealand. He died on 23 Jun 1996 in Greytown, New Zealand.

They had the following children:

301	M	i.	**Stuart John PAYNE** was born on 25 Mar 1949 in Lower Hutt, New Zealand. Stuart married[10] **Cynthia Marrion Roberts** on 11 Jul 1970 in Christchurch, New Zealand. The marriage ended in divorce. Cynthia was born on 26 Jun 1948 in Australia.
+ 302	F	ii.	**Sandra Alice PAYNE** was born on 17 May 1950.
303	F	iii.	**Susan Decima PAYNE** was born on 17 May 1950 in Lower Hutt, New Zealand. She died on 23 May 1950 in Lower Hutt, New Zealand.
304	F	iv.	**Heather Laureen PAYNE** was born on 12 Dec 1951 in Lower Hutt, New Zealand. Heather married **John William Bowness** on 7 Mar 1970. John was born on 13 Apr 1950.
305	M	v.	**Dean Alistair PAYNE** was born in 1954 in Lower Hutt, New Zealand.

261. **Clive ROWE** (Henry Graham Rowe, Mary Ann Graham, Mary Ann Graham, John Graham, Alexander Graham, Robert Graham, Alexander Graham, Robert Graham, James) was born on 27 Dec 1934 in Wellington, New Zealand. Clive married Faye Brandon in 1964. Faye was born in 1938. They had the following children:

306	M	i.	**Michael Berry ROWE** was born in 1962 in New Zealand.
307	M	ii.	**Perry Martin ROWE** was born in 1964 in New Zealand.
308	M	iii.	**Quentin Wayne ROWE** was born in 1966 in New Zealand.
309	M	iv.	**Steve Manu Clive ROWE** was born in 1969 in New Zealand.
310	F	v.	**Karina Faye ROWE** was born on 13 Nov 1970 in New Zealand.

Sources

1. Joy Alexandra (Rattray) Campbell, Personal communication, email dated 2/13/2004.

2. Joy Alexandra (Rattray) Campbell, Personal communication.

3. Sheila (Graham) Rattray, Personal Communication.

4. Sheila (Graham) Rattray, Personal Communication.

5. Sheila (Graham) Rattray, Personal Communication.

6. Sheila (Graham) Rattray, Personal Communication.

7. Sheila (Graham) Rattray, Personal Communication.

8. Sheila (Graham) Rattray, Personal Communication.

9. Sandra (Payne) Blake, Personal Communication, 22 Nov 2009.

10. Sandra (Payne) Blake, Personal Communication, 22 Nov 2009.

Charles L. Graham racing his own car

Book published by David A. Graham on sheet metal working, resting on a metal storage box made by same.

Chuck Graham with grandson Connor, Sep 1989

Eleventh Generation

270. **Kenneth BRADLEY** (Linda Carol Graham, Robert David Graham, David Alma Graham, David Alma Graham, James Campbell Graham, Alexander Graham, Robert Graham, Alexander Graham, Robert Graham, James) was born on 25 Feb 1973 in Norwood, NJ. Kenneth married Michele Ann Tomicich on 12 Dec 1998 in Colorado Springs, CO. Michele was born on 24 Jan 1969 in Pueblo, CO. They had the following child:

311   F   i.   **Taylor Nicole BRADLEY** was born on 3 Mar 2004 in Denver, Adam, Colorado.

278. **Dana Lamparter** (Jean Fuller, Ruth Lenora Graham, George Forbes Graham, David Alma Graham, James Campbell Graham, Alexander Graham, Robert Graham, Alexander Graham, Robert Graham, James) was born on 18 Jun 1979 in Syosset, NY. She had the following child:

312   F   i.   Lilly was born in Sep 2009.

Dana, Lilly, Ruth (Graham) Fuller, and Jean, ca 2010

279. **Michael Charles SMAIL** (Agnes Helen Graham, Charles Lord Graham, William Melville Graham, Charles Iconaclast Bradlauch Graham, James Campbell Graham, Alexander Graham, Robert

Graham, Alexander Graham, Robert Graham, James) was born on 2 Nov 1966 in Jersey, Channel Islands, England. Michael married Amanda Wright on 31 Dec 2004 in Thornhill, Dumfries & Galloway, Scotland.

They had the following child:

313   F   i.   **Georgia SMAIL** was born on 18 Apr 2007.

280.   **Jonathan William SMAIL** (Agnes Helen Graham, Charles Lord Graham, William Melville Graham, Charles Iconaclast Bradlauch Graham, James Campbell Graham, Alexander Graham, Robert Graham, Alexander Graham, Robert Graham, James) was born on 7 May 1968 in Jersey, Channel Islands, England. Jonathan married (1) Julia Barnes in Aug 1996. The marriage ended in divorce.

They had the following child:

314   M   i.   **Jake Charles SMAIL** was born on 27 Jan 1998.

Jonathan remarried Mairi Brown on 5 Sep 2004. Jonathan and Mairi had the following children:

315   M   ii.   **Finlay SMAIL** was born on 15 Jan 2007.

316   M   iii. **Billy SMAIL** was born on 3 Jun 2008.

282.   **Rona Margaret BARCLAY** (Rosalyn Mary Rattray, Sheila Graham, Charles Graham, Charles Iconaclast Bradlauch Graham, James Campbell Graham, Alexander Graham, Robert Graham, Alexander Graham, Robert Graham, James) was born on 10 Jan 1980 in Glasgow, Lanark Scotland. She had the following child:

317   M   i.   **Craig Kenneth BARCLAY** was born on 8 Apr 1996 in Rutherglen, Lanark, Scotland.

Rona married James Temple 18 Jul 2010.

Ken, Ros and Craig on his 13th birthday

302. **Sandra Alice Payne** (Yvonne Ngaire Sidey, Ethel Inez **ROWE**, Mary Ann Graham, Mary Ann Graham, John Graham, Alexander Graham, Robert Graham, Alexander Graham, Robert Graham, James) was born on 17 May 1950 in Lower Hutt, New Zealand. Sandra married[1] Ian Barry Blake on 15 Nov 1975 in Caterton, New Zealand. Ian was born on 6 Jun 1951 in Caterton, New Zealand.

They had the following children:

318 F i. **Nicola Lee Blake** was born on 30 Aug 1978 in Masterton, NZ.

319 M ii. **Kieran James Blake** was born on 1 Feb 1981 in Masterton, NZ. Kieran married[2] **Sarah-Jane Nesta Cameron** on 14 Mar 2009 in Masterton, New Zealand. Sarah-Jane was born on 24 Feb 1981 in Masterton, New Zealand.

320 M iii. **Brendan Michael Blake** was born on 3 Apr 1983 in Masterton, NZ.

Mary Ann "Molly" Graham #172

Sources

1. Sandra (Payne) Blake, Personal Communication, 22 Nov 2009.
2. Sandra (Payne) Blake, Personal Communication, 7 Feb 2010.

The Graham Girls - Claire, Kirsten, Jane, Laura and Wilma

Where We Came From – Places of Origin

The Mearns – St. Cyrus, Marykirk and Surrounding Parishes

The title of this family history points us toward our earliest origins in the Mearns, or lower Kincardineshire on the north east coast of Scotland a few miles north of Montrose. The Mearns was and remains primarily an agricultural area overlooking the North Sea. Though without formal designation, the area could be said to comprise the parishes of St. Cyrus, Marykirk, Garvock and Benholm, all small villages that served as focal points for the rural, agrarian inhabitants of the area. The river North Esk, which forms its southern border, flows swiftly toward the sea. At one time, on land a little south and west of St. Cyrus, were lands belonging to the Grahams of Morphie. Grahams were granted land around the Montrose Basin and one particular Graham, James Graham the Marquis of Montrose gained fame in the 1640's for his leadership on behalf of King James II against the Covenenters. Early in my research I held out the hope that we might be related to the Great Montrose, who was probably born in Montrose or surrounding area, but further investigations revealed that our lineage cannot be a direct descent from this noble Scot as his sons died without male heirs. It is our misfortune as the Great Montrose, though no favorite of the powerful Scottish Covenanters, was a man of unusual insight, courage, and principle. Though captured, hanged and quartered in 1650, the Marquis now celebrated in St. Giles Cathedral in Edinburgh, would have been a hero in any age so true was he to his principles and the monarchy that he gave his life to its cause.

But let us return to the Mearns where our less noble Graham ancestors can be traced. The North Esk was a place for fishing, especially salmon during the spawning season and later became a source for textile mills which no longer exist. The principal town is St. Cyrus which sits on a high, windswept bluff above the sea. The bluff itself drops to sea level and today this area at the cliff base is a nature preserve filled with sea birds of various types. It also contains a small cemetery that was part of a small kirk now destroyed where many Grahams of Morphie and some of our own ancestors are buried. The crypt for the Grahams of Morphie can be seen in the photo – a tree is growing up out of the crypt today.

Southern Kincardineshire — from a survey in 1774

During my second trip to Scotland in June 2006, Nancy and I spent a day driving up from Dundee to Montrose and St. Cyrus where we visited the Nether Kirk, the Hill of Morphie, Pitbeadlie and Marykirk, the home of our earliest Graham ancestors. From the base of the cliffs, or heughs, at Nether Kirk up the bluff and over to Morphie, Pitbeadlie and westward onto Marykirk is not more than two or three miles in total. The area is nearly all farmland though I didn't ascertain what crops were being grown. Our earliest confirmed ancestor, Alexander Graham (#15) was a cotterman in Pitbeadlie and then Hill of Morphy according to the Old Parish Registers that recorded the baptisms of his nine offspring. Cotterman were tenant farmers who worked larger landholdings in exchange for their own small plots and undoubtedly experienced a meager living. The Statistical Account of Scotland 1834-1835 listed the population of the entire parish at roughly 1,600 people, a number that remained surprisingly constant from the late 1700's through the 1841 census. During this period the main industries were farming, and operations connected with a lime-quarry and valuable salmon fishing along the coast and in the North Esk.

In the 1750's, William Graham, laird of Morphie, was noted for planting clover to feed his horses before becoming a cattleman. He also experimented with other crops such as turnips and became known for his agricultural daring and prowess. He may well have been the benefactor of our own

Grahams by subletting them small portions of the land in exchange for farmwork. Interestingly, this William Graham was not a Graham by birth at all. Instead, he was William BARCLAY of nearby Balmakewan who was granted the land if he retained the Graham name. BARCLAY's mother was a Graham but her brothers died without male heirs and so the deal was struck. The castle of Morphie no longer exists, its stones being carried away to build other houses or field fences. But there is an old Scottish fairy tale of sorts regarding the Kelpy, a seaweed encrusted equine denizen of the deep that lived in the North Esk (and other rivers and streams). According to legend, the kelpy (or kelpie) was 'captured' by the laird of Morphie to move stones from the river to his property for building but was put off by the hard work and put a curse on the laird for his difficult treatment.

> *Sair back and sair banes,*
> *Drivin' the laird o' Morphie's stanes!*
> *The laird o' Morphie'll never thrive*
> *As lang's the kelpy is alive!*

The present-day village of St. Cyrus was originally a combination of three smaller hamlets – Ecclescraig, Roadside and Lochside - that converged when it came time to support a single parish kirk. The village of Marykirk lies to the west of St. Cyrus and a few hundred yards from Pitbeadlie just north of the North Esk. So it came as no surprise that Robert Graham (#39) would have had his illegitimate son Alexander (#55) registered in this parish, and Alexander would ultimately marry and have his family in this same parish. Nancy and I looked at every headstone in the Marykirk cemetery surrounding the local church but found no evidence of Graham relations, much to my dismay.

By the 1841 census, his wife Ann Lindsay and children were south across the river in Logie-Pert where two large mills had been established. According to the 'New' Statistical Account of Scotland [1834-1835], Logie-Pert was said to have had a population of 1,360 in 1831 with 260 families at an average size of 5 per family.

> *The ordinary food of the peasantry is oatmeal, milk and potatoes....there are two manufacturing establishments in the parish, namely those at Logie and Craigo. The Logie works comprise a bleachfield and a flax spinning mill...the number of hands employed varies from 40 to 50...the average working time is eleven hours a day.*

Today, Logie-Pert is nothing more than a few small homes that would hardly be classified as a farming village or hamlet. The mills, of course, are long gone.

Pitbeadlie, view looking west toward Woods of Canter, Jun 2006.

Forfar

Another town of import to us Grahams is Forfar which lies about twenty miles southwest from Marykirk and Logie Pert. It was here that James Campbell Graham (#99) met and married Catherine Wilkie who was born and raised in town. Her father David Wilkie was a flesher

Grahams o' the Mearns

(butcher) and the family lived at 23 Castle Street in the center of town as listed in both the 1841 and 1851 censuses though Catherine was not in the household in 1841 and was married to James Campbell Graham by the 1851 census. The Wilkie family is buried in Forfar which I learned through an exchange with a gentleman genealogist by the name of Ian MacKenzie. His investigations of the Forfar cemetery records opened the door to several Wilkie connections though it is not at all clear that Catherine maintained close contact with her siblings once married. Nancy and I spent only little time in Forfar but it appeared to be a small town that was an agricultural center in years past but has outgrown that reason for being. It was the county seat for Angus, previously known as Forfarshire.

Dundee – Migration to the Big City

While our earliest Graham ancestors can be traced to the Mearns, Alexander the Tailor exhibited a propensity to travel throughout present day Angus before finally settling in Dundee by the 1851 census. Many of his children both male and female also lived there, at least at some point in their lives. And though James Campbell Graham and Catherine Wilkie married in Forfar, they were in Liff & Benvie in 1851 before migrating throughout Scotland before eventually returning to Dundee between the 1861 census (New Monkland) and the birth of George Heron Graham in Dundee in 1864. That Dundee would become a focal point for employment in the nineteenth century seems obvious in retrospect as woolen mills gave way to linen and then jute that could then be exported from the city's docks. Dundee, established as a royal burgh in the 1200's, became the fourth largest town/city in Scotland, a position it maintains to this day. The emergence of the industrial age no doubt swept up the rural population, which would have caused simple tradesmen, for example tailors such as Alexander and his sons, to move into the cities as well.

Dundee was once noted for its three "J's" - jute, jam and journalism - Jute manufacturing became the primary industry in the mid-1800's but it also became famous for Keiller's marmalade when a Spanish ship sold its Seville oranges to avoid spoilage, and then at the beginning of the 20th century the publisher DC Thomson emerged and continues to this day with many famous titles. Dundee is now promoted as the 'City of Discovery', a title that reflects not only its links with exploration and Captain Scott's research ship Discovery, but the city's post-industrial role as a center of scientific research, education and tourism.

1893-1894

1899-1900

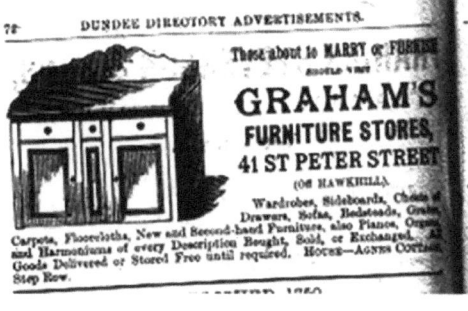
1903-1904

1909-1910

But let us focus on Dundee in the nineteenth century. Our Grahams seemed to have their earliest lodgings on the Westside around Hawkhill. Today, the University of Dundee claims much of that area but Charles IB Graham lived and worked in that neighborhood as shown by the various Dundee Trades Directories on the previous page. If you read carefully, in the 1903-04 version, Charles IB was living at Agnes Cottage (which I presume is 39 Step Row) but by 1909-1910 his house (named Ellenbank, perhaps as no street exists by that name today) is way out in Errol, a small town to the west of Dundee, birthplace to his second wife Agnes Dickson Soutar. Perhaps it was her family home. Though he started as a joiner or carpenter and had a thriving furniture making business for many years, he also became a property owner. Below I list a series of addresses where our ancestors lived in Dundee and at what time.

Shop of Charles IB Graham, ca 1882 probably at corner of Perth Road and St. Peter Street.

(not listed) Doigs Entry Overgate, home to Alexander Graham in the 1851 census

(1) 2 Park Entry, Alexander Graham home in the 1861 and 1871 census

(2) 41-43 St. Peter Street, shop of Charles IB Graham

(3) 9 St. Peter Street, home to Charles IB and first family with Agnes Candow

(4) 39 Step Row, CIB Graham residence in the 1901 census

(5) 224 Blackness Avenue, home to Catherine (Wilkie) (Graham) Watson in the 1881 and 1891 census

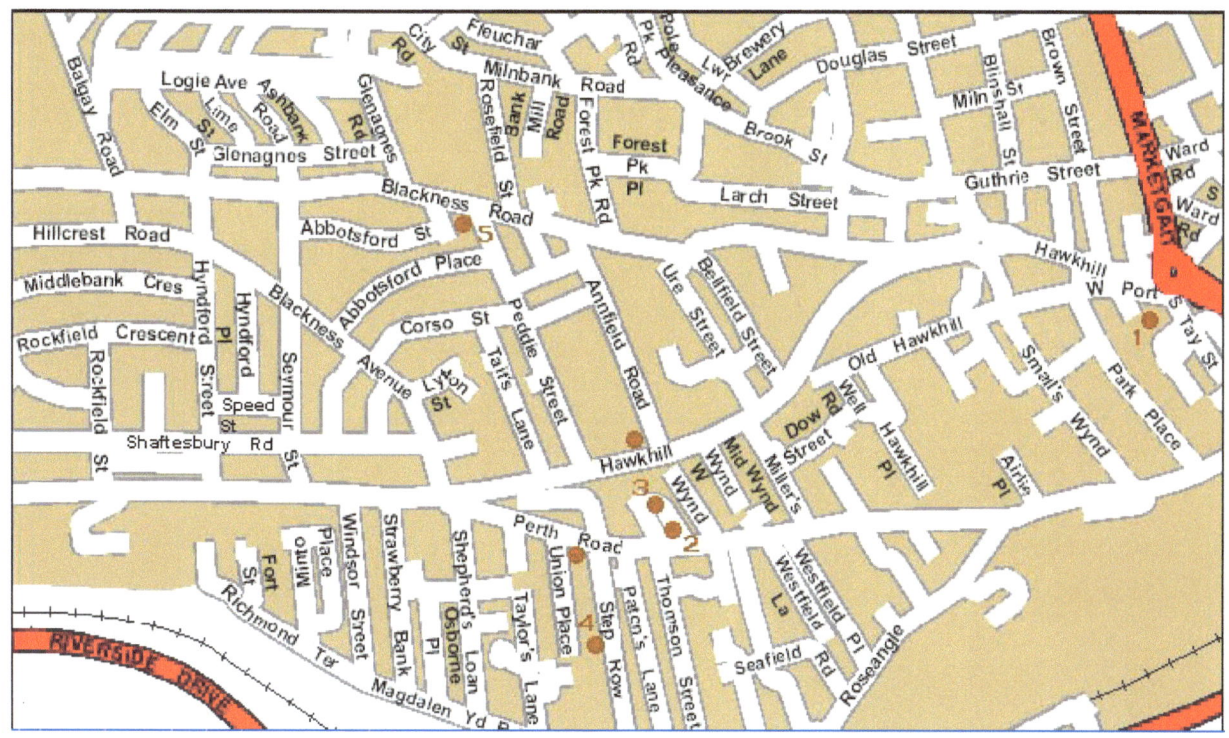

Charles IB Graham, Agnes "Nan", David, William, Charles, Agnes (Soutar) Graham, ca 1905

Brooklyn NY – The Starting Point for Grahams in America

NOTE: The following was written by the author in September 2004 after taking a family trip to New York City. This visit afforded him the chance to walk the streets where David Alma Graham and his family set down roots once they reached America in 1885.

When my younger son CJ (age 13) announced that he wanted to see NYC, I recognized this as an opportunity to get back to the area where the families of David Alma Graham (DAG1) and Agnes Cuthbert Graham landed and expanded after emigrating from Scotland in 1885. August is not the best time to visit New York City, but off we went. Knowing that Graham family history is not a passion shared by my wife or sons, we agreed that they would do the 'tourist thing' in Manhattan and I would venture off on my own to walk the streets of Brooklyn in search of homes lived in by various Graham family members. Previously, I had identified seven locations in Brooklyn/Queens that had come up on US census data or other family records. With the exception of the first one, I made it to the other six, several of which I was accompanied by George. As a youngster, I recall visiting the George Street location many times and it sure brought back memories to walk through this neighborhood. But what was once an area filled with German or Scottish immigrants is now a mixture of Hispanics, Russians, and a variety of other newer immigrant groups.

1. 53 Hope Street, Brooklyn NY — DAG1, 1900 Census location — DNV
2. 1270 Madison Street, Brooklyn — DAG1 from ~1914 to 1930, wedding location DAG2 — Visited
3. 1723 Putnam Avenue, Brooklyn — DAG2, 1920 Census — V
4. 1724 George Street, Ridgewood — DAG2 & family from 1924-1978 — V
5. 435 Etna Street, Brooklyn NY 11208 — Presbyterian Church — V
6. Jamaica Ave & Crescent St, NE ¼ Lot 792, sect 14 — Cypress Hills Cemetery — V
7. 6729 Metropolitan Avenue, Flushing Lutheran Cemetery — Public 1, Map 3A, row 23, Grave 41 — V

(LEFT) 1270 Madison Street

Home to David Alma Graham and Agnes Cuthbert Graham from ~1914 through ~1930. Also the location of the wedding of David Alma Graham (#2) and Emma Frances Schwarz 25 Nov 1914.

RIGHT) 1724 George Street (maroon door with gold trim), home to David Alma Graham (#2) and Emma Schwarz Graham from ~1924 through 1978 when Emma died. Home to my father Charles James Graham and Uncle Robert David Graham.

I had taken the subway out to Ridgewood early that morning but it was already hot and humid. After locating the three houses which were within a 5-10 block walk from one another, I then began a longer walk over to the Cypress Hill cemetery and the Presbyterian Church where DAG1 was an elder. This church was founded in 1902 though the building on this site wasn't completed until 1911.

Now Presbyterian Church of East Brooklyn – the Redeemer, previously Cypress Hills Presbyterian Church, 435 Etna Street, Brooklyn NY

After a three mile walk, I came upon this place, and after taking a few pictures, ventured in to the basement where a group of elderly folks, mostly women, were speaking Spanish. Of course, they stopped to see what this gringo outsider wanted and when I explained that my grandparents and great grandparents worshipped there, they were delighted to show me around. Unfortunately, it appears that historical Session records have been lost to time, though I may try and contact a church leader again in hopes of finding some entry of birth, marriage or death of any of our Graham ancestors. But I must say that it was a treat to see this building and know that some of our Graham ancestors worshipped there decades ago.

It was then that I walked back to the Cypress Hills Cemetery and met up with second cousin George and we began exploring our past together. From the photos you can see that the Graham family headstone is now being overtaken by a cypress bush on the right. In addition to the headstone, there are three markers, one for David Alma Graham (b. 1854 Dundee, d. 1933 Brooklyn), one for Agnes Cuthbert Graham (b. 1857 Dundee, d. 1922 Brooklyn) and one for both David Alma Graham (b. 1888 Brooklyn, d. 1955 Brooklyn and his wife Emma Schwarz Graham (b. 1893 Brooklyn, d. 1978 Brooklyn). It's also worth noting that at the left hand base of the headstone, there are inscriptions for Jennie F. Graham (b. 1886 Brooklyn, d. 1969 Brooklyn)

Grahams o' the Mearns

and her younger sister Agnes Cuthbert Graham (b. 1890 Brooklyn, d. 1955 Queens). The two unmarried sisters rest with their parents, brother and his wife.

Perhaps the most amusing thing I discovered was based upon the will of David Alma Graham Sr. (DAG1) that George is in possession of. The will was executed on 30 Sep 1929 just weeks before the great stock market crash of 1929. Below is an excerpt.

"FOURTH, Inasmuch as my children David A. Graham, Jr. and my daughters Jennie F. and Agnes C. Graham, since the death of their beloved mother Agnes C. Graham, have not shown the proper love and respect due me, I give, devise and bequeath to each of them the sum of One Dollar.

FIFTH, I direct my Executors hereinafter to divide all the rest, residue and remainder of my estate, both real and personal, of whatsoever kind and nature and wheresoever same may be situate, of which I shall die seized or possessed, or to which I may in anywise be entitled at the time of my decease, into two equal parts and I give, devise and bequeath on such equal parts to my beloved son George Forbes Graham."

So it would appear that DAG1 had some kind of 'problem' with his three eldest children and favored the youngest one George. Unfortunately, we have no record of what might have been the cause of the conflict. Ruth (Graham) Fuller, granddaughter to DAG1, has informed me that 'he may have been hard to get along with' though she was young at the time all this occurred. I wish we had some other record or oral tradition that would help explain this situation. Suffice it to say, the George Forbes Graham branch of the family became the beneficiary and repository for a myriad of early Graham family memorabilia

George C. Graham, at Graham Gravesite, Aug 2004

including photos, documents (such as the will), and a Bible printed in Dundee in the 1860's (but without any notes or markings). Again, I thank 2nd cousin George for surveying this treasure trove of items.

And on the subject of unusual documents, George showed me a copy of a Summons or Complaint in a Civil Cause that was in his possession. The complaint was made by Catherine (Watson) Marshall and her sister Minnie (Watson) McDonald and directed against Charles I.B. Graham on 7 Jun 1898. These two half-sisters to the four Graham brothers were seeking a burial plot certificate (*"certificate No. 1515 being the title to Lairs No 98 A.b. Compartment III in Western Cemetery Dundee which belonged to Pursuers Father James Watson, which certificate is dated 24 April 1866 and now belongs to the Pursuers jointly"*).

Apparently, they were accusing half-brother Charles (listed as Charles Graham, Furniture Dealer, 308 Perth Road) of not delivering the certificate which was valued at £12 sterling. Note that Catherine (Wilkie) Graham Watson had died 21 Feb 1898 of burns to head, neck and extremities. I suspect that the sisters wanted to insure a burial with their father James Watson but can only speculate on this. The available records do not indicate where Catherine Wilkie Graham Watson was buried. How this document ended up in America, and whether or not the claim was ever met, is not known. However, the document does give a family historian like me new clues. For example, I knew that Catherine Watson had married James Marshall, tailor 1 Jan 1892 and had at least one child by him. I had not yet found evidence that younger sister Minnie had married, but according to the summons she was listed as Minnie McDonald, wife of Alexander McDonald living at 9 Watson's Lane Dundee.

39 Step Row, Dundee, home to CIB Graham Family according to 1901 Census (photo taken Jun 2006)

There was still one more adventure that George and I embarked upon, and that was trying to see if there was a gravesite for two infants born to DAG1 and Agnes in the late 1800's. My family lore held that two infants, perhaps one named Charles and one James had been born but died young. A 1900 census entry for DAG1 and family indicated five children in the household including a Charles born Apr 1899. Earlier this year, cousin George provided me with information and a scanned image of a burial plot deed in the Lutheran Cemetery for two infants – an Alexander J. Graham and Charles Graham. From the image on the right, we learned that Alexander was buried on 3 Apr 1889 and that Charles was buried on 18 Jun 1904. Prior to the trip, I had contacted the cemetery and they confirmed the information and the location. George and I then drove over to this place and a staff member provided us with a map of the cemetery and directions to the burial area. We made our way out into an open field with very few markers and began our search. Given the paucity of headstones, I would have thought it quite easy to locate Row 23 Grave 41 but it was not. After many minutes of searching and beginning to think that there might not even be a headstone or marker, I looked up and spotted it! I was rather surprised and amazed, first that any headstone existed and second, that it was in such fine shape. We stood there and pondered it for quite some time.

The quality of the headstone was quite intriguing. We speculate that the stone may have been purchased and laid by the sisters some time after the actual deaths. The engraving is precise and shows no weathering.

Headstone for Graham infants buried 15 years apart.

If you will indulge me one more family history comment, I find it intriguing that what would have been the second son born to David Alma Graham and Agnes Cuthbert Graham was named Alexander J Graham. First, I suspect the J stands for James, a thesis I hope to confirm by seeking out a birth or death record for the child. Second, it suggests that Alexander was a family name of some kind. Assuming that I have the right "Alexander" Graham as father to James Campbell and grandfather to David Alma and Charles Iconaclast Bradlauch, he may have been known to his grandsons who would have been 17 and 10 at the time of his death in 1871.

Upon returning to the cemetery office, we learned that though no records of headstone placements existed, there were records of gravesite maintenance paid for by family members from 1955 through 1972. Apparently, Agnes C. Graham took responsibility until her death in 1955, and then Jennie took over until her death in 1969 and finally youngest brother George from 1969 to 1972 when he died. Somehow, at his death, this plot and task was overlooked and has been dormant ever since. Amusingly, what started out at $1.50 per year in the 1950's became $3.00 by the late sixties and today modest gravesite maintenance costs $30 per year. George and I declined to undertake the cost.

George C. Graham by headstone in Lutheran Cemetery, 20 Aug 2004

At this point, it was lunch time and we headed off to a nearby German restaurant for a nice meal together. Certainly it made sense that a Lutheran cemetery would be located near a German restaurant as this was undoubtedly an area once highly populated by German immigrants. Why did David and Agnes decide to bury their two sons here? This part of the cemetery was for infants and children and may have been the only place nearby available to them. Regardless of the reasons, it is intriguing to note that two distant offspring were on hand 100 years after the burial of Charles James Graham. This may have been the first time any of us has visited this place since the 1960's!

View from Empire State Building looking east over Queens and Brooklyn. The green hills in the mid-distance include the Cypress Hills Cemetery, home to the Graham family plot.

After lunch, George and I drove back to the Ridgewood area to visit some of the homes that I had been to earlier in the day. We even spent time hunting down an address on the back of a photo from the late-1920's that had DAG1 in it. It was most amusing to have some black kids playing out front and want to look at the old B&W photos of their home. Overall, I thoroughly enjoyed spending that hot, humid day in Brooklyn tracking down family history sites. Second cousins met and we exchanged several family history stories and documents. It was strangely engaging to roam the area where the David Alma Graham family first established themselves after coming to America in 1885.

Connor, Dave and CJ Graham atop Arthurs Seat, 29 Jun 2001
The day this family history quest began!

Grahams Down Under

Throughout this Graham family history research, there have been many fascinating discoveries and connections or reconnections. Perhaps one of the most intriguing was finding that first cousins Joseph Blyth Graham and Mary Ann Graham met, married, started a family and then immigrated to New Zealand. Actually, her younger sister Amelia and her husband Robert Oswald William Stewart were the first to immigrate to New Zealand, arriving in Port Chalmers (Dunedin) in October 1874. None of this information would have been uncovered had I not posted our family tree on some public family history sites and gotten inquiries from 'distant' cousins in New Zealand and Australia. I wish to acknowledge Margaret (Wright) O'Connor, Sandy Payne Blake, and Clive Rowe as living relations that shared my family history interests and helped us build connections between Scotland and the commonwealth countries of Australia and New Zealand.

Joseph Blyth Graham was the son of Andrew Graham and Ann Blythe born in Dunblane in 1852. Like his father and grandfather (Alexander Graham), he too took up the tailoring trade. In the 1871 Scottish census, he was living with his uncle Renwick Graham, also a tailor, in Dundee, perhaps apprenticing with him. Shortly thereafter, we found a marriage between him and Mary Ann Graham, the illegitimate daughter of John Graham (his uncle) and Mary Milne. They married in Montrose, had one daughter there, Mary Ann Graham (27 Nov 1873, Montrose, Angus), and then migrated to New Zealand on the Jessie Osborne which left Glasgow 7 Nov 1875 and landed in Lyttleton Harbor on 31 Jan 1876. They landed off Christchurch on Ripa Island just in time for their second child, Charles Riper Graham (31 Jan 1876) to be born, and then went on to have six other children for eight in total. I cannot but wonder if Charles Riper Graham was actually born at sea and then had his birth recorded upon arrival but this may never be confirmed. These cousins-german as indicated on their marriage entry were probably not the first Grahams to immigrate 'down under.'

Marriage Registration for Joseph and Mary Ann Graham, Montrose 1871

It's likely that John Graham, father to both Mary Ann and Amelia, though out-of-wedlock with Mary Milne, took off for Australia in the 1850's. We know that Mary Milne married Alexander Towns 5 May 1848, three months before Amelia was born on 2 Aug 1848. I must say, Alexander Towns was either a very gracious and forgiving man, or a dupe. That Mary Milne bore him five children and stayed married to him for another 62 years before her death suggests to me the former.

Investigative efforts into John Graham in Australia uncovered several interesting facts but only the barest of details of his life appear on the one document found thus far - his Queensland Australia death registration. I was able to locate a gravesite based upon information obtained from Margaret (Wright) O'Connor, a relative of Amelia (Graham) Stewart. Her family data showed a John Graham buried in Toowoomba Cemetery (see photo on p 30). With hope that their might have been a marriage with an Aussie family, I wrote for his death certificate but was disappointed to learn upon its arrival that John had no relatives listed on his death registration and that he died of dengue and senile decay on Neil Street, Toowoomba, was listed as a merchant/shopkeeper and had immigrated to Australia about 50 years earlier. Interestingly, the marriage registration of his second daughter Amelia offered up information that he was known as John Peter Graham and was a plumber at the time. Why would John (or John Peter) be the only brother that did not take up the tailoring trade like his dad Alexander? Who knows, but clearly he marched to the beat of his own drummer. I would have thought there was a better than even chance that John Graham might have married once he got to Australia but that doesn't seem to have happened or been recorded.

Marriage Registration Amelia Graham and ROW Stewart, 1872

Possible portrait of Mary (Milne) Towns, mother to Mary Ann and Amelia Graham

The people whose names are highlighted helped build our connections between Scotland and New Zealand.

Given my preference for patrilineage descent, I wrote for death certificates for the male Grahams born to Joseph and Mary Ann. Sadly, several of their sons died young and without issue. In fact, the New Zealand Grahams were not without serious heartaches. Charles Riper Graham committed suicide in 1931 at the age of 55. Sons Joseph Ivon and Ernest Graham died at young ages. Edwin Allen Graham lived a long life but never married (as far as I could tell). Only Charles and Herbert married and had children. I remain very curious about two sets of Grahams on this list: the Joyce and Charles Graham born to Charles R. Graham and Edith Margaret Emma Spencer, as one or both may have offspring; and also the pair of children born to Herbert Rowell Graham and Clarice MacAlindon. There may yet be Grahams in New Zealand or Australia that are blood relations.

L to R: Greta (Hopper) Rowe holding son Trevor, Decimus Rowe, Molly (Mary Ann Graham) Rowe, Greta's husband Henry (Harry) Rowe, my grandmother Inez (Sidey) Rowe, Marjorie (Wainwright) Rowe and husband Charles Rowe. In front, my Mum, Yvonne Sidey, Cynthia Rowe (daughter of Marj and Charlie), Marion Rowe, also their daughter and the girl on the end their 3rd daughter, Suzie. Dale Rowe and Clive Rowe are children of Greta and Harry, seated in front. This photo would have been taken about 1940/41. (Photo and caption courtesy of Sandra (Payne) Blake.

Charles Ripa Rowe with wife Edith (Spencer) and their two children, Joyce 4 and a half and Charles 11 months, taken about 1923. Don't know who the older woman is, possibly Edith's mother. (Photo and caption courtesy of Sandra (Payne). Note: due to privacy laws, I have not been able to determine if young Charles Graham married, had children, or is still alive.

Grahams o' the Mearns

Descendants of John GRAHAM

1. John GRAHAM (b.Abt 1824-Marykirk,Kincardineshire,Scotland;d.5 Jun 1905-Brisbane,Queensland,Australia)
 sp: Mary MILNE (b.8 Sep 1824-Logie-Pert,Angus,Scotland;m.Not married;d.25 Mar 1910-Logie-Pert,Angus,Scotland)
  2. Mary Ann GRAHAM (b.1 Dec 1844-Logie-Pert,Angus,Scotland;d.13 Aug 1938-Wellington,New Zealand)
   sp: Joseph Blyth GRAHAM (b.1852-Dunblane,Perth,Scotland;m.27 Jun 1871;d.24 Dec 1915-Wellington,New Zealand)
    3. Mary Ann GRAHAM (b.27 Nov 1873-Montrose,Angus,Scotland;d.30 Jul 1955-Christchurch,New Zealand)
     sp: Decimus ROWE (b.27 Aug 1875-Christchurch,New Zealand;m.23 Mar 1899;d.21 Sep 1946-Wellington,New Zealand)
      4. Ethel Inez ROWE (b.2 Mar 1900-New Zealand;d.27 Jul 1980-Masterton,New Zealand)
       sp: Albert John SIDEY (b.1884;m.26 Dec 1923;d.11 Jan 1935-Lyall Bay,Wellington,New Zealand)
        5. Denzel Molly SIDEY (b.1924-New Zealand)
         sp: Percy MILLAR
          6. Kenneth Albert MILLAR (b.May 1945)
         sp: Frank PAYNE (b.Abt 1915-Lower Hutt,New Zealand;d.2000-Lower Hutt,New Zealand)
        5. Rodney Graham SIDEY (b.18 Feb 1926-Wellington,New Zealand;d.2000-Papamoa,Bay of Plenty,New Zealand)
         sp: Mary Angela BYRON-WOOD (b.9 Jun 1921;m.(Div);d.19 Feb 1983-Waihake Island,Auckland,NZ)
          6. Sharon Gail SIDEY (b.21 Jan 1945)
          6. Kevin Graham SIDEY (b.25 Oct 1947-Lower Hutt,New Zealand;d.1979)
          6. Rodney Desmond SIDEY (b.11 Dec 1950-Lower Hutt,New Zealand)
          6. Michael Dennis SIDEY (b.1 Jul 1951-Lower Hutt,New Zealand)
          6. Geoffrey Colin SIDEY (b.28 Jan 1954-Lower Hutt,New Zealand)
          6. Keith Robert SIDEY (b.25 Aug 1961-Lower Hutt,New Zealand)
        5. Yvonne Ngaire SIDEY (b.31 Oct 1930-Wellington,New Zealand;d.1 Jun 1987-Greytown,New Zealand)
         sp: Gordon Alister PAYNE (b.28 Aug 1924-Lower Hutt,New Zealand;d.23 Jun 1996-Greytown,New Zealand)
          6. Stuart John PAYNE (b.25 Mar 1949-Lower Hutt,New Zealand)
           sp: Cynthia Marrion ROBERTS (b.26 Jun 1948-Australia;m.11 Jul 1970(Div))
          6. ==Sandra Alice PAYNE== (b.17 May 1950-Lower Hutt,New Zealand)
           sp: Ian Barry BLAKE (b.6 Jun 1951-Caterton,New Zealand;m.15 Nov 1975)
            7. Nicola Lee BLAKE (b.30 Aug 1978-Masterton,NZ)
            7. Kieran James BLAKE (b.1 Feb 1981-Masterton,NZ)
             sp: Sarah-Jane Nesta CAMERON (b.24 Feb 1981-Masterton,New Zealand;m.14 Mar 2009)
            7. Brendan Michael BLAKE (b.3 Apr 1983-Masterton,NZ)
          6. Susan Decima PAYNE (b.17 May 1950-Lower Hutt,New Zealand;d.23 May 1950-Lower Hutt,New Zealand)
          6. Heather Laureen PAYNE (b.12 Dec 1951-Lower Hutt,New Zealand)
           sp: John William BOWNESS (b.13 Apr 1950;m.7 Mar 1970)
          6. Dean Alistair PAYNE (b.1954-Lower Hutt,New Zealand)
      4. Charles Francis ROWE (b.10 Mar 1901-New Zealand;d.25 Oct 1994-Upper Hutt,New Zealand)
       sp: Marjorie Rowsell WAINWRIGHT (b.Abt 1901;m.1926;d.3 Oct 1995-Upper Hutt,New Zealand)
        5. Cynthia Graham ROWE (b.30 May 1928-Lower Hutt,New Zealand)
         sp: Hugh Hector NANKIVELL

Descendants of John GRAHAM

```
            ├─ 5. Marion ROWE
            └─ 5. Suzie ROWE
         ├─ 4. Henry Graham ROWE (b.7 Nov 1904-New Zealand;d.1 Sep 1977-New Zealand)
         │     sp: Greta Mary HOPPER (b.21 Feb 1909-Wellington,New Zealand;d.20 Aug 1988-Auckland,New Zealand)
         │     ├─ 5. Clive ROWE (b.27 Dec 1934-Wellington,New Zealand)
         │     │     sp: Faye BRANDON (b.1938;m.1964)
         │     │     ├─ 6. Michael Berry ROWE (b.1962-New Zealand)
         │     │     ├─ 6. Perry Martin ROWE (b.1964-New Zealand)
         │     │     ├─ 6. Quentin Wayne ROWE (b.1966-New Zealand)
         │     │     ├─ 6. Steve Manu Clive ROWE (b.1969-New Zealand)
         │     │     └─ 6. Karina Faye ROWE (b.13 Nov 1970-New Zealand)
         │     ├─ 5. Dale Irene ROWE (b.23 Oct 1936-Wellington,New Zealand)
         │     │     sp: Clifford BRANIGAN
         │     ├─ 5. Trevor ROWE (b.Jan 1938-Wellington,New Zealand)
         │     │     sp: Elizabeth GRAY
         │     └─ 5. Linda Kathryn ROWE (b.26 Dec 1950-Wellington,New Zealand)
         ├─ 4. Sidney Eric ROWE (b.21 Dec 1911-Wellington,New Zealand;d.3 Jul 1997-Dunedin,Otago,New Zealand)
         │     sp: Ethel Friday MCKAY (b.Abt 1916-Dunedin,Otago,New Zealand;d.29 Nov 1994-Dunedin,Otago,New Zealand)
         └─ 4. Lottie Joan ROWE (b.1913-New Zealand)
      ├─ 3. Charles Riper GRAHAM (b.31 Jan 1876-Ripa Island Lyttleton,New Zealand;d.18 May 1931-Wellington,New Zealand)
      │     sp: Edith Emma Margaret SPENCER (b.Abt 1897;m.1919)
      │     ├─ 4. Joyce GRAHAM (b.Abt 1919-New Zealand)
      │     └─ 4. Charles GRAHAM (b.Abt 1922-New Zealand)
      ├─ 3. John Harland GRAHAM (b.1881-Dunedin,New Zealand;d.17 Jul 1952-Palmerston North,New Zealand)
      │     sp: Annie Elizabeth BURKETT (b.20 Nov 1887;d.21 Jun 1984-Palmerston North,New Zealand)
      ├─ 3. Ernest GRAHAM (b.1885-New Zealand;d.Apr 1917-Wellington,New Zealand)
      ├─ 3. Edwin Allen GRAHAM (b.27 Oct 1886-Dunedin,New Zealand;d.17 Apr 1975-Dannevirke,New Zealand)
      ├─ 3. Joseph Ivon GRAHAM (b.Aft Apr 1888-New Zealand;d.5 Apr 1908-Palmerston North,New Zealand)
      ├─ 3. Herbert Rowell GRAHAM (b.1890-Dunedin,New Zealand;d.26 May 1947-Palmerston North,New Zealand)
      │     sp: Clarice Mary Claire MCALINDON (b.Abt 1892;m.1925;d.9 Nov 1959-Palmerston North,New Zealand)
      │     ├─ 4. ???? GRAHAM (b.Abt 1927-Palmerston North,New Zealand)
      │     └─ 4. ???? GRAHAM (b.Abt 1928-Palmerston North,New Zealand)
      └─ 3. Alice Elizabeth GRAHAM (b.14 Aug 1892-New Zealand;d.1988-New Zealand)
            sp: Reginald Lewis HULSTON (m.1914)
└─ 2. Amelia GRAHAM (b.2 Aug 1848-Logie-Pert,Angus,Scotland;d.4 Aug 1917-Wanganui,New Zealand)
      sp: Robert William Oswald STEWART (b.Abt 1845-Dumfries,D,Scotland;m.7 Jun 1872;d.30 Jun 1927-Kogarah,NSW,Australia)
      ├─ 3. Wilhelmina GRAHAM (b.23 Apr 1869-Dundee,Angus,Scotland)
      ├─ 3. Robert William Oswald STEWART (b.30 Jun 1873-Partick,Lanark,Scotland;d.20 Oct 1873-Partick,Lanark,Scotland)
```

Descendants of John GRAHAM

- 3. George STEWART (b.1876-New Zealand)
- 3. Amelia Gillespie STEWART (b.1878-New Zealand)
- 3. John Taylor STEWART (b.1879-New Zealand; d.1941-New Zealand)
  - sp: Florence Jane THOMSON (m.1918)
- 3. Mary Eleanor STEWART (b.22 Jul 1880-Hampden, Otago,New Zealand;d.11 Feb 1934-Hurstville,NSW,Australia)
  - sp: Charles Arthur BOWEN (b.5 Dec 1877-Kaipoi,New Zealand;m.24 Apr 1900;d.5 May 1948-Botany Bay,S,NSW,Australia)
    - 4. Gwendoline BOWEN (b.22 Dec 1901-Wanganui, New Zealand;d.1973-Blacktown,Australia)
      - sp: Alfred WRIGHT (b.14 Dec 1897;m.12 May 1923;d.1980-Sydney,NSW Australia)
        - 5. Robert WRIGHT (b.25 May 1924-Lidcombe, NSW,Australia)
        - 5. Helena WRIGHT (b.14 Oct 1926-Sydney, NSW,Australia)
        - 5. Maxwell Stewart WRIGHT (b.29 Jul 1927-Sydney, NSW,Australia;d.1993)
        - 5. Margaret WRIGHT (b.1936-Sydney, NSW,Australia)
    - 4. Charles BOWEN (b.30 Nov 1905-Wanganui, New Zealand;d.1937-Botany Bay,Sydney,NSW,Australia)
    - 4. Maxwell BOWEN (b.25 Jun 1911-Willoughby, NSW Australia;d.1958-Sydney,NSW Australia)
- 3. Jessie Anna STEWART (b.1882-New Zealand;d.1885-New Zealand)
- 3. Andrew Duncan STEWART (b.1883-New Zealand;d.1911-New Zealand)
- 3. James Sinclair STEWART (b.1885-New Zealand)
- 3. Louisa Carter STEWART (b.1887-New Zealand;d.1945-New Zealand)
  - sp: John DALZELL (m.22 May 1906)
    - 4. Howard DALZELL (b.4 Aug 1906-Wanganui, New Zealand;d.6 Oct 1981-Hamilton,New Zealand)
      - sp: Grace Elizabeth GWYNN (b.21 Feb 1902-Ilford,London,UK;d.17 Jul 1965-Wanganui,New Zealand)
        - 5. Margaret Priscilla DALZELL (b.13 Jun 1946-Wanganui,New Zealand)
- 3. Elizabeth Florence Maude STEWART (b.1890-New Zealand; d.1978-??,Victoria,Australia)
  - sp: Frederick BYRON (m.1929)
- 3. Ruby Valerie Castlemaine Ballance STEWART (b.1895-New Zealand; d.1973-New Zealand)
  - sp: Norman Herbert MCEWEN (m.1918)

Trades and Professions - How Grahams Supported Themselves

Looking back through available family history records, we see an interesting progression of trades, careers and professions. One thing seems quite clear – our Grahams were not of noble birth but rather common laborers. Trades and professions included farm laborers, tailors, stone masons, tinsmiths, woodworkers, insurance agents, teachers, electrical engineers, business executives, attorneys, and bankers just to name a few. Several male Grahams were military veterans, the first of which – Robert Graham – made a career out of the British Army before returning closer to home in the early 1820's. Other male Grahams served admirably in WWI, WWII and beyond but none that made a full career in the military.

Alexander Graham, our earliest confirmed ancestor was listed as a cotterman in the church baptismal records. No doubt he worked the land for a larger landowner, perhaps the Grahams of Morphie, and then had a small patch to care for himself and his large family. Some of his sons continued to work the land but we begin to see a shift toward non-agricultural trades (e.g., tailoring, stone masonry, plumbing and carpentry) before exhibiting another shift in the twentieth century toward white collar trades such as teaching, insurance and engineering. While I have mainly tracked the males of our lineage, this is not to say the women did not work. In fact, it's quite apparent that many spouses were fully engaged in a variety of labors required to put food on the table along with clothing and shelter. But in the table below, we present a cursory overview of stated trades and professions of many Graham ancestors

Alexander Graham #15	1743-??	Cotterman, OPR
Robert Graham #39,	1778-??	Ploughman, military, OPR, archives
Mary Nicol	??-??	Farm servant, OPR
Alexander Graham #55,	1797-1871	Tailor, journeyman, OPR, census
Ann Lindsay Graham	~1795-~1845??	Mill worker, 1841 census
Alexander Graham #100,	1821-1843	Mill worker, 1841 census
Mary Ann Graham #101,	1822-1902	Mill worker, various censuses
John Graham #102,	1824-1905	Plumber ?, dau marriage registration 1873, storekeeper (death regn)
Andrew Graham #103,	1828-1902	Tailor, upholsterer, censuses
Renwick Graham #104,	1830-1904	Tailor, censuses
James Campbell Graham #99,	1822-1865	Stone mason, journeyman, census & death regn
Catherine Wilkie Graham Watson	1823-1898	Housekeeper Worked after being twice widowed
David Alma Graham #135,	1854-1933	Tinsmith, gasfitter, censuses
James Talford Graham #136,	1856-??	Tinsmith, gasfitter, 1871-81 censuses
Charles IB Graham #137,	1861-1943	Joiner, property owner, various
George Heron Graham #138,	1864-??	Factory worker (age 16), 1881 census
Joseph Blyth Graham, #143	1852-1915	Tailor, census
John Blyth Graham, #144	1854-1942	Tailor, census
Wm M. Graham #165,	1889-1961	Insurance, WWI veteran, family
David S. Graham #167,	1893-1965	Advertising Agency Owner, WWI vet, family
Charles Graham #169,	1895-1979	Insurance sales & mgmt, WWI vet Town councilor, church organist, family

David Alma Graham #159,	1888-1955	Teacher, NYC public schools, drafting and metal working, family
George F. Graham #162,	1892-1972	Insurance industry executive, WWI vet
Charles L Graham #183,	1911-2000	Insurance sales & mgmt, WWII RAF vet
Charles R. Graham #173	1876-1931	Tailor, burial registration
Ernest Graham, #175	1885-1917	Clerk, burial registration
Edwin Allen Graham #176	1886-1975	Retired sheepfarmer, burial registration
Duncan M.H. Graham #200	1883-1942	Elevator operator, dynamite worker
John Graham #202	1892-??	Veteran of Black Watch, laborer?
Robert D. Graham #204,	1921-2004	Engineer, GE mgmt, WWII US Navy vet, Pacific
Charles J. Graham #205,	1929-1991	Engineer, GE and telecom industry executive, US Army 1951-53
George C. Graham #206,	1921-1996	Physician
Donald C. Graham	1938-present	Insurance executive, RAF vet
Donald M Graham	1938-present	University professor, chemistry

Military Service

While Robert Graham had a long career first in the Angusshire militia followed by 24 years in the Royal Regiment of Artillery, other Grahams have played parts in the military though none from a career standpoint. World War I saw Grahams on both sides of the Atlantic participate – all of Charles IB Graham's sons and one of David Alma Graham – his youngest son George F. Graham. Images of draft registrations shown on this and the following page have been located on the internet in various repositories though I have been unable to find every single draft registration card. I've been told that George F. Graham served in France in WWI and received an injury to his shoulder that couldn't be addressed for fear that he might lose his arm.

World War II was a time of service in the US Navy for Robert D.

Grahams o' the Mearns

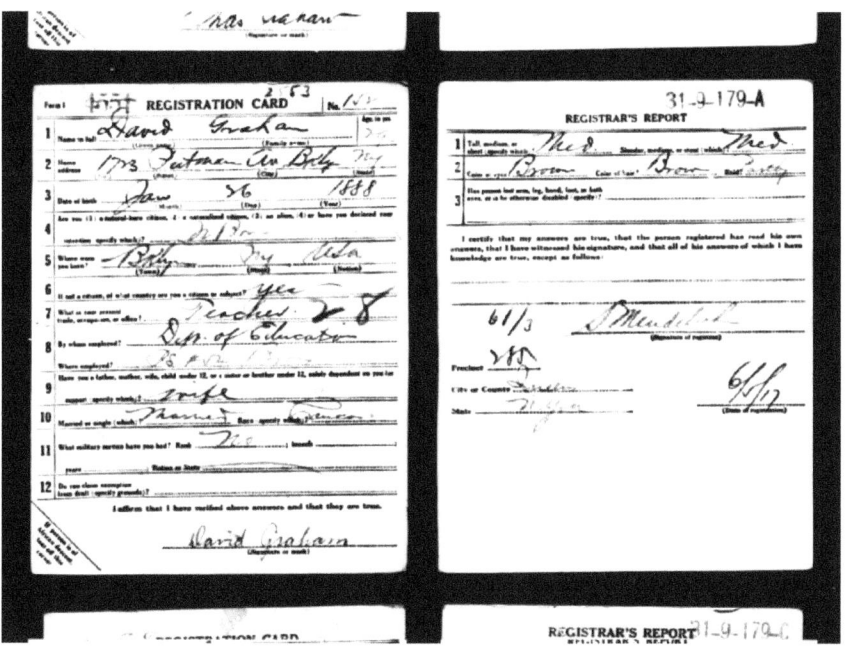

Graham though I am not sure if other Grahams participated also. My own father spent two years in the US Army from 1951 to 1953 working as an engineer at what was then called Cape Canaveral and is now known as the Kennedy Space Center on the Atlantic coast in northern Florida.

Who Were We, Really? – Personal Essays on Our Family and Ourselves

In the pages ahead, we present a collection of brief essays or remembrances of various family members that responded to my infrequent requests for such information in the spring of 2009. The impetus for such stories comes from the author/editor who, throughout the multiyear process of pursuing Graham family history, lamented the lack of real knowledge of who our ancestors were as people, parents, and citizens. We can surmise much from public records like census data, but really – who were our ancestors? What were they really like? What were their political views? Did they even have any political views? These and a myriad of other questions plague me to this day. Hence, I feel it an obligation to capture more about those of us alive today so that future generations – our children's children's, children will have some written record to goes well beyond birth, marriage and death dates. Yes, it is difficult to write about ourselves, our values and beliefs, our seminal life experiences, but what have we to lose? Indeed, we offer a gift to future Graham descendents that help them know more about their distant ancestors than many families might ever attempt.

Sheila (Graham) Rattray

I was born on 19th July, 1926, in Maidstone, Kent, England to a Scottish father and an Irish mother, so you could call me truly British. I was christened Sheila Mary Graham and we all moved to Dundee in Angus, Scotland when I was one year old. My brother and sister have written about my father, Charles Graham, a kindly even-tempered man. He had met my Irish mother, Mary Constance Fox, when they worked together in the Dublin office of the General Accident Insurance Company. May, as she was known, the daughter of an Irish farmer, must have been a lovely young woman. The villagers where she lived used to say "You have a face like the Madonna, May."

My Scottish grandparents, Charles Graham, and his wife Agnes, lived in Newport in Fife in a house called "Ashcliffe" on the edge of the River Tay. We used to visit them every weekend, crossing the river on a passenger boat nicknamed the "Fifie."

I have given Dave all the information available about my grandfather, a master joiner. My Grandma was a dear little woman, quiet and kindly, and I loved my Auntie Nan who would play with me on the pebbly beach. My mother spent two and a half years attending to my little brother Gordon who was ill with tubercular meningitis, so I often stayed at "Ashcliffe", cosseted by my grandmother and aunt, spoiled with cocoa and biscuits before going off by candle-light to the cozy feather bed, listening to the waves break on the shore.

Gordon died when I was six years old, and Maureen arrived when I was seven in 1933. Our summer holidays were spent at "Windgates House" in County Wicklow in Ireland, about fourteen miles from Dublin, where my grandfather, Richard Fox, had a farm. He was a big cheery fellow, my grandmother Annie Frances rather austere. The farm and woodlands surrounding it provided a wonderful holiday playground; the old farmhouse was intriguing with its dairy laden with bowls of cream waiting to be churned by hand into butter, later spread on the home-made soda bread, eaten at breakfast with eggs and bacon from the farm, mushrooms picked in the fields. At night the house was lit by paraffin lamps, an evocative smell of my childhood.

Donald arrived in 1938, just before the war. Friends invited me to stay with them in Glasgow, considered a safer area than the east coast, frequently visited by German planes. My parents thought it a good idea, rapidly discarded when Clydebank near Glasgow was blitzed. I came home and returned to school at Grove Academy in Broughty Ferry.

At the age of seventeen I was greatly tempted by an advertisement asking for a girl required to train in journalism, and joined the staff of D.C. Thomson in Dundee, a famous newspaper and magazine firm. I worked in the fiction department as a sub-editor and later, at the tender age of twenty-one, became the agony aunt on one of the firm's magazines.

At a dance on 20th November, 1947, to celebrate the wedding of Princess Elizabeth to the Duke of Edinburgh, I met my future husband, Ronald Rattray, who worked in the local council office under the burgh surveyor and who later qualified as a civil engineer. We married on 11th October, 1951 and settled in Yorkshire where Ronald worked in Pudsey. Rosalyn was born there in 1953 and we moved to Dumfries when she was one year old. Joy followed in 1956 and Howard in 1961.

In 1969, we moved to Uddingston near Glasgow when Ronald became Technical Services Manager for Hamilton District Council, followed by a move several years later to Paisley where he was appointed Director of Technical Services. In Dumfries Ronald became an elder in the Church of Scotland and I followed in his footsteps in Uddingston. We are very proud of our family and their achievements - Rosalyn trained as a nurse and eventually became a sister midwife, Joy took an honours degree in English and Philosophy and teaches English, Howard graduated in Law and now works as a legal adviser in Glasgow District Court.

We had many happy holidays with the family - travelling to France, Austria, Italy and of course exploring Scotland. Our family are now all married and the next generation of Graham descendants takes its place on the branches of the family tree, the first three girls honours graduates - Rosalyn's Rona, Joy's Rachel and Sonia, the latter perhaps having the most intriguing job at the moment working for an M.P. in the House of Commons and meeting occasionally with famous figures such as Prime Minister Gordon Brown. Howard has two children at school, Georgia and Gavin, and Rona's son Craig is now thirteen.

Ronald has been retired for over twenty years and we have had some wonderful holidays to America, Canada, Alaska, the Mediterranean, the Baltic capitals. And of course it was a great thrill to meet our distant American cousins Dave Graham and his sister Nancy when they came to Scotland on a family history expedition three years ago.

How does one sum up? I have had a blessed, fortunate and happy life. For many years I regretted not going to university but in my forties I started to study with the Open University and took a Bachelor of Arts degree in Fine Art and Literature, two of my main interests. I used to write articles for the local paper in Dumfries, and have painted in watercolour for many years and am still exhibiting. Any regrets? - not writing in a more serious vein, not painting masterpieces, not helping others more. So? - I'm only eighty-two, going on eighty-three. Hope springs eternal...

Charles IB Graham

Copy of letter from Charles to his older brother David in the USA three months before David's death in 1933.

Ashcliffe West Newport Fife

Dear Brother,   13 of July 1933

just a few lings to Let you Know that I Received your Letter all Right. Sister Minnie must have had a verry Bad time in Clifornia Sah must been verry Bad here famley are all Well and Working Wee have no Work here for any one.

I was sorry to hee that your legs are not Right yet. I hope you be all Right Soon,

I am sorry to say Mrs Graham is not Keping Well She was away for 2 week But is not any Better yet I was Glad to here that your sons famley ar all Well and Working David and Charly and aggu are all Working and doing verry Will, as for me I am just Lik a Boy of 18 year old I can Make 5 myes every day.

your Loving
                    Brother Chas Graham

Maureen Graham-Graham Family Memories

I shall tell you a little about my father, Charles Graham, who died in 1979, aged 84. As a young boy he learnt to play the organ and became the church organist in Errol Parish Church, near Dundee at the age of 14. He continued to play church organs and also became a church elder in the Presbyterian Church of Scotland.

At the outbreak of the 1st World War he joined the 53rd Highland Field Ambulance and served in France and Belgium.

He worked in insurance companies all his life and met my mother in Ireland while he was Chief Clerk of General Accident Fire and Life Assurance Company working in Dublin. In 1934 he became manager of the Scottish General Insurance Company in Dundee. As a young married couple they lived in Maidstone, England and then came to Scotland where they lived in Dundee, Monifieth and latterly, after retirement some years earlier, they moved to Castle Douglas, in the Stewartry of Kirkcudbright.

He enjoyed golf and also became very involved in the local community, as councillor, magistrate, treasurer of Monifieth Town Council and member of the Angus County Council.

From his daughter Maureen Frances Graham, born 30 December 1933 in Dundee, Scotland

****

Donald Charles Graham

My father was born in 1895. He was forty three when I was born; and that gap always remained.

During the first world war he became an Acting Sergeant in the Royal Army Medical Core. I asked him many boyish questions about the war, but the only thing he ever told me in response to my questions was, "It's a terrible thing to have to cut a man's leg off without anaesthetic!!"

Dad had huge ability in many sports. He played cricket for Maidstone in England and played cricket, billiards and badminton at county level and was the East of Scotland champion at badminton. I never beat him at golf, in spite of him giving me two "bisques," (a point taken when desired) and he continued to be a low handicap player until he gave up golf in his late

Mr Charles Graham retiring

At the end of this year Mr Charles Graham, A.C.I.I., manager of the Scottish General Insurance Co., Ltd., will retire from the position he has held for 26 years. Ad. 2/12/60

Mr Graham, who lives at Hillcrest, Hill Street, Monifieth, is a native of Dundee.

He was educated at Harris Academy before beginning work in 1910 at the Dundee branch of the Edinburgh Insurance Co., just across the way from his present offices in Panmure Street.

One of the managers under whom he worked at the Edinburgh Insurance was Mr (later Sir) William Y. Darling.

During the first world war Mr Graham served with the 53rd Highland Field Ambulance in France and Belgium. He returned to Edinburgh Insurance for a short time, before joining the General Accident Fire and Life Assurance Company.

He was chief clerk at Gaflac's branches in Dublin, Maidstone and Dundee, before taking over the

post of manager of the Dundee branch of the Scottish General Insurance Company (an associate of Gaflac) in 1934.

Church organist

In his younger days he was a keen cricketer and badminton player.

He is a member of Broughty Golf Club at Monifieth, has a keen interest in cinematography and is organist at South Church, Monifieth.

He was formerly a councillor, magistrate and honorary treasurer of Monifieth.

He was also on the Angus County Council.

Mr Graham's successor will be Mr John McCaig, chief inspector at the company's head office in Glasgow. He will take over on January 1.

A farewell function is being held for Mr Graham in Nicoll & Smibert's rooms on December 15.

seventies. I did once beat him at draughts (checkers)!! Although I went fishing with him a couple of times, it was always only as an observer.

In old age he once said to me "you diddled (got the better of,) me when you were young!!" On asking how, he reminded me that I had once asked for a new bicycle (costing about £14.00). Certain that his money was safe, he replied that if I saved up half, he would buy it for me. Where we lived was a great raspberry growing area, and I went to work picking with such energy, that I had earned £7.00 pounds in a fortnight!! Dad was not best pleased, but I got my "Raleigh Trent" sports bycycle!!

Dad was Chief Clerk or Office Manager with the General Accident Fire and Life Assurance Corporation (or GAFLAC) in Dublin where he met my mother. After they married they moved to Maidstone in the South of England, a move I know my mother enjoyed. Later he became Branch Manager with an associate company the Scottish General, in Dundee. He remained in Dundee all his career until he retired at age sixty-five. I know that a previous boss told him he would become Chief General Manager, and although he undoubtedly had the ability, and a huge grasp of the English language, and an amazing vocabulary, that never happened. Sad. I was with the same group at the time, and attended his retirement dinner. I was pleased that he made some subtle cutting remarks in his retirement speech about the less able General Manager, who was present!!

My dear mother suffered from multiple sclerosis for many years and I was glad for her sake, that after retirement dad gave up all his connections in the East of Scotland, and moved home to Castle Douglas in the Borders, which has a milder climate, was closer to Sheila and Ronald, at that time, and is flat, allowing her to walk a little in town and attend church. Dad did join another Golf Club and continued to play the organ (something he had done since age 13!!), so becoming part of the community. Mum died in 1974 and dad went to live with Sheila and Ronald in Uddingston, where Wilma and I had also bought a house following my first promotion. It was about this time when he wistfully mentioned to me that he had been offered by his employers, The General Accident, a post in Rio De Janiero, but having just married he declined. That could have been life changing! My sister Sheila and her stalwart husband Ronald were wonderful in the way they looked after dad who as the years went by became a frail old man until he died in 1979. Both of them would deny that they were either long suffering or stalwart, but I think they were brilliant! During this time occasional respite for them was provided by us!

On looking back I regret that for what ever reason, we didn't get to know each other better.

Barbara (Graham) Pate

It's been 17 years since I lost my mom, Dottie, and almost 5 since dad passed away. Moving to Scottsville was a welcome change since we no longer had a reason to stay in Chesapeake.

I never realized how much I would miss my parents and what an impact they had on my life. I was always told, "you're just like your mom", but in reality I am "Bob Jr.". Maybe not as business savvy as he but I have the reflective and stubborn side of him.

As for Terry and I, we have been married sixteen years now. It's hard to believe. Terry will become a grandfather for the second time in September. His son, Dylan, and wife, Kristy, are expecting a baby boy. Guess that makes me a step grandma. They live near Fredericksburg, VA, so we do get to see them on occasion.

East Main Street Garage is still busy despite this poor economy. People are hanging on to their vehicles and getting them repaired rather than buying something new. This is good news for us!

Linda and Tom are still living in Colorado and enjoy spending time with Ken, Michele and Taylor. They celebrated their anniversary early this year with a cruise to Hawaii in February rather than to wait until June.

Ken, Michele and Taylor are returning from Costa Rica on June 8th. It was a welcome and much needed escape as Michele lost her mom in February and took it quite hard.

Bob & Dottie Graham, ca 1990

Well, I guess that's all the family news I can give you at this point in time. We have our house on the market but have not sold it to date. We have had a lot of interest and one serious bite, but that' so been it. We'll keep you all posted. We are looking for a ranch home on more acreage and have a few places in mind.

Our best to all of our relatives near and far.

Barbara (Graham) & Terry Pate

Robert Schwarz

Stories About my Uncle Dave (David A. Graham, born 1888)

"Willie Off the Pickle Boat"

When I was very young, I would visit my Aunt and Uncle on George St. in Brooklyn. It was about a ten-block walk to their house, down 62nd St, around the corner along Cooper Ave., down St Felix to Seneca and along Seneca past Decatur, Summerfield, Norman, Stephen and then George St. We could walk it in about 20 minutes. There was a Delicatessen on the corner of Seneca and George St., which my Aunt would send me to occasionally to buy a loaf of Pumpernickel bread for her and my Uncle Dave. It cost about a dime. When we got to 1724 I would eagerly climb the steps and yell, "we're here". My uncle would always be sitting on the front porch smoking or scraping out his pipe. As soon as I entered the door and said "Hi Uncle Dave" he'd greet me by replying "Hello there Willie off the pickle boat." I never knew where that expression came from, but I'll never forget it.

The biggest Lionel Trains I ever saw.

As a small boy, my Mother Edith, Father Robert and Sister Ruth would visit frequently during Christmas time. There was something very special going on in the Graham basement at Christmas time. When I descended the basement stairs I heard a roar getting louder as I went down each step. As I neared about the halfway point I could look to my left and see that the entire basement had been transformed into the most amazing sight I had ever seen. There were huge trains on a platform that covered the whole basement. My uncle Dave was right in the middle of the layout standing in a hole in the middle, his body showing from the waist up. He had an Engineers hat on and was controlling the trains with the biggest Lionel transformer in existence. There was a bridge in the middle that the train would traverse that was about two or three feet long and the whole thing was mind boggling to a four or five year old. I'm guessing that is how old I was at the time. It would have been 1951 or 1952. There seemed to be lights all over the layout.

Car trips

I remember a few outings we went on with my Aunt and Uncle. They had a car and we would go for rides with them, to "Squeedunk". That was one of his favorite places. I don't know where that is or if it even exists. We didn't get a car till somewhere around 1950 or '52. It was a '49 Buick and of course it was black. We called it Black Beauty.

Bad News

One day my mother was at home and very upset. She told me my Uncle Dave had died. I was very sad. I seem to remember her saying she had gone to visit and she had found him lying on the floor of the front porch. Needless to say, it was a very sad day.

Stories About my Aunt Emma (Graham)

The "Conditta" what?

One day my Aunt Emma gave me 25 cents and some very detailed instructions. She wanted me to go to the corner of Seneca and George Streets to get some bread for her and the next-door neighbor. I was somewhat confused as to exactly what she wanted, but I thought I could handle it. I entered the Bakery and proceeded to tell the proprietor that I needed a loaf of Pumpernickel and a Conditta Rye. He replied "What?" I repeated the order and he promptly broke out in the jolliest laugh I had ever heard. I was very embarrassed when he told me to go back and "get better instructions", because Konditorei means "Pastry Shop" in German. I had asked for a whole lot more than I could buy. When I had tucked my tail between my legs (so to speak) and returned to my Aunt, she too had a chuckle and promptly gave me written instructions, probably in German.

"Slice it thin"!

My Aunt Emma used to visit us for dinner after my Uncle had passed on. She, as many older folks, had shown her years by growing out rather than up. In a psychological effort to remain within certain physical boundaries, would try to economize input of caloric sustenance. After one particular meal at which my wife was present, she was offered a slice of pound cake for dessert. She initially refused the cake, but upon momentary reconsideration, asked for a piece from my wife. She also immediately followed the request with the qualification "Slice it thin". Immediately after it was consumed, another request for the cake was issued, and the qualification was reissued "slice it thin, no thinner". We all appreciated what she was trying to accomplish and proceeded to annihilate the entire cake.

Cookies and Grape Juice

As a young man, I rode my bicycle all over the Brooklyn Queens area. My friend Fred and I were probably the champion bicycle riders of the city. We would often depart the neighborhood on a Saturday morning and not return until evening. I knew my Aunt Emma loved to be visited and we would therefore make it a point to stop by her house to get a drink on the hot summer days. She would always be very glad to see us and treat us to a cookie and a drink, As a very frugal person and living alone after her husband David had passed on, she would buy just enough of things to take care of her needs. She frequently went to her refrigerator, which was one of the first ones ever made, and when I was eleven or twelve years old, it was an antique. It had the condenser on top of the unit and appeared as a white cylindrical appurtenance worthy of interstellar travel. From this intriguing box she would obtain the smallest can of Welch's' grape juice ever made. It was enough to make about 4 glasses of juice and it sure was good to a couple of thirsty riders. I remember those cans cost seven cents each, because I would request that my mother buy them when she went grocery shopping. Somehow they just weren't as good when made at home, so you know where I went to drink them. I think we most always left a seven-cent tip on the kitchen table.

The Brewery

There was a brewery about two blocks from my Aunt Emma's house. I believe it was Pabst Blue Ribbon Beer, because I can remember a giant blue sign on top of the building. It went out of business somewhere around 1958 (a guess). Every time my Father and I went to visit my Aunt, the wrecking ball had done more of its work. One evening I was advised not to go to the playground of the school across the street. When I asked why, I was told the reason I had been seeing so many small dogs running around the neighborhood during that demolition. They were rats, which had used the empty vats for their home and were being evicted. I wisely listened to that advice.

Tar the roof again?

My Father took care of his Sister Emma, quite well. I spent many weekends in the summer doing house projects on George Street. I'll never forget two summers (not consecutive ones) we selected to put a coat of black tar on the roof of the house. The five gallon buckets were heavy all right, but the fun didn't start until we made it up through the closet to the roof. It was mid summer and about ninety-five degrees. Just right to make the tar flow smoothly on the two six foot long-handled brushes we used. After thoroughly sweeping up the debris on the roof and precision bombing it to the yard below, the job could commence. I pried open the first bucket tab and then the rest to expose the messiest pile of goop you ever saw. We had to stir it because the lighter elements would rise to the top and separate. After obtaining an even consistency we could dip our brushes into the mess and spread it on the roof. It was heavy and smelled like an oil field in New Jersey. Unless you've driven through refinery area on the New Jersey Turnpike in summer you can't appreciate it. After six or seven hours we could scrub up and get back to looking white again. Upon carting our empty buckets to the curbside for disposal a man stopped to talk to us and offered to pay us Eighty dollars to do his roof on Central Avenue. The next weekend we did it all over again. That time it had a slightly different flavor.

Magical Mystery Tour. The Cousins.

One of the most indescribable, mystical, experiences of my life was the rare occasion when I could see my cousins. My Aunt Emma's oldest son Robert, and his wife Dotty had the great fortune to have been blessed with the two most wonderful girls ever put on the face of the earth. When I heard my Father say that we were about to go to Aunt Emma's house to visit Linda and Barbara the Earth stopped turning. That's about the most inadequate terms I can use to describe what it was that I felt every time they briefly came into my life. Those two girls always had a smile on their face and I hope were almost as glad to see me as I was them. We would have the greatest fun running up and down the stairs of my Aunt's house and playing "hide and seek" and other neat games. We had so much fun. We shut the world out from early afternoon until late at night. Then the saddest hour came. I had to go home and spend eight hours asleep. Every once in a while I would get to return the next morning until their departure in the early afternoon. I felt as though my heart had been ripped out when we had to say goodbye. I can still feel that sensation as I write this. As we grew older, the most wonderful thing happened, and at the right time. They had moved from Warwick, Rhode Island, (the Moon) to Wayne, New Jersey. My favorite place to go in the summer and on any weekend I could, was through the Holland Tunnel to N.J. and visit my cousins, Linda and Barbara. I love them dearly to this day, and always will.

Pittsfield what?

Almost as wonderful were my other cousins who lived in Pittsfield Massachusetts. I can't believe I spelled that right. I got to see them less frequently but what swell folks. My cousin Chuck had the same priceless smile on his face, you'd have thought he was the one who invented it. Every time I saw him I knew I would not be disappointed. He had that wonderful glow about him that few people will ever know. His wife Marilyn was his equal in grace and beauty and they always treated me as someone who was very special to them. The feeling was *always* mutual. We visited them in Massachusetts one winter after a snowy trip up the Connecticut Turnpike. I knew I would get to see my cousin David and now there was a new addition to the family. Her name was Nancy. How in the world could one family get all the good looks? David was a fine looking boy and Nancy was as cute as a bug's ear. In 1968 before I married my wife Linda, we learned that Chuck and Marilyn would be in Dallas Texas. I was attending College in Durant Oklahoma at the time, so Linda and I drove my Fathers '54 Buick to a small town north of Dallas to meet them for lunch. We had a great visit and caught up on the latest events in each other's life. That was the last time I saw them.

That's all I have to say about that.

Sincerely, Bob (Robert) Schwarz

Jeanine Graham

Whilst thinking about their wedding day, I remembered a lovely story about that day which you may feel will add a bit of 'colour' to the statistic. As you know, Dad was car mad but being a true Scot, he never treated himself to a really good machine, always watched the pennies and contented himself with his racing cars until his 50th year. As you can imagine, our family cars were always in tip top condition mechanically so the following story was hilarious to us kids when it was told to us:

Ethel & Charles caravaning in the Highlands

Dad was driving to his wedding in Glasgow from Lesmahagow where his parents lived at the time, when the car broke down!! Don't think this had ever happened to him before or since. Despite being dressed in his full wedding regalia, tail coat, stripped trousers etc. and being the mechanical genius that he was, he got out, lifted the bonnet and proceeded to repair the problem. The result was a fully functioning car but the bridegroom's hands were black with motor oil! The breakdown had delayed his arrival at the church so there was no time to find soap and water. He was married with oil stained hands - this must have given Mum fair warning of what was to come - every weekend her husband lived in his garage at the back of the house building his racing cars. A lovely footnote to this story is that when Mum & Dad celebrated their Golden Wedding Anniversary in 1988, my husband Nikos, visited Scotland for the first time. When we were leaving, Dad presented Nikos with the kid gloves he had worn on his wedding day (he HAD to wear them in the photos to cover the oily hands). In the plane home I told Nikos the story so we turned the fingers of the gloves outside in and low and behold, lots of dark smudges!! There were no "wet-wipes" in those days!!

David Alma Graham

Letter to his younger son, Charles J. Graham while Chuck was in the military during the Korean Conflict.

Bob, Emma, David and Charles, ca. 1943

car again. It is too bad that this illness had to happen at this particular time.

Our government seems to be in an awful mess and I do not know how long the American people are going to put up with it. Lets hope that the people will put in enough protests that they will have to do something about it. The people all over seem to be dissatisfied with the way things are being run.

I hope and pray that something turns up that this whole mess all over the world will be cleaned up quickly

I am writing this letter so when mother goes to the bank to cash my pension check and deposit yours that she will be able to mail this letter

I have been feeling pretty good and take good care of yourself

love,

Dad.

Auntie Nan

On the following pages is a copy of a letter written by Agnes "Nan" Graham Fairweather back home to Sheila & Ronald Rattray in Jun 1957 while Nan and Frank Fairweather were on a visit to America and Canada. I have known for years that these two Scottish cousins came to my christening in May 1957 in Pittsfield and that 'Aunt Jenny' drove them up and back from New York City for the event. Frank's son Howard immigrated to Canada and lived in Toronto, presumably at the address given.

at 14 Servington Crescent,
Toronto 7,
Canada.

Friday 14/6/57.

Dear Sheila & Ronald,

Thank you for my birthday gift received when we returned from New York on ~~Tuesday~~ Wednesday. I hope you are not meaning me to sing any of the songs, but it will be useful to have, and it was good of you to remember my birthday. I sent off a handbag for you, Sheila, for the 19th July, and I hope you like it. As I said in my accompanying note, that type is very much used here. I may buy myself one some day, if I have any money left. I hope you don't have to pay duty. I didn't put on the full price.

We left New York at 11:15 on Tuesday night, and arrived here 12:30 ~~~~ Wednesday. The bedrooms on the trains are very comfortable, and I was amazed because I slept off and on all night. I never sleep at all at home. The train stopped ¾ hr. at Buffalo, and we had a wander round the Station. When we returned to our compartments the top bed was tucked away, and the over one converted into a lovely wide settee.

I forgot to say thank you for your air letter also awaiting us. The snaps are very good, and we both think Joy is very like Rosalyn. I note she is to be lazy at walking, - takes after her mother!

2.

You will be galavanting around Monifieth, Carnoustie or Aberdeen by the time this reaches G.B. so I'll address it to Hillcrest.

Certainly I have enough material for several articles. All I lack is the ability to write them. I am supposed to give a talk to the D/dee U.F. Church's Women's Guild when I return, so that will have to be jotted down. I don't intend to try to describe scenery &c. They can get that from Guide Books. What I thought of doing was telling about the little differences in customs, which appealed to us. Every restaurant, business, office, hotel, insurance Co., bank &c. &c. have match books with their names printed on them, and I started to collect them. I haven't counted them, but I'm sure I must have between 50 - 70 different ones. Another custom which intrigued us is that wherever you have a meal, there are peppermints provided as you leave. Frank thought that looked as if the meal was so indigestible that mints were required, but I said you were expected to order drinks, and the mints were meant to hide the smell! If you order a dish with spaghetti (?) in it, or lobster, a waiter comes and ties a huge paper feeder round your neck. That is true, and I kept one of mine to illustrate my talk. It is about 18" deep, and 15" wide. The first time I saw a man with lobster, having this bib tied round his neck, I wondered what was happening. I haven't risked lobster yet, as the nut-crackers and array of implements scares me.

3.

The majority of Americans (not so much Canadians) are very slovenly in their speech and grammar. In fact we have been complimented several times on our speech. Practically every-one say nothin' and somethin', and the use of double negatives is common even by college students. "They don't know nothin'." is almost universal, and Dr. George Graham and his wife, also a Doctor, thought our perfect English was outstanding, and they said they had noticed in their rounds, that British people, even of the poorer class, had very few grammatical errors in their speech, - especially Scottish people. Good old Scottish education. "Foist" for first, "Thoisday" for Thursday and so on is ordinary pronunciation, even from the pulpit.

Frank says to tell you about the "No smoking" notices. They are in shops of all kinds, sub-ways, street cars and buses, cinemas &c., and you simply couldn't imagine the litter of cigarettes at entrances to these places. Frank said over and over again when we would see dozens of almost-whole cigarettes on the streets "What a gold mine for the Dundee dowpie pickers!" Being a Scottie, he didn't enter the sub-way &c. until his cigarette was almost finished.

We go on to Milo, Alberta, a week on Sunday, arriving the following Tuesday. We are quite looking forward to meeting Elvera, Laurine, Lloyd & Floyd &c. you know who they are? If not, ask your Father!!

Love to all, &again Happy Birthday,
Auntie Nan & U.F.

> I have often wondered if the names – Elvera, Laurine, Lloyd and Floyd are somehow related to the Grahams since the comment is to "ask your Father"

Life with my Father: David S. Graham
January 24, 1893 – May 19, 1965
by Donald M. Graham

David Soutar Graham was my father, and no-one still alive knew him better than I did. He was an ardent Scottish Nationalist, and wrote and spoke extensively and passionately on the subject, first under the name Sandy M'Intosh (sometimes Sandy McIntosh), then later under his own name. I have what I believe to be a nearly complete archive of writings to, by, and about him in the form of three booklets and hundreds, perhaps thousands, of newspaper clippings pasted into a large volume along with carbon copies of many of the original typescripts. The earliest clippings date back to 1914, and appear under the nom-de-plume Doksa. I can't say for certain that he was Doksa (nor do I know the origin of the name), but it seems plausible. One section of the volume has been cut out for some reason, and I have no idea what it included. He was a skilled and articulate writer and public speaker.

Many of his earlier writings were in Scots, but he later switched to English.

He used to carry paint and brushes with him in his car, and paint **HOME RULE FOR SCOTLAND** on rocks all over the countryside. He had a rubber stamp saying the same thing, and used it to stamp the slogan on every official document and the back of every banknote that passed through his hands. Once he was charged with defacing currency, but defeated the charge on the grounds that he stamped only the backs of the banknotes, not the faces.

To make a living, he and my mother owned and ran Graham's Advertising Services in Dundee. Most of their work consisted of newspaper and magazine ads for shops, small businesses, and department stores. Once they got the contract for the Edinburgh Tattoo, and at one point an ongoing contract with Baxter's Foods in Fochabers, which at that time was on the verge of going international with its array of gourmet-quality jams, sauces, soups, and other assorted items. Once in a while my mother would go up to Fochabers for meetings with Ena Baxter, and come back with a huge hamper that Ena had given her, with samples of everything they produced.

My father was also an outstanding chess player, a brilliant debater, and as a young man a world-class middle-distance runner, having told me that he once held the British Army record for the mile at 4 minutes 12 seconds. However, I am unable to reconcile this with what records I can find for that event during the time that he would have been in the army (probably ca. 1911-1918).

In my younger days, he usually wore a tailored suit, often with a trilby or fedora, and even at home rarely took off his tie. When he got older, and more relaxed about his clothing, his usual garb was either a kilt with a Balmoral, or a tweed suit with a deerstalker. After he retired, he either stayed with the kilt or tweed suit, or dressed casually.

On the other side, as his son, I can testify that he was severely deficient in what today would be called "parenting skills." My friends used to tell me that they wished they had my mother, and were glad they didn't have my father. My feelings about their parents were the reverse.

His main way of dealing with me as a child was to bark orders at me, demanding instant unquestioning obedience, hemming me in with innumerable pointless restrictions, and constantly reprimanding me for offences ranging from trivial to imaginary. When he wasn't doing that, he was muttering *sotto voce* how useless, incompetent, careless, lazy, unreliable, stupid, untrustworthy, etc. I was. He would surreptitiously monitor my reactions to this until I was ready to explode with rage, at which point he would suddenly stop, leaving me stranded with simmering anger, just short of achieving release from it by losing my temper. My tension manifested itself in the form of frequent severe headaches and bellyaches.

He was forever ordering me to stand up for my beliefs, by which he meant *his* beliefs. He loved to tell me to "Dare to be a Daniel, dare to stand alone," but what he really wanted was for me to stand with him. When I did stand up for beliefs that were different from his, he would shout me down or use debaters' tricks of rhetoric to "prove" me wrong.

I had certain daily chores I was expected to do, most of which I didn't mind, since they were not onerous. But if he happened to notice that I was making a move towards starting one of them, he would then immediately order me to do it, then tell me that I would never have done it if he hadn't told me to. The only one I really didn't like was being expected to get on my hands and knees to keep the long gravel pathway from the front gate to the door free of weeds. No weed, however tiny, escaped my father's scrutiny when he carried out his regular inspections. Once I got some weed-killer and used that. This enraged him, since it was "lazy." To him, work, no matter how pointless, was a moral imperative, whereas to me, work is what I do to achieve a desired result. Doing something more efficiently frees me to do something else.

I had to ask permission for anything I wanted to do, which he usually refused, and if he did grant permission, often put impossible restrictions on it. For example, he once gave me permission to go swimming with my friends, and when I had everything ready and was about to leave the house, he told me I had to be back in an hour. When I pointed out that the travel time alone to get to the pool and back was an hour, he did not relent.

One of his favourite tricks was to wait until we were all seated around the table for a meal, then he would order me to fetch something. When I had brought it to the table and seated myself again, he would order me to fetch something else. After a while, I started asking him, before I had sat down again, if there was anything else he wanted me to fetch while I was still on my feet, to which he would always answer "no." Then when I was seated, he would do it anyway. He had lots of other malicious little tricks in this vein, but you get the idea.

I was allowed a single token protest, to which he never listened, and if I persisted, he snapped at me, "You've had your say." I once sarcastically asked his permission to breathe. I don't remember his response, but the asthma I developed after that lasted until puberty.

There was always active conversation around the dinner table, both when I lived only with my parents, and also when my maternal grandparents lived with us. He allowed me limited participation in this, but when I had reached what he considered to be my allotted limit, he would snap at me to tell me I had said enough, even – perhaps especially - if I was in the middle of the final sentence in which I would have made my point. If I continued to talk after he interrupted me, he would reprimand me for having interrupted *him*.

He was constantly telling me how important it was to get an education, which I wanted to do anyway, but when I applied to the university, his response was to say, "Why can't you get a job instead, like other boys, and bring some money into the house?" When I had had part-time or summer jobs in the past, he made me hand most of my pay over to him.

When I was in high school, he tried to insist that I do my homework and studying in the same room where he and my mother were talking, so that he could monitor me to make sure that I was actually doing it. When I protested that their conversation - mostly political discussions in which I had no interest - was such a distraction that I couldn't concentrate, he said that I was just nosy and wanted to eavesdrop. (If I wanted to eavesdrop, why did I insist on working where I wouldn't be able to do it?) With my mother's support, I was eventually allowed to study in another room, but wasn't allowed to listen to music while doing so, because according to him that *was* a distraction. Once in a while he would tiptoe to the room where I was working, then suddenly open the door to see whether or not I really was studying, which I always was. Since his failed attempts to prove that I wasn't hard at work gave him no satisfaction, he eventually gave up on that.

Part of his reason for reversing his stand on my getting an education was his inability to deal with the possibility that I could be better at anything than he was. A case in point: he loved puzzles, and was always coming home with illustrated, written, or mechanical ones. One day he showed me two identical oddly-shaped plastic polyhedra, and said that the puzzle was to fit them together to form a tetrahedron. I played around with them for a bit, then suddenly saw the solution, said, "Ah! I got it!", and started to show him. Before I could do so, he grabbed them from me and said, "No, you couldn't have done it," then demonstrated the solution, with evident relief that he had been able to do so before I could show him. When I protested that that was what *I* had been about to do, he insisted that I couldn't possibly have solved it if he hadn't shown me. He had had to look up the solution. Despite that, I still derive great pleasure from puzzles, and one of my favourite books when I was growing up was *The Puffin Puzzle Book*, intended for children. I still collect books of puzzles, and sometimes find Puffin puzzles in books intended for adults.

I don't mean to suggest that my father was dim-witted. His mind was quick and agile, which served him well in debates, whereas mine is slow and careful, geared more towards dealing with complex, multi-faceted problems through prolonged and detailed thought. To this day I never express opinions on things that I haven't thought through – or if I do, I make it clear that this is a preliminary assessment, which could change if I were to get more information or give it more thought. When he used his debating skills on me to "prove" that I was wrong about something, I was usually able to *detect* the flaw in his reasoning, but by the time I was able to identify and articulate it, the opportunity to counter it was lost. By both temperament and my training as a scientist, my intellectual focus is on clear thinking with the aim of finding objective truth through careful evaluation of as much evidence as I can find, whereas his was on winning arguments. He would have made an outstanding trial lawyer. When I *was* able to articulate the flaws in his reasoning, his method of dealing with it was not to reason with me, but to shout me down. Once he had taken a position on something, he would never back down from it, no matter how much evidence there was against it, although to be fair to him, when he got older and had mellowed a bit, he sometimes revised his opinions on his own.

One of his favourite debating tricks was to leave a deliberate hole in one of his arguments, then wait for his opponent to jump through it. Of course, he knew ahead of time what the opponent would say, and he was waiting on the other side to pounce. But it didn't stop there; he would do this about three levels deep, by which time his opponent would be floundering at a total loss as to what to say. However, I don't recall his ever having used that on me.

At that time in Britain, the official government policy on higher education was that it should be available to anyone capable of benefiting from it, which in practice meant passing all courses. Towards that end, government grants were available, intended to cover all education expenses, such as fees, textbooks, food, and accommodation. The amount was scaled according to one's parents' income, but if the parents did not want to supplement a grant that was diminished according to what they earned, they could sign an affidavit to that effect, so that the student could get the maximum grant. His income was such that I qualified only for a reduced grant, but he refused either to supplement the grant or to sign the affidavit, saying, "What would it look like if I said that I was unwilling to support my own son?" (!)

In high school, I worked hard at my studies, which meant that at the end of each term I was mentally exhausted, but when my father tried to insist that I continue to study just as hard as ever during the break to get a flying start on the next term, my mother intervened on my behalf, and I got a reprieve. When I came home one day, and told him proudly that I had taken the second place in class on a mathematics test, his only response was to growl, "Why can't you be first?" When I did take first place in the next test, he said, "Why can't you be first in everything?" Nothing was ever good enough for him.

On a lighter note, he had a tendency to utter accidental spoonerisms, which I appear to have inherited and passed on to my daughter Nicole. Once he said that it was time to "fight the liar," and on another occasion, which my mother and I never let him live down, we had had raspberry mousse for dessert, which he really liked, so he asked my mother for more of the "stink puff." My own unintentional masterpiece in that genre was a three-way spoonerism during a discussion of how restaurants divided tips among the staff, in which I referred to their "ship-scaring team."

A peculiar incident one day made it clear that at some level my father had some insight into his behaviour. He came home from work, and said that he felt strange. He was uncharacteristic-ally cheerful and good-natured, and advised me to take advantage of it while it lasted, because whenever this condition wore off, he would be unable to prevent himself from going back to being his usual abusive self. This lasted for the rest of the evening. The next day he did revert, and had no recollection of anything that had happened the day before. I have no idea what brought this about. My mother suspected that he had bumped his head and suffered a mild concussion. Perhaps he had had a minor stroke. Who knows?

Although he was abusive towards me, he and my mother had a very close relationship, and I never once witnessed their ever having arguments or fights. Many years after he died, I asked my mother about this, and she told me that although they did occasionally argue, they tried to protect me from it. Every evening, she would curl up in his lap in an armchair and they would both have a nap. I sometimes felt a bit left out.

I don't mean to suggest that life with him was a total disaster. He may have been an opinionated petty tyrant much of the time, but we did have some good times together. He introduced me to photography, and when we visited scenic areas, he brought along his binoculars, pointed out interesting features of the landscape, and showed me how to identify birds and wildlife from a distance. He also had a 400× microscope, and introduced me to a whole world of microscopic life and other things from the world of the very small. On our walks in the countryside, he drew my attention to all kinds of plant and animal life and explained whether or not it was edible and what it was good for. We often brought things home to examine under the microscope.

On weekend evenings, we always sat around the sitting-room fire and played board, card, word, or paper-and-pencil games. For some reason, his attitude during our game sessions was diametrically opposed to what it was at other times. When I won, he congratulated me, and when I lost, he would encourage me to keep trying, and wish me better luck next time. These regular games had a lot to do with sharpening my wits. Although both he and my mother consistently beat me at chess and he also at checkers (draughts), which my mother didn't play, I did better at the other games we played. My father was the second-best player in his chess club, and apart from his nemesis, Arthur Smart, who lived a few doors away from us, and *always* won, the only person I knew who could match him was my mother. Although I played chess from an early age, I never developed any feeling for the game, and played only by plotting out individual moves as far ahead as I could, which wasn't very far. In fact, in my entire life I have met only one person who is an even worse chess player than I am. Sometimes we would play billiards or snooker, and occasionally table tennis. He was better at the slow careful games of billiards and snooker, and I at the fast-reacting game of table tennis – the reverse of our mental capabilities. He was also good at golf, a game I never played.

Although we played a lot of card games, there was no gambling, even for token stakes. My father considered gambling to be immoral, so was vehemently opposed to it. I never even *heard* of poker until I was in my teens. However, he made an exception for himself by playing the quintessentially British gambling game of "football pools" every week – predicting the outcomes of all the professional football (soccer) games to be played in Britain in the week to come. When I asked him about the inconsistency, he said that it was acceptable since he never bet more than he could afford. So far as I am aware, he never won anything. For my part, I have no moral objection to gambling; it just doesn't interest me. He also thought that dancing was immoral, but the only music he ever listened to was Scottish country dance music. However, he probably meant whatever kind of dancing was currently popular with young people. But that didn't affect me, since I didn't like dancing anyway.

Every evening, we all went for a walk outside Newport-on-Tay (usually just called Newport), where we lived, and in the summer, we drove to some point in the country every Sunday for a picnic, sometimes with friends or other family members. There were a number of favourite scenic spots we went to, always isolated, and often reached by some seldom-travelled back road. If the weather was inclement, we would drive instead to some picturesque little town like Crieff or Dunkeld, and eat in a restaurant.

On one of these picnics, we went fishing in a stream in Glen Ogle, and I caught a trout, which we ate that evening. The only other time I went fishing with my father, off Balmerino pier, about 10 km west of Newport, all we caught was the biggest crab I had ever seen. But it fell off the line before we could land it. I remember my mother later teasing us about fishermen's tales. My father used to tell me about "guddling" for trout when he was young – stroking the trout's belly to relax it, and catching it by hand.

Every year we took a vacation for a week or two. At first, while my parents were building their advertising business, they took separate vacations - my father alone, my mother with me, to different places every year - so that one of them was always around the office, but once the business was established, they hired some help, and all three of us would go, by now usually to the same place each year: a centuries-old hotel called Inverarnan, about a third of the way from the north end of Loch Lomond to the highland village of Crianlarich. The hotel had a spectacular view of a beautiful waterfall on the mountainside to the east. It was a popular spot with mountaineers, including Scottish climbing legends Bill Murray and Ben Humble.

The atmosphere in the hotel was such as to encourage interaction among the guests. There was a lounge where we would all congregate around a fire in the evenings. Some people would talk, some would play games or read from the supply of games and books in the corner, and sometimes someone would play the piano. My father liked to demonstrate magic tricks to the children. One small boy was utterly mystified when my father made something disappear, then happened to find it in some unexpected place. After three or four repetitions, the boy's face suddenly lit up as he said, "Now I know how you do it – it's a *trick*!"

My father was a religious fundamentalist who never went to church, and a passionate politician who never ran for office. Although neither of my parents ever went to church, I was sent there every Sunday as soon as I was old enough to walk there unattended, probably when I was about five.

He had extraordinary powers of concentration, and was able to shut out distractions to such an extent that if you had set off a bomb beside him while he was working, he probably wouldn't have noticed. However, if he was asleep, the slightest sound would elicit a violent startle reaction – a consequence of the shell shock he suffered in World War I. When he wasn't writing copy for the advertising business, he was writing political speeches, articles, or letters to the editor, which usually got published. He made his notes in shorthand, and typed them out only when the final draft was ready. The only place you are likely to see a typewriter nowadays is in a museum, but when I was growing up, there were always four or five of them around the house. I got my parents' most recently cast-off ones when they upgraded to newer models, and started to type when I was about five years old. I didn't learn to touch-type until I was fifty. Both of my parents were lifelong two-finger typists – but very fast nonetheless.

Whenever we got together with family or friends, and later in the lounge of the small hotel my mother ran after my father retired, he loved to pontificate. From time to time, my mother used to remind him that he was in a social gathering, not addressing a public meeting.

At home, my parents rarely spoke about anything but politics, and I would just tune out. To this day I have such a distaste for politics that I don't even vote. However, that is also because political issues are so complex that voting intelligently requires more intensive study than I am prepared to carry out. My father encouraged me to sell Scottish Nationalism to my friends, but my heart wasn't in it, and I had no real understanding of it anyway. While I was growing up, a number of prominent Scottish Nationalists were guests in our home, including Arthur Donald-son, who later became leader of the Scottish National Party, and Wendy Wood. I remember Wendy Wood as a very tweedy lady dressed all in brown, including some kind of knitted cap, which she kept on the entire time she was in our house, and Arthur Donaldson as a kindly old gentleman in a white shirt and dark suit and tie. Both were awarded the place of honour by being seated in my father's personal armchair.

When I was an undergraduate at Queen's College in Dundee, which at that time was a college of St. Andrews University before it separated from St. Andrews to become the University of Dundee, I sometimes travelled by ferry from Newport, and sometimes by train, which crossed the river via the Tay (rail) Bridge. At the time of its completion in 1887, this was, at about three and a half kilometres, the longest bridge in the world. This was in the late 1950s, before the 1965 completion of the Tay Road Bridge. The ferry no longer exists. Once in a while I used to share a compartment on the train with Douglas Young, a former leader of the SNP, who lived in Tayport, about five kilometres east of Newport. He was Professor of Classics at Queen's College, well-known as a translator of ancient Greek literature into Scots. His best-known translation is *The Puddocks* (in English, *The Frogs*), from Aristophanes' *Βάτραχοι*. He was an extremely tall, thin man with a full black beard, and always wore some kind of flat round hat with a wide brim. However, although he and my father knew each other, I don't specifically recall his ever having been a guest in our home (although I have a vague recollection that he may once have been when I was very young). We never spoke when we shared a compartment, and I don't think he knew who I was. He always read or did some writing during the trip. My father told me that the reason for the beard was that he had hæmophilia, so couldn't risk cutting himself while shaving.

Decades later, long after my father died, my mother worked as office manager for yet another leader of the SNP, Gordon Wilson, who was about my age, and to whom she introduced me while I was visiting Scotland with Nicole, who was then seven years old.

I have a vivid recollection of an incident that took place around 1950, when I was about 12. Newport is in the north-east corner of Fife, an area known as the East Neuk. A couple of thousand years earlier, the region had a number of Roman settlements, and some of the local names are of Roman origin, including a picturesque bit of wilderness called Chesterhill, the "Chester" part of the name being derived from the Latin word "castra," meaning a camp. One day a hole about 30 cm across appeared in a patch of lawn in our front yard at 4 Kerr Street, and as the edges crumbled and fell into the hole, the opening became larger and larger, exposing a hollow the size of a small house, with a deep pool of water at the foot of it. Apparently this had been an old Roman well that someone centuries later had covered over with logs or thick planks so that houses could be built around it. Eventually the wood rotted, and this exposed the well. It took something like 20 truckloads of dirt to fill the hole. Since we had all walked over that spot every day for years, it is a miracle that no-one had fallen into it.

654 years earlier, a 152-kg rock called the Stone of Destiny (also known as the Stone of Scone – pronounced "Scoon"), its origins lost in antiquity, and with heavily symbolic value to the Scots as the seat upon which its monarchs had traditionally been crowned, had been forcibly removed from Scotland by England's King Edward the First, and placed into a wooden chair called St. Edward's Chair in Westminster Abbey in London, upon which many English and British monarchs were later crowned.

Around the same time that the hole appeared in our yard, four Scottish students broke into Westminster Abbey, liberated the Stone, and brought it back to Scotland.

Although no-one had as yet actually said the Stone was in Scotland, it was the obvious area for the authorities to look for it. As a prominent Scottish Nationalist, my father was, of course, a prime suspect. One day there came the inevitable knock at the front door. My father answered, with me standing behind him, looking past to see and hear what was going on. It was a heavy-set middle-aged police sergeant with a tall thin young constable accompanying him. The sergeant harrumphed, put on his best official voice, and a conversation took place, somewhat as follows:

Sergeant: "Are you Mr. Graham?"

My father: "I am."

Sergeant: "Do you know who stole the Stone of Destiny?"

My father: "I do."

At this point, both the sergeant and the constable became instantly alert, and the sergeant's notebook came out, with his pencil poised over it. The conversation continued.

Sergeant: "Well? Who was it?"

My father (straight-faced): "King Edward the First."

Both the sergeant and the constable looked distinctly startled, then as if they were about to explode as they suppressed their laughter. With the gravity of the moment disrupted, the questioning continued in a noticeably different tone as they tried to maintain their composure.

Sergeant: "Hmph, well, do you know where it is now?"

My father: "Do you see that hole over there?"

Sergeant (craning his neck to look at it): "Ye-e-e-es."

My father: "It's at the bottom of the hole."

The sergeant took a few cautious steps towards the hole, briefly looked into the deep pool of muddy water at the foot of it from behind the safety barrier that had been placed around it, came back, looked quickly to the left and to the right, then leaned conspiratorially towards my father with the back of his hand shielding his mouth as if to thwart eavesdroppers, looked him straight in the eye, and said, quietly and very seriously, "Bloody well keep it there!", folded his notebook, gestured with his head to the constable, who hadn't said a word during the entire exchange, to follow him, and left. That was the sum total of the police investigation into my father's possible involvement.

I think he was secretly hoping that the police would send a crew to search through the water, mud, and dirt, and waste a lot of manpower on looking for the Stone, which had in fact never been anywhere near the hole. Ian Hamilton, one of the students who had retrieved the Stone from Westminster Abbey, later told him that several duplicates of the Stone had been made, and that the one eventually taken back to England after an anonymous phone call told authorities where to find it was not the original, so that the stone on which the current Queen was seated during her Coronation is a forgery. I have no way of knowing whether or not this is true, but it seems unlikely.

Since that time, the (or a?) Stone has been repatriated to Scotland, with the understanding that it may be borrowed any time it is needed for a Coronation in England.

My father was a vehement anti-evolutionist, stemming from his religious fundamentalism, and loved debating scientists on the topic. Since the primary focus of scientists is to find verifiable objective truth, and his was to win arguments, he always won those debates by using tricks of rhetoric, including his hole-in-the-argument trick, that were sufficient to convince the largely uninformed audiences who voted on the debaters' skills. He knew my high school mathematics teacher, Dr. Inglis, and loved to tell about how he had defeated him in an evolution debate.

As with his Scottish Nationalism, he tried to recruit me to spread the anti-evolution doctrine among my friends. I didn't have any success, largely because I was recycling his second-hand arguments on a topic about which all my information came from him. Unlike with politics, in which I had no interest, I had a passionate interest in science, so later set about learning as much as I could about evolution. I started at the source by reading *The Origin of Species*, which my father told me he had read, and went from there to general biology textbooks, then on to more specialized ones in genetics and evolutionary theory, which he hadn't read. That was when I discovered that nearly everything my father and the anti-evolution books in his library had taught me about evolution was nonsense, and that solidly confirmed evolutionary mechanisms were the only known way to explain how life developed, with no credible evidence whatsoever against it. Lots of specific details remained to be discovered, but the basic principles were well understood. And progress in the field was such that things that had not already been explained soon would be. By now even more of that work has been done, and progress continues to be made. As of this writing, there is only one remaining major gap in our understanding: although the spontaneous formation of simple biological molecules from inorganic precursors is well understood, we do not as yet know how to get from there to self-reproducing molecules, nor from there to the first cells. But the gap is steadily closing.

This, however, was after I had left Scotland for Canada, so he never found out about the reversal in my stance. It wouldn't have done any good anyway; if I had pointed out to him what I had learned, he would have tried to use either his debating skills or his old argument-by-intimidation trick on me to "prove" the error of my ways.

This apparent conflict between science and religion is completely unnecessary. The purpose of (institutional) religion is to provide moral and spiritual guidance to those who feel the need for it, and that of science to find verifiable objective truth. Neither is equipped to do the job done by the other. However, although you don't find scientists using their expertise to try to provide spiritual guidance, fundamentalist religions routinely try to foist their ideas about objective reality on others, despite their complete lack of competence to do so. This does a grave disservice to both science and religion.

My father was a strict teetotaller, but a heavy smoker. He would not allow alcohol in the house, even a small quantity of sherry to go into the Christmas cake, despite my mother's pointing out to him that all the alcohol would evaporate out anyway during the baking process. He explained many times how this came about. His father, Charles Iconaclast Bradlauch Graham, had also been a strict teetotaller and a religious fundamentalist (directly contradicting the radical atheist father who had given him those unusual –and unusually spelled - middle names), and my father followed his lead. However, my father served in the army trenches in World War I, and suffered from what was then called shell shock, later known as combat fatigue, and currently as post-traumatic stress disorder, or PTSD (which was the probable primary cause of his irrational behaviour). To calm him down, the army medics ordered him to get drunk and started him on cigarettes. This was decades before the health hazards of smoking had been discovered. He said that after he woke up from his drunken stupor, he had no recollection of anything that had happened, but his friends told him that he had been the funniest drunk they had ever seen. After that, he never again touched alcohol, but became addicted to tobacco. He ordered me not to drink, and advised me not to smoke. I had no interest in smoking anyway, since I hated the smell of cigarette smoke (and still do), so never smoked, but I do drink moderately. As a student, I went through the customary rites of passage involving getting drunk, but didn't like the feeling of losing control of my body and mind. Now I am usually content to stop at one drink, don't drink at all if I expect to be driving, and don't drive if I have had more than one drink.

But back to my father. It should be clear by now that critical thinking was not his forte. He frequently made egregious errors in reasoning, such as false syllogisms, generalizing from limited data, relying on anecdotal evidence, and misunderstanding statistics. For example, since individual air accidents often had large numbers of casualties, so got a lot of publicity, he concluded that air travel was unsafe, despite the fact that crashes are extremely rare compared with the millions of uneventful flights. I soon learned that when he did this, it was a waste of breath to try to point out the mistakes. One day he told me that an article he had read in one of the Sunday newspapers proved that space travel was impossible. I was curious to know which of the common errors leading to this conclusion the author of the article had made, so I asked him where the newspaper was so that I could read it. He said he had used the newspaper to start the fire, but since it had proved its point, there was no point in my reading it to find out how. I asked him to summarize the reasoning used, but he was vague, saying something to the effect that since space was empty, it was impossible to travel through it. I didn't understand the argument then, and still don't. I suspect it may have been the old fallacy about rockets being unable to work in space because there is nothing to push against. This was in the late 1950s, a few months before Sputnik I went into orbit.

When I told him that one day there would be machines that could play chess, he snapped at me, "There will never be a machine that can play chess; it's much too complicated." I wonder what he would have made of the facts that today the two greatest chess grandmasters the world has ever seen are machines, you can buy chess-playing machines of more modest capacity off the shelf in any electronics store at easily affordable prices, and chess-playing programs for personal computers are readily available free of charge over the Internet.

For a while, he became interested in tracing his ancestry, and spoke of little else. After some time, I noticed that he hadn't mentioned it for a while, so I asked how his researches were going. He mumbled something that sounded like an evasion, so I later asked my mother what was going on. She said, in a kind of stage whisper, *"Don't ask!"* I guessed that what had happened was that he had found English ancestors, which of course had been bound to happen eventually, but when our somewhat distant cousin Dave Graham tracked me down decades later after having had considerably more success in the same task, unencumbered by the same prejudices, I found that it was much worse: he had found *Campbells*, which to my father was the worst disgrace imaginable. He used to love telling Campbell jokes. To this day anti-Campbell prejudice is common in Scotland, deriving from the 1692

Massacre of Glencoe, even though only one captain and six privates among those responsible were Campbells, and the event took place centuries before any present-day Campbells were even born. Again, considering that Campbell is one of the largest Scottish clans, he was bound to have found some sooner or later. However, he never seemed to make the connection between the abstract notion of the Campbells he despised on principle and the real flesh-and-blood Campbells he actually knew, who to him were no different from anyone else.

Although my father told me he had two brothers and a sister, I had never, so far as I knew, met any of them. The only Graham family member I was sure of having met while growing up was my grandfather with the unusual middle names, although I have carried with me throughout my life a vague memory of having met my first cousin Donald Charles Graham, son of my father's younger brother Charles, when we were both six years old, and having been washed along with him in the same bathtub. When we finally met when we were in our late 60s, he said he had no recollection of this, and his older sister Sheila said it never happened. Still, I wonder where the memory came from.

I have two memories of my grandfather. The first was when he came to visit when I was about five, and took me for a walk around Newport. We went to Windmill Park, which was quite a long walk for a small boy – not to mention for a man in his 80s. On our way home, we stopped by the drinking fountain on Tay Street, which overlooks the River Tay, and he gave me a drink of water from a rusty iron cup secured by a chain. When my parents found out about this, they were horrified that he had allowed me to drink from such an unhygienic source.

Charles I. B. Graham

The second was when my father took me to visit him in the nursing home where he spent his last days. He was very feeble, and his head kept falling back onto the pillow. I asked my father, "Is he dead?", and a moment later he opened his eyes. A few days later, my father came home and said, "The old man's dead." I remember my father setting off for the funeral in a top hat and tails.

He had a story he liked to tell about Grandpa in the nursing home. According to the story, a tree just outside Grandpa's room had a branch that kept blowing back and forth between the sun and the window in his room, and the flickering was annoying him. Grandpa, who made furniture for a living ("Furnish your house for five pounds"), climbed out the second-floor window of the nursing home, down a drainpipe, and home to his workshop, where he picked up a saw, climbed the tree and sawed off the offending branch before taking the saw back home, returning to the nursing home, up the drainpipe, and back to his room. Having seen Grandpa's feeble condition in the nursing home, I seriously doubt the veracity of this story, but I still like it.

My father occasionally described his life as a boy growing up in the village of Errol, on the north shore of the River Tay about half-way between Dundee and Perth. When his father lost patience with him and his siblings creating havoc in the house, he would tell them to go play in the woods so he could have some peace and quiet – "Awa tae the wid," meaning "Away to the wood." When my father got into mischief with his friends, they would have a lookout to watch for the local police constable. The signal was "ABC," meaning "a bobby comes."

There was apparently a village drunk, who owned a horse and buggy, and frequently drank himself into a stupor. When he passed out, the bartender would load him into his buggy, then the horse would take him home and wait patiently outside his house for him to recover consciousness. My father said that one time he and his friends came across him in this comatose state, gently removed him from his buggy, disengaged the horse, dismantled the buggy, reassembled it within a courtyard accessible only by a passageway too narrow to accommodate the assembled buggy, led the horse inside, reattached it to the buggy, and lifted the drunk back into his seat. This seems to me to be about as likely as the tree branch story. But still entertaining.

Sometimes my grandfather would borrow the horse and buggy to carry out some errand. On his way home, the horse would always stop at the pub and refuse to continue until it had seen my teetotal grandfather go into the pub and come out again.

My father sometimes spoke of his brother Bill, to whom he referred when talking to me as "Uncle Bill." He told me that Bill was managing director of Armstrong Whitworth. I don't remember his ever having told me anything about his other brother Charles or his sister Agnes, beyond the fact that they existed.

I once asked my mother why I never met any of my father's family, and she told me that it was because he was the black sheep of the family. Part of this was his extreme Scottish Nationalism, which annoyed some other members of the family, who falsely perceived Scottish Nationalism as being anti-Royalist. It wasn't until I was 19 that I learned more about the rift with the family.

My father often mentioned his other son, my much older half-brother Kenneth, whom I had never met, and whose photograph as a young boy was prominently displayed in our house. He never spoke of Kenneth's mother. Although I have no memory of having given the matter conscious thought, in retrospect I am sure there must have been questions simmering away just below the surface of my mind, which is why, when I was working in Lancashire, I decided to contact Kenneth, whom I somehow knew to be living in the Manchester area, with the intention of finding out more.

I found a Kenneth Graham in the Manchester phone book, with an address in the suburb of Sale, so I called. I got his wife, who seemed mystified when I identified myself. He called back the next day, and we arranged to meet at a railway station somewhere between Sale and Widnes, where I was working.

He was a very tall man with a forbidding manner, thick curly black hair, and a bristling black moustache. He made it clear that he was not pleased to see me, and would not introduce me to his family. I felt foolish and somewhat intimidated. He told me he had a teenage son and daughter, that he had never mentioned his father to his family, and no-one had asked. We exchanged a few horror stories about him, and Kenneth seemed to want to outdo me by pointing out that when he was a teenager and still lived with his father, he was a much younger man and had a lot more of what Kenneth called "zip." He said, "Well, I was a big fellow, and after things came to a head, we left and never went back."

Kenneth was astonished when I told him that our father was very proud of him, and that his photograph as a child was prominently displayed in our house. I can relate to that, since after he died *I* was astonished when my mother told me that he was very proud of me also, but never told me because he didn't think it was good for children to be praised. He thought it would make them conceited.

Kenneth told me that there were things about the family situation that I had obviously never been told, and suggested that I ask our father about them. So I did. I wrote to him and told him that I had met Kenneth, and what had transpired. He wrote back and told me that although my mother went by the name Mrs. Grace Graham, they had never been formally married, so that that their relationship was codified under Scots common law. He told me that except for Norman Robertson, the family solicitor, nobody outside the family knew of this. My mother later told me that the reason was that Kenneth's mother had refused to grant him a divorce. She told me that according to his solicitor he could have divorced her on the grounds of desertion, but that for some reason he didn't want to do that. He did, however, continue to provide her with financial support, which was why, despite his better than average income, we always seemed to be short of money. Eventually Kenneth's mother died, and my parents planned to get formally married, but my father died before this could take place. Kenneth himself died in 2006 at the age of 86.

It wasn't until Dave Graham tracked me down and told me of his family researches that I learned about the extended family I knew nothing about. I was flabbergasted to learn that my father's sister Agnes had lived with her husband Frank Fairweather at 4 Struan Place – about a seven-minute walk from us - in Newport while I was growing up there. As a teenager, I even delivered newspapers to their home without ever knowing that Mrs. Fairweather was my aunt.

When my father died in 1965, at the age of 72, I was close to finishing my Ph.D. in Edmonton, and I didn't really feel much of anything when I heard the news. I couldn't afford to go to Scotland for the funeral, return to Canada to finish my degree, then back to Scotland, so I waited until I had my degree in hand before returning. I went to visit my mother in Arrochar, at the head of Loch Long, where she and my father had purchased and run a small waterfront hotel called Greenbank after they retired from the advertising business. My father is buried in the cemetery there, but I still didn't feel much when I visited his grave. My mother, who died in 2002, shortly after celebrating her 90th birthday, is now buried alongside him.

When I returned to Arrochar in 1991 with Nicole, who was then seven years old, I spent some time alone at his gravesite in order to make my peace with him. Even then, I didn't feel much of anything, but at least the old ghosts of our troubled relationship were now buried along with him.

February 18, 2010

Don and Nicole, Oct 2009

Ethel (Eccleston) Graham

I was very fortunate to have correspondence with Ethel (Eccleston) Graham in 2004 and 2005 after I sent her a letter and earlier version of my research upon her 90th birthday – this at the request of Sheila Rattray.

Nethona
35, Strathfield Road.
Lanark
SCOTLAND.
ML11 9BS.
4th Nov. '04.

Dear David,

Thank you very much indeed for the lovely surprise delivered to me on my birthday. I do appreciate the kind thought & have enjoyed reading all the wonderful family information you have gathered. What a task!

I know nothing about computers so I do everything in the old fashioned way!

My marriage to Charlie was a long & happy one. He worked with Prudential Assurance Co. first in Dundee on his first agency & was then promoted to the DUMFRIES DISTRICT in 1937. Our first bungalow was built for us getting married in 1938 in THORNHILL, DUMFRIES. We bought the land from the Duke of Buccleugh who has a castle there.

Chas. was called to the R.A.F. the year Manette was born 1940, & I lived in Lanark with Chas.' parents with the baby until 1946 when we returned to THORNHILL & later built a second house there. I nursed Chas.' Dad there after he had been in hospital, until he died. Grandma stayed on with us for a bit & then returned to Lanark & her own home. Chas.' Dad was with the Pru' too.

Chas. was always keen on cars & motor racing & after the war I encouraged him to go racing as he hated his job with the Pru'. He enjoyed a few years in the sport – he bought his first car from Stirling Moss & afterwards built his own cars in our garage (I was the assistant). Snap enclosed.

Chas.' health was causing anxiety & after a long spell in hospital in Edinburgh he retired in 1966 at age 55. Rid of the stress we enjoyed a long & happy retirement. Went caravanning to the Highlands of Scotland in June & South to some lovely English areas in Sept. & to Jersey, Channel Islands where Fred & Manette lived for a time & Jonathan & Michael were born there.

When we retired we built another bungalow in Lanark, our present house, as Bhas' Mother & some of her family were getting old & needed some caring.

Monette trained as a Physiotherapist at Glasgow Royal Infirmary & worked in Jersey & later in Dumfries Royal Infirmary. She retired in 2000.

Jeannine took a degree in Company Law & Accountancy & worked in Jersey for a few years & then took off to travel in Europe, North Africa, Switzerland & Greece, where she met Arios, who is a Doctor. She came home to Scotland a few years ago & now works in a Call Centre. She speaks Greek & other languages.

Bhas. died four years ago & since then I live alone, have a huge garden which I enjoy & the girls visit regularly & take me shopping. I drove my own car until this year.

Have enclosed a few pictures which may interest you. I think seeing 'faces' helps to 'know' someone better. Sorry I have no up to date pictures of the family.

Just regret not asking more questions about the Graham family & the old days. Sheila & Maureen know a bit more than me.

Aunt Mon & Uncle Frank used to visit us in Thornhill at times. Frank always drove a big heavy car. They were well travelled & I think were in America & Canada but whether they visited relatives I don't know. Frank was a keen philatelist & had a big collection. He had a son, Howard & daughter Margarite who both lived in Canada.

Sorry I have no Birth or Death Certificates of Bhas' parents.

When we were on holiday with our caravan we always went to the cemetery at ARROCHAR to see Uncle David's grave. Bhas. arranged to have the headstone cleaned up & letters replaced on one occasion.

I do hope this has been some help to you & again thank you for sending me so much information.

Elizabeth Ethel Graham

The Tale and Trail of Minnie Watson, Half-Sister

One fascinating aspect of genealogical research stems from the random discoveries and clues that pop up along the way. The story of Minnie Watson serves as a fine example. The photo to the right is, I believe, a photo of a widowed Minnie (Watson) MacDonald, probably taken in 1907 shortly before she immigrated to the USA with her three children. Though Minnie does not appear on the Graham lineage we do share an important common ancestor – Catherine Wilkie, the wife of James Campbell Graham.

Early in my research, I acquired the 1881 census entry for David Alma Graham showing him (and his youngest brother George) to be living with their now twice-widowed mother Catherine (Wilkie) (Graham) Watson. Catherine was now a housekeeper and had two of her four Graham sons and both her surviving Watson daughters living in the household – Catherine and Wilhelmina or Minnie.

Source: FHL Film 0203480 GRO Ref Volume 282-1 EnumDist 28 Page 13

175152 Liff & Benvie, Forfar, Scotland H

Dwelling: 224 Blackness Rd George GRAHAM Son N/A 16 M Factory Worker Dundee, Forfar, Scotland

Dwelling: 224 Blackness Rd David GRAHAM Son Unmarried 26 M Tinsmith Stirling, Stirling, Scotland

Dwelling: 224 Blackness Rd Catherine WATSON Daughter N/A 13 F Scholar Dundee, Forfar, Scotland

Dwelling: 224 Blackness Rd Catherine WATSON Head Widowed 53 F Housekeeper Forfar, Forfar, Scotland

Dwelling: 224 Blackness Rd Minnie WATSON Daughter N/A 11 F Scholar Dundee, Forfar, Scotland

As ever, research efforts waxed and waned. But the 2004 New York City trip enabled me to reconnect with second cousin George Graham for a day. We drove around Brooklyn and Queens checking out houses and cemeteries where David Alma Graham and his extended family established their early roots. On that hot August day, George provided me with a copy of a first interesting document and clue. The document, in his family's possession, was an official Civil Complaint and summons dated 7 Jun 1898 to Charles IB Graham from his two half sisters, Catherine (Watson) Marshall and Wilhelmina (Watson) MacDonald. Apparently, the sisters wanted him to deliver the title to the Watson burial plot where their mother Catherine was buried some four months earlier. It seemed odd that such a document would be in the possession of David Alma Graham in Brooklyn NY but this was most certainly the case.

Thinking little more about it, other than having new clues as to the marriages of the two Watson half-sisters, I did little else until I received the following email from George in Dec. 2005.

Dave

I mentioned that I had a letter to DAG, Sr and that it might be of interest to you. I am sorry that I hadn't written about this to you sooner. It's postmarked June 29, 1933 and written to 90-40 205st, Hollis, LI, Brooklyn, New York. I suppose that was where he lived with my grandparents for a time. The letter starts out "Dear Brother" and has the return address E.W. Hayward, 5'10 8 St, Hermonia, CA. It reads:

"Dear Brother

"I received your kind and welcome letter and was ever so pleased to hear from you again. was very sorry to hear you were not feeling so well again on account of your back and legs bothering you so much. It is just too bad you cant get them doctored up so as you can feel fine and dandy again. I only wish that you were out here enjoying the sea breezes along with me. I came down here to let Dave move into my house in Los Angeles on he is only working 3 days a week and couldn't pay much rent. California rated wet yesterday along with the other states back east so they thing that business will be better on that account. some things are inching up here but there are lots here living on the county and has been for the past 2 years. we are all well except agnes there were in an auto accident last thursday set got her shoulder marked up and their car wrecked sot their is always something to worry about. I hope your family are all well and that you are feeling better now that the warm weather is in. Remember me to all the folks and hope they have all a good time during their vacation. I am sorry about charles wife not feeling so good. I haven't heard from him in quite a long time but I guess he writes just when the spirit moves him. I am pretty near as bad myself at writing to folkds.

"With best love and wishes from your loving brother and sister, Ed & Minnie

"address 510 8 st, Hermonia Beach"

There is also an address listed in his memo book for a Mrs Mallette, 3168 W 10th St, Los Angeles California. I guess we have some sort of relations there, living or dead.

Obviously, this transcribed letter raised many questions. Is this the Minnie (Watson) MacDonald from 1898? How and when did she get to California? What happened to her first husband Alexander MacDonald? These and many other questions were ultimately answered but we also gain a brief but intriguing picture of life during the height of the Great Depression. I assumed that George's transcription was reasonably accurate suggesting that Minnie was not a particularly good grammarian.

With this new clue, I was able to search US Census and California Vital Records data and I returned again to Scottish Peoples to see what I could learn about Minnie Watson and her family. Below, I will summarize Minnie's life chronologically, but the research discoveries certainly did not arise in the same step-by-step fashion. And it should be noted that it would take nearly two years of off-again, on-again research before the entire story unfolded.

Minnie Watson was born to James Watson (ship's carpenter and later property manager) and Catherine (Wilkie) (Graham) Watson in Dundee 2 Nov 1869. She grew up at 224 Blackness Avenue in Dundee with her step brothers in 1881 and then with her mother and sister in the 1891 census entry. She and her sister were listed as jute weavers. Minnie married Alexander MacDonald, third child and second son of Alexander MacDonald and Agnes Simpson, on 14 Jun 1895 in Dundee. Young Alexander and Minnie were both listed as a 23 years old showing that lying about one's age began in the nineteenth century. Alexander's occupation was as a plasterer. The young couple had three children in quick succession: Alexander b. 6 Dec 1896; Agnes Wilkie b. 15 Oct 1898; and David Watson b. 16 Oct 1900. Husband Alexander then signed up to the military and was sent to fight in South Africa during the Boer War. Alas, he died of the flu there in Apr 1903.

For reasons unknown, the young widow and her three children immigrated to America leaving Glasgow on 6 Sep 1907 aboard the SS Laurentian heading for Ludlow, Massachusetts after docking in Boston. The manifest lists another Dundonian family, James and Davina Connal with four children heading to the same place and both families were listed as 'friends of J. Lindsay James', presumably a Scottish connection. Minnie's description on the manifest was having fair complexion with brown hair and blue eyes. In the 1910 US Census, Minnie and children were living in Methuen, MA where her occupation was listed as 'housework.' By 1920, however, Minnie was living in Los Angeles, California. In a confusing entry found only when searching for her sons, there was the following:

[Census record image]

Note that Edward Mallete and wife Anna W. were living with Alexander and David MacDonald. My supposition is that Mina Watson sounded like Anna to the census taker and that she had remarried to Edward Mallette and had her two sons living with her. She was listed as hotel chamber maid, Edward was a house painter, Alexander was an auto mechanic and young David was a druggist in a drug store though his career later in life was also as a mechanic, limo driver and finally foreman for Mobil Oil Company.

Additional research revealed the whereabouts of daughter Agnes Wilkie MacDonald who was married to Albert James Neville at the tender age of seventeen and quickly had their one and only son, Robert R. Neville, who was over three years old in the 1920 census. Albert Neville was ten years her senior and though listed as a bookkeeper in 1920, reportedly went on to become a dentist. Refer back to the letter and it appears that Agnes and her husband were in some kind of auto accident in June of 1933. Agnes Wilkie MacDonald Neville, died October 1970 at age 72 in Deerfield IL and her husband Albert died four years later at the age of 86. Their son Robert was an auto executive with General Motors and moved a great deal throughout his career and was in the greater Chicago area at that time, so presumably his parents were moved closer to him and his family. [Note: I was able to locate the third wife of Robert R. Neville who provided me with his daughters' names and contact information, but they never responded to my inquiries.]

Unfortunately, the 1930 US census is not completely available online and we are without further records on Minnie or her children. But from the letter, we know that she was now married to Edward W. Hayward and living in Hermosa Beach, CA (the transcription reads "Hermonia Beach" but this was probably a matter of poor penmanship. Other than the June 1933 letter, we have little to indicate the direction of Minnie's life. However, as noted elsewhere in this history, Agnes Cuthbert Graham purportedly spent several years in Los Angeles managing a notions store. I wonder if she worked or lived with her aunt Minnie.

Wilhelmina Watson MacDonald Mallette Hayward died 5 Sep 1942 of chronic myocardial degeneration. The entry lists her as Minnie Hayward living at 510 8th St. Hermosa Beach, CA – the same address as the 1933 letter. It appears that Edward Hayward, who was born in England in 1866, lived until 1962 before passing in San Diego, CA. In the 1920 census he was listed as steam railroad painter.

At the same time that I obtained Minnie's death registration, I also got her son David's entry. Again, referring to the 1933 letter transcript, Minnie refers to having her son Dave's move into her house in Los Angeles because he could not afford the rent to live on his own. David died 11 Oct 1972 in South Pasadena, CA of congestive heart failure following a heart attack two weeks prior. His wife was listed

Laura (MacDonald) Peters, Kayla Peters, Joy Campbell, Sheila (Graham) Rattray, Willie Campbell and Sonja Campbell in Glasgow 28 Jun 2008.

as Lorraine Leque. They were married in 1928 and had two sons: Larry David (b. 1935) and Neil Willam (b. 1940). Using available online resources, I located an address for Neil and gave him a call in November 2007 followed by a letter with the MacDonald family history and its link to Catherine Wilkie. I didn't hear back for several months and thought that I had reached another dead end but in February 2008 I received a call from one of his daughters Laura (MacDonald) Peters. She was keenly interested in what I had discovered and passed along but said that her dad had suffered a mild stroke many months before I spoke to him and was reluctant to talk on the phone. But he did provide her with my letter and she excitedly made contact. In our exchanges, Laura indicated that she and her younger daughter Kayla were going to Scotland as a high school graduation gift. A few emails to the Scottish Grahams and they proved yet again to be exceedingly gracious hosts for such distant family members.

It is intriguing to contemplate how Minnie, Charles IB and David Alma managed to maintain a relationship over many decades and through difficult personal events and trying times. Though the letters are terse and to-the-point, they reflect the times and the cordial if not deeply rooted familial relationships that must have existed. The one letter from Minnie and two others from Charles to David convey a sense of obligatory connectedness, respect and a shared family experience in Dundee for roughly fifteen years (~1870-1885), but no real warmth. Perhaps it was the fate of the nineteenth century Grahams to lead lives of quiet independence when, in nearly all cases, the family patriarch was missing or dead. Nonetheless, I am grateful that we have evidence in letters and documents of a relationship between Minnie and her two step-brothers, David and Charles, which allowed us to make a living connection to Laura (MacDonald) Peters and her family. Though Laura and I are 4th cousins, her enthusiasm for family history and the research provided was gratifying. And we can live in the knowledge that all of us Grahams and MacDonalds share Catherine Wilkie as our common ancestor.

Laura (MacDonald) Peters by the Watson gravestone, Western Cemetery, Dundee. 2 Jul 2008. This was the site of the original Civil Complaint between the Watson daughters and Charles IB Graham.

UNDER "THE SMALL DEBT AMENDMENT (SCOTLAND) ACT, 1889,"
AND RELATIVE STATUTES.

COPY SUMMONS OR COMPLAINT IN A CIVIL CAUSE.

SECTION 2. JOHN COMRIE THOMSON, ESQUIRE, ADVOCATE, SHERIFF of the SHIRE of FORFAR.
To Officers of Court,
and other legal Executors hereof, jointly and severally;
WHEREAS it is humbly complained to me, by Mrs. Catherine Watson or Marshall, wife of James Marshall, 52 West Port, Dundee with his consent & concurrence, and Minnie Watson or Macdonald wife of & residing with Alexander Macdonald, 99 Watson's Lane Dundee with his consent & concurrence Pursuers.

THAT Charles Graham, Furniture Dealer, 308 Perth Road Dundee

Defender, ought to deliver to the Complainer the ~~subjects specified in the List hereto annexed~~ Certificate No. 1515 being the Title to Lairs No. 98 A.C. Compartment III in Western Cemetery Dundee which belonged to the Pursuers Father James Watson, which Certificate is dated 26th April 1866, and now belongs to Pursuers jointly

which subjects do not exceed Twelve Pounds in value, and which the said Defender refuses or delays to deliver; and therefore the said Defender ought to be DECERNED and ORDAINED to deliver the said subjects to the Complainers and failing delivery to pay to the said Complainers Twelve pounds sterling

with Expenses: HEREFORE it is my Will, that on sight hereof ye lawfully Summon the said Defender to compear before me, or my Substitute, in the COURT-HOUSE, at Dundee upon Tuesday the fourteenth day of June current at Half past Ten o'clock afternoon, to answer at the Complainer's instance in the said matter, with certification, in case of failure, of being held as confessed; requiring you also to deliver to the Defender a copy of any List of subjects pursued for; that ye cite Witnesses and Havers for both parties, to compear at the said place and date, to give evidence in the said matter.—Given under the hand of the Clerk of Court, at Dundee the seventh day of June Eighteen Hundred and ninety eight years.

(Signed) A. J. Findlay Depute Sheriff-Clerk.

CITATION FOR DEFENDER.

Charles Graham

Defender, above designed, you are hereby Summoned to appear and answer before the Sheriff, in the matter, and at the time and place, and under the certification set forth in the above copy of the Summons or Complaint against you. This Notice* posted upon the seventh day of June Eighteen Hundred and ninetyeight years, by me,

J. Grafton Lawson
Enrolled Law Ag
61 Reform St Dundee

Copy of the Civil Complaint levied by half-sisters Catherine (Watson) Marshall and Winnie (Watson) MacDonald.

Loose Threads - Mysteries to Be Solved

Despite the time and effort put in by myself and many other family members, there remain many mysteries and dead ends. Perhaps we can describe these as 'loose threads.' Blood relatives appear in selected records and then can no longer be found in the usual places. Scotland's Old Parish Records (OPR) are a great though sometimes limited resource. The census records which began in 1841 and continued every ten years along with the country's the civil registration for births, marriages and deaths which began in 1855 provide the framework for our family tree. Unfortunately, some of our Grahams dropped off the radar screen so-to-speak. And even when we have records, they open questions about why and how someone might be here or there. From a family history perspective, we are fortunate that the Church of Scotland proved to be an excellent documentor of births and marriages in what has been called Old Parish Registers. And Scotland again proved helpful when it implemented civil registrations of births, marriages and deaths beginning in 1855 in addition to the British census program which began in 1840. Nonetheless, many times we are left to ponder what happened in their lives between appearances in official rolls or where someone might have gone off to. I list some of them here with the fervent hope that future efforts will yield new discoveries and perhaps lead us to even more blood relations.

1. ***What ever happened to James Talford and George Heron Graham and what is the significance of those unusual middle names?*** Brothers two and four born to James Campbell Graham and Catherine Wilkie cannot be found past the 1881 Scottish census – no marriage, census or death entries, at least in Scotland. If my research is correct, James was living at age 26 as an unmarried lodger at 75 Park Street Aberdeen as a tinsmith while George was a 16 year old factory worker living at home 224 Blackness Road Dundee with his widowed mother Catherine Watson, his older brother David a 26 year old tinsmith and his two half-sisters, Catherine and Wilhelmina. James' age is off by a year or two but census data for age is notoriously 'off' especially if respondents wanted to appear older or younger for whatever reason. No further marriage, census or death records have yet been located for these two brothers in Scottish records though I do have a Canadian death entry in Toronto for a James Graham, age 35, 9 Feb 1894 whose occupation was listed as tinsmith born in Scotland (but not a more precise location). Given that we have evidence that David Alma and Charles IB maintained contact for nearly fifty years after David and his wife Agnes headed for America, it puzzles me that we have no evidence of contact with brothers' number two and four.

   As to the names, we are left to speculate. For example, there was a famous Scottish stone mason/architect/engineer of that era by the name of Thomas Telford. Given the misspelling of Charles Iconaclast Bradlauch Graham, we might assume that James worked on behalf of Telford but that the transcription on the birth registration was made in error. As for brother #4, the middle name of Heron was not widespread in Scotland but it did exist. One point in my research yielded a Wilkie-Heron connection but further investigation did not support this as a source for his middle name. We can only wonder if James Campbell Graham had a wry sense of humor or simply was interested in current events and personalities and used these to name his sons.

2. *What happened to Henrietta Law and Archibald Douglas Graham the first wife and son of Robert Graham?* In 1824, Robert returned to Scotland from 21 years of military service leaving Donaghdee Ireland for Portpatrick in Scotland but there is no mention of his wife and son. Robert made his way back to the Montrose area and in 1829 married Elizabeth Gove who may have had one illegitimate child already (Elizabeth McKenzie). I found no trace of Henrietta, Archibald or even Robert and Elizabeth and their son Robert (born 1833) in the 1841 census. Perhaps as camp followers they died during his military tenure, or perhaps he left them somewhere during his travels.

3. *Who raised Alexander Graham, the tailor? If Mary Nicol, whatever happened to her? Where was she from?* I found no birth, baptism or marriage evidence for Mary Nicol other than the church records in Marykirk. But she must have been a major factor in Alexander's life. Certainly his father Robert was not spending time with him having committed to the military from 1799 to 1824. That Alexander named his first daughter, though illegitimate, Margaret Nicholson Graham speaks to some bond that must have existed. Alexander is the first Graham to be identified with the tailoring trade. The fact that he was born and married in Marykirk parish suggests that he didn't stray far from home, but we can only wonder how he acquired this skill and who might have taught him the trade. He did move easily around Forfarshire, especially in his early twenties. Though most of his children were born in Marykirk, our common ancestor – James Campbell Graham - was born in Glamis and appeared to live with his mother Christina Doig there until he reached the age of majority.

4. *What relationship did Alexander Graham have with his extended family?* The evidence points to a man that moved around Forfarshire, present day Angus, throughout his early adult life before settling in Dundee from 1851 until his death in 1872. He was not listed with his wife in the 1841 census in Logie Pert but rather in Tannadice about 15 miles away and appeared to have an apprentice, fifteen year old William Cummin living with him there. I find it intriguing that Alexander's death registration was witnessed by his oldest child, Margaret (Graham) Watt who traveled from Keithbank, Rattray despite the fact that there were several sons and grandchildren living in Dundee when he passed away. In fact, his address in Dundee for 20 years was not far from his son Renwick's address. Did Renwick maintain a relationship with his father Alexander Graham? Both were tailors. Interestingly, one of Alexander's other sons Andrew was also a tailor then turned upholsterer in Dunblane; and Andrew's oldest son Joseph also became a tailor, so there is some suggestion that the father's profession became a skill or trade for several of his offspring. Unfortunately, we have no other evidence upon which to judge Alexander as a father. It's possible that Margaret N. Graham Watt was the *de facto* head of the Graham children and that the task of registering his death fell to her.

5. *Why did Mary Ann Graham not appear to be as close to her dad?* Mary Ann Graham (#101 - second legitimate child born to Alexander the tailor) died in 1902 in the Combination Poorhouse Stonehaven though listed as pauper from Logie-Pert. But we are left to ponder why Mary Ann, Alexander's oldest legitimate daughter, died a pauper in Fetteresso, Kincardineshire without family members nearby. Her half-sister Margaret had already died by this time but her brothers Renwick and Andrew were alive and living in Dundee and Dunblane respectively. There doesn't appear to be much connection between them. And yet, the name Mary Ann or

Mary Anne was used by several of her brothers when they had daughters. There were four other Mary Ann Grahams born after the first suggesting that she was an integral member of the family.

6. *What happened to some of the grand and great grandchildren of Alexander Graham?* Our infamous tailor had five sons and three daughters. Of the sons, one died young without issue (Alexander #100), one married twice but had no children (Renwick (#104), one (James Campbell #99) had four sons; one moved and established himself and family in Dunblane (Andrew #103), and one immigrated to Australia after having two daughters illegitimately (John #102). Some offspring of these male Grahams have 'gone missing' after birth entries suggesting that they either died young or moved away before marrying. Four intriguing candidates present options: James Talford Graham, George Heron Graham (both previously discussed and 'missing in the ether,' John Graham (#102) who moved to Australia and John Alexander Graham (#203) who might have had family after marrying Ann Henderson in Stirling in 1921.

7. *What caused David Alma Graham and his new bride Agnes Robb Cuthbert to immigrate to America within a month of their marriage?* They were married in Dundee on 20 Aug 1885 and arrived in New York 28 Sep 1885 on the SS Furnessia via Greenock-Moville. There was some American family folklore that her relations weren't happy with the match but upon investigation this theory doesn't hold up well. The Cuthbert family was renowned as manufacturers of coaches and then rail cars. The patriarch was John Cuthbert and several sons, grandsons and extended family members appear to have worked for Cuthbert Coach Manufacturing. But David's bride, Agnes R. Cuthbert, was the middle child of George Cuthbert and Agnes Robb Kidd who also had two sons one older and one younger. Agnes R. Cuthbert was born 6 May 1957 but lost her father to a stroke in 1861 when she was four and half years old. George was listed as a coach painter on his death registration and the witness was his oldest brother and primary owner of the firm in 1861. Research then showed that widow Agnes [Robb] (Kidd) Cuthbert and her three children spent at least two different stretches in the Dundee Poorhouse (1863 and 1865). Clearly, they were not the wealthy Cuthberts who lived on Dudhope Lane and one wonders why the family might not have supported them better in such trying times. I can only surmise that David and Agnes sought a better life in America. They must have planned this for quite some time because savings were no doubt required for passage and for establishing themselves in their new home. That David and Charles were reasonably close as brothers is supported by Charles and Agnes Candow listed as witnesses to David's marriage. We also have documented evidence (photos and ship manifests) that David Alma (#135) returned to Scotland at least once in 1907 with his youngest son George (#162).

8. *What caused David Alma Graham to get angry with his three oldest children and cut them out of his will?* This was accomplished in the late 1920's after his wife Agnes (Cuthbert) Graham had died. We have a copy of the will but no rationale or even family folklore to explain this peculiar turn of events. David Alma spent the last years of his life (roughly 1929-1933) living with his youngest son George and family in Hollis, Long Island. However, the family plot at Cypress Hills Cemetery has the remains of David, his wife Agnes, his son David and his wife Emma, and daughters Agnes and Jennie. Perhaps they are squabbling still.

9. *How did David Soutar Graham develop his political leanings toward Scottish Nationalism and his anti-evolutionary views, especially since he was reputedly not a practicing Christian?* Don Graham has a large scrapbook containing numerous letters to the editor written by David Graham most of which were directed toward Scottish nationalism but also included heated debates against the concept of Darwinian evolution. David was a prolific writer and wrote two tracts on the cause of Scottish independence which he self-published. In addition to his life as a political gadfly, David was estranged from his Graham family when he left his wife Margaret Gardiner "Meg" Brand for his secretary, Grace Winters. Meg would not grant him a divorce and we can only guess at the scandal it must have caused. When David and Grace had their only child, Don, he grew up with almost no awareness of his older half-brother and the extended Graham family. Don does recall meeting his brother Kenneth in the mid-1950s near Salford, England when he was about eighteen years old but that was the one and only time the two met.

My uncle David Soutar Graham, born 24th Jan, 1893, was married to Meg and had one son, Kenneth. But David and Meg parted and he suffered the opprobrium of many family members when he went to live with a lady named Grace. The following information I got from Grace whom I contacted in 1994, when I first began my genealogical research. She and David never married but they had a son, Donald, whom I mentioned before and now lives in Canada. Apparently he is a doctor, who will be 66 in April this year (if still alive) was married and divorced from Melinda and later married to Mary, a politician's daughter. When I told Grace about family members and questioned the name Alma she quoted the battle as its source with no further information. Now there's a mystery to be solved. My beloved Auntie Nan (Agnes Graham, born 24th May, 1897) once told me when I was a young girl that a soldier in the family had run off or eloped with a girl belonging to a wealthy sugar firm. No names - sorry!

Regret we lost touch with Kenneth. Did try to contact him years ago but to no avail. Would you consider trying to trace Donald? His father David as I've suggested was an unusual man, and also an iconoclast of sorts! He was fiercely nationalistic, desperate for Scottish Independence, separate from the rest of the United Kingdom, and greatly irritated my mother, a southern Irish Protestant, loyal to the Royal Family, when he wrote regularly to the local newspaper signing off - Yours for Scotland, Sandy McIntosh. Source: email from Sheila (Graham) Rattray 8 Mar 2004.

David, Donald, Claire and Nancy, Jun 2006

The Grahams
By Archie McKerracher

From the greed of the Campbells,
From the ire of the Drummonds,
From the pride of the Grahams,
From the wind of the Murrays,

Good Lord Deliver us, prayed a 17th century laird whose land was bordered by all four. And indeed, the pride of the Grahams was famous throughout Scotland for they were a close knit race deeply loyal to kith and kin. The also took pride in their unswerving devotion to their monarch even when this was sometimes rewarded with scant thanks. And lastly, they took pride in following their personal conscience, whatever the consequences.

Tradition says the first Graham was a Caledonian chief called Graym who attacked and burst through the mighty Antoine Wall which divided Scotland in two, and drove the Roman legions back to Hadrian's Wall on the English border. More likely, the chiefs spring from an Anglo-Norman family who originally came to England with William the Conqueror in 1066, and are recorded in his Doomsday Book as holding the lands of Graegham or Grey Home.

David I, king of Scots, was brought up in England and given a Norman education. He married a Norman heiress and through her acquired vast estates in England. Thus when he succeeded to the Scottish throne in 1124 he brought with him many of his Anglo-Norman friends to help create order in what was then a very primitive and savage land. He granted them large estates in the Lowlands and without exception these barons then intermarried into the local Celtic aristocracy. Within a generation or two they had become totally integrated with the older race and were soon exclusively Scottish.

William de Graham, the first recorded of that name, was granted land around Dalkieth and Abercorn in Midlothian and appears as a witness on David I's charter of 1128 founding the Abbey of Holyroodhouse. His descendant, Sir David Graham, acquired the lands of Dundaff in Strathcarron in 1237, and built a castle there. This was probably a wooden fortification on a motte or artificial earth mound in the Norman style. The remains of the later stone castle can still be seen. Sir John de Graham of Dundaff was William Wallace's right hand man and close friend in the first struggle for Scottish independence in the late 13th century. The contemporary poet Blind Harry calls him ''Schir Jhone the Grayme'' and records his brave death at the battle of Falkirk in 1298 when the small, ragged Scottish army was crushed beneath the hooves of the heavy armoured cavalry of the English army of Edward I. Sir John's gravestone and effigy can be seen today at Falkirk Old Church and bear the inscription '"Here lyes Sir John the Grame, baith wight and wise, Ane of the chiefs who rescewit Scotland thrise, Ane better knight not to the world was led, Nor was gude Graham of truth and hardiment".

Although principally a Lowland and Border clan the Grahams never forgot the Highlanders who had fought for them. The 3rd Duke of Montrose, when Marquis of Montrose and a Member of Parliament, was responsible in 1782 for the repeal of the law forbidding the wearing of Highland dress. Mugdock was the principal seat of the Graham chiefs until 1680 when they acquired the lands of the Buchanans and moved to Old Buchanan House near Drymen. In 1707 James Graham, 4th Marquess, was created the 1st Duke of Montrose by Queen Anne. He is perhaps better known for being firstly the partner, and then the foe, of the Highland folk-hero Rob Roy McGregor.

The Grahams had become the largest landowners in Stirlingshire by Victorian times and in 1857 built the huge Gothic Buchanan Castle on the foundations of a much older fortification. This became the residence of the Dukes of Montrose until the beginning of the Second World War when it was requisitioned as a military hospital. Here was kept Rudolf Hess, Hitler's deputy, after he made his mysterious flight to Scotland in 1940. The roof was removed after the war and the castle is now a ruin. James Angus Graham, b. 1907, was the 7th Duke of Montrose and was also Earl of Kincardine; Viscount Dunduff, Lord Graham; Aberuthven; Mugdock and Fintry. He became a farmer in Rhodesia (now Zimbabwe) and was a cabinet minister in the Rhodesian Government of Ian Smith. He moved to South Africa and later returned to Scotland before his death in 1992. His son, James, the 8th Duke of Montrose lives on the ancestral estates, at Auchmar near Loch Lomond. The name of Graham is an honourable one not only in Scottish history but also in more modern times. For example, it was the

6th Duke of Montrose who invented the aircraft carrier during the First World War. Others of note include the evangelist Billy Graham; Kenneth Graeme who wrote the classic "Wind in the Willows:; Admiral Sir Cunningham Graham of the last war and many others too numerous to mention.

The "pride of the Grahams" is perhaps best summed up in the famous verse by James Graham, the Great Montrose,

He either fears his fate too much,
Or his deserts are small,
Who dare not put it to the touch,
To win or lose it all.

Sir John's elder brother, Sir Patrick Graham, had fallen two years before at the battle of Dunbar in 1296 while carrying the royal banner of the King of Scots. Their father, Sir David Graham, had married into the ancient Celtic Earldom of Strathern and acquired land around Kincardine in south Perthshire. He was also the first to acquire land around Loch Lomond on the verge of the Highlands, still held today by the present Duke of Montrose. Sir Patrick's son, also Sir David, supported the cause of Robert de Brus, another Anglo-Norman-Scot whose mother was a Celtic countess and he descended from the younger son of David I. When de Bus or Bruce became King Robert I, and independence was achieved, he granted Sir David land around Montrose in Angus in exchange for Graham lands near the River Clyde. The hero king built a fortified house for himself at the latter where he died in 1329. A branch of the Graham – the Cunningham – Grahams – continued to live nearby until recent years.

The Grahams continued a steady rise. They had acquired land at Mugdock to the north of Glasgow and began to build a huge castle here from about 1370. This became the principal seat of the chiefs until the beginning of the 18th century. In 1445 Sir Patrick was created Lord Graham and in 1460 gave his land around Loch Lomond to the chief of the Buchanans in exchange for some land around Mugdock. These lands were regained later when the bankrupt Buchanan chief was forced to sell his ancestral estates to the Grahams in 1682.

An unfortunate episode began in 1413 after the then chief's half brother, Patrick Graham, was murdered by the Drummonds. He had been created Earl Palatine of the royal Earldom of Strathearn after marrying the grand-daughter of Robert III, and had acquired the vastly rich estates. He had left his infant son in the care of his younger brother, sir Robert Graham of Kilpont but in 1427 King James I seized the wealthy earldom and gave the boy only the poor Highland parish of Aberfoyle and the empty title of Earl of Menteith. He also sent the unfortunate child as a hostage to England where he was imprisoned for nearly twenty five years.

The Grahams always resented injustice and Sir Robert Graham of Kilpont protested loudly. He tried to arrest the king in Parliament, and then publicly renounced his allegiance to a tyrant. On February 21, 1437, Sir Robert led a band of Highlanders to Perth where they trapped the king in the cellar of the Blackfriars Monastery and stabbed him to death. For this crime Sir Robert and his sons were tortured and executed in a most horrible manner at Stirling.

William, 7th Earl of Menteith, was restored to the Earldom of Strathearn in 1603. He rose to high office as Justice – General of Scotland and President of the Scots Privy Council. But the pride of the Grahams was his undoing. His casual remark that he had a better right to the crown than the king reached the ears of Charles I who promptly stripped him of the Strathearn earldom. In 1680 the last Earl of Menteith, childless and in debt, left all his estates to his chief, the Marquess of Montrose, who thus regained all the old Graham land around Loch Lomond plus the lands of the Buchanans and also the land in Menteith. The Grahams now held a vast estate stretching right across Scotland from Loch Lomond to near Perth, and roughly comprising the ancient earldoms of Strathearn and Menteith. There were many cadet families established throughout these lands on the very verge of the Highlands. William, 3rd Lord Graham, chief of the Clan, had been created Earl of Montrose in 1504 but had died with the rest of the Scottish nobility around their king James IV on Flodden field in 1513.

The Graham Crest

But without doubt the most famous Graham was James, 5th Earl, born in 1612, and created a Marquis in 1644. He was the first to be given the Gaelic patrynomic An Greumach Mor, The Great Graham, or as he is better known to history, The Great Montrose. He was a poet and intellectual who was happiest in his study in one of his many castles or stately homes in Angus, Perthshire or Stirlingshire. In 1638 he was persuaded to sign the National Covenant which declared its opposition to the Episcopalian religion King Charles I wished to force upon Scotland. He then actively fought against the king's forces who tried to enforce the king's edicts. But as time went on James Graham became increasingly uneasy about the motives of the ultra-Protestant party headed by Archibald Campbell, Marquess of Argyll. In 1643 the Solemn League and Covenant was drawn up which declared the Scottish Covenanters would assist the English Parliament in a Civil War against the king provided England would adopt a Presbyterian form of worship. This was more than James Graham could stomach. He left the Covenanters and offered his services to the king. He was created Captain-General of the King's army in Scotland although this comprised a mere 400 men, mainly Grahams. Then they were joined by a 1000 Highlanders led by Alasdair MacColla MacDonald, a giant of a man and a fearsome fighter from the western isles.

During 1644 – 45 James Graham won a series of brilliant victories against far superior odds and became renowned as probably the finest strategist the world has ever seen. Unfortunately, with all Scotland almost conquered, the Highlanders slipped away to harry the Campbell lands in Argyll. James Graham's small force was cut to pieces at Philiphaugh in the Borders and he was forced to flee into exile. He returned in 1649 but was captured and taken to Edinburgh where he was hung, drawn and quartered. His quiet dignity on the scaffold won him the respect of all who watched. In 1660, when Charles II was restored to the throne, David Graham of Gorthie took his kinsman's head off its spike and had the other remains gathered together for honorable burial in the Montrose Aisle of St. Giles Cathedral in Edinburgh. All the various branches and cadets of the family attended the funeral – the Grahams of Inchbrakie; Orchill; Morphie; Balgowan; Cairnie; Deuchrie; Drums; Duntroon; Fintry, Killearn; Monzie and Potento.

Another Graham entered the history books in 1689 when John Graham of Claverhouse raised a Highland army in the name of the exiled Stuart king James VII. He was created Viscount Dundee and was variously known as

"Bonnie Dundee" or "Bloody Claverhouse", depending on which side one was on. He met a government army on the hill above Killiecrankie gorge in Perthshire on July 27, 1689, and within minutes his screaming Highlanders had devastated the enemy with their claymores. But in the moment of victory Dundee fell dead. It is said he was killed by a silver button fired from a gun because his enemies believed he was the Devil incarnate and only silver would kill him. It is remarkable that although the Grahams were really a feudal Lowland family only these two were able to bring out the highland clans in a national cause and devise strategies which used their peculiar fighting methods to advantage.

The other principal Graham area was in the Borders. Sir John Graham of Kilbride, one of the cadet families, fell out of favor with the king towards the end of the 14th century and led his followers south into the Border country where they settled in Eskdale. They met violent opposition from the other unruly Border clans and also from the hostile English in this disputed area. Yet the Grahams not only flourished here but became the largest and strongest family in the Borders. By 1552 they held over thirteen Border towers and could raise over 500 mounted troopers. They continued to dominate the Borders by right of the sword until the early 17th century when measures were taken against them by the Commission for the pacification of the Borders. In truth this was an attempt by the English Earl of Cumberland to seize their lands for no action was taken against the other unruly Border families of Maxwells, Elliots, Armstrongs, Scotts and Kerrs. The Grahams were hanged, transported, banished and imprisoned. Some came back with assumed names and the McHargs and Mahargs in Scotland and Northern England are simply Border Grahams with the name reversed.

The coat-of-arms of Sir David de Graham appears on the earliest known roll of Scottish arms dated 1332. These shows three scallop shells, used as pilgrim's begging bowls, and indicate an early Graham had made the pilgrimage to the shrine of Santiago de Compostella in Spain. The scallops are also found on the earliest known Graham seal dated 1230.

The personal arms of the Duke of Montrose shows three scallop shells in the 1st and 4th quarters, and in the 2nd and 3rd quarters the rose for the title of Montrose The crest below, entitled to be warn by clansmen, shows a falcon killing a stork. The motto is "Ne oublie", (Forget Not).

**Cousins George & Robert back, Ruth and Charles front
ca 1935**

Descendants of James GRAHAM(E)

1. James GRAHAM(E)
 sp: Isoble HILL (c.6 Jun 1680-Dun,Angus,Scotland;m.23 Oct 1698)
- 2. Robert GRAHAM (c.30 Aug 1696-St. Cyrus,Kincardine,Scotland)
- 2. John GRAHAM (c.15 Sep 1700-St. Cyrus,Kincardine,Scotland)
   sp: Margaret NICOLL (m.26 Jun 1729)
- 2. Janet GRAHAM (c.20 Sep 1702-St. Cyrus,Kincardine,Scotland)
- 2. James GRAHAM (c.8 Oct 1704-St. Cyrus,Kincardine,Scotland;b.27 Feb 1786-Brownhill,St. Cyrus,KCD,Scotland)
   sp: Isobell NICOLL (m.16 Jun 1732)
  - 3. James GRAHAM (c.23 May 1735-St. Cyrus,Kincardine,Scotland)
     sp: Ann DORRAT (m.Not listed)
    - 4. Helen GRAHAM (c.27 Oct 1754-St. Cyrus,Kincardine,Scotland)
    - 4. John GRAHAM (c.4 Mar 1759-St. Cyrus,Kincardine,Scotland)
  - 3. Margaret GRAHAM (c.13 Mar 1737-St. Cyrus,Kincardine,Scotland)
  - 3. Mary GRAHAM (c.5 Aug 1739-St. Cyrus,Kincardine,Scotland)
  - 3. John GRAHAM (c.5 Jun 1742-St. Cyrus,Kincardine,Scotland)
  - 3. Alexander GRAHAM (c.15 Jul 1744-St. Cyrus,Kincardine,Scotland)
  - 3. David GRAHAM (c.18 Oct 1747-St. Cyrus,Kincardine,Scotland;d.17 Sep 1820-Montrose,Angus,Scotland)
     sp: Mary BRAND (m.16 Jun 1781)
- 2. Robert GRAHAM (b.14 Dec 1707-St. Cyrus,Kincardine,Scotland)
   sp: Janet WHITE (m.28 Jun 1739)
  - 3. Robert GRAHAM (c.30 Mar 1740-St. Cyrus,Kincardine,Scotland)
  - 3. Alexander GRAHAM (c.28 May 1743-St. Cyrus,Kincardine,Scotland)
     sp: Jean or Jane MITCHEL (m.24 Jul 1768)
    - 4. Janet GRAHAM (c.3 Sep 1769-St. Cyrus,Kincardineshire,Scotland)
    - 4. Mary GRAHAM (c.11 Mar 1771-St. Cyrus,Kincardineshire,Scotland)
    - 4. Anne GRAHAM (c.4 Oct 1772-St. Cyrus,Kincardineshire,Scotland)
    - 4. Alexander GRAHAM (c.26 Sep 1773-St. Cyrus,Kincardine,Scotland;d.8 Apr 1840-St. Cyrus,Kincardine,Scotland)
       sp: Jean BLACK (m.7 Apr 1799;d.22 Oct 1837-St. Cyrus,Kincardine,Scotland)
      - 5. Betty GRAHAM (b.11 Nov 1799-Montrose,Angus,Scotland;d.17 Oct 1866-Montrose,Angus,Scotland)
      - 5. Ann GRAHAM (b.21 Sep 1801-Montrose,Angus,Scotland;d.7 Jan 1824-St. Cyrus,Kincardine,Scotland)
      - 5. William GRAHAM (b.11 Aug 1803-Montrose,Angus,Scotland;d.14 Apr 1881-St. Cyrus,Kincardineshire,Scotland)
         sp: Jean DONALD (b.Abt 1801-Monymusk,Aberdeenshire,Scotland;d.Aft 1881-St. Cyrus,Kincardineshire,Scotland)
        - 6. Jean GRAHAM (b.30 Nov 1833-Laurencekirk,Kincardine Scotland;d.1914-Garvock,Kincardine,Scotland)
           sp: David SUTTIE (b.28 Mar 1841-LB&I,Angus,Scotland;m.8 Dec 1860;d.11 Jul 1921-Garvock,K,Scotland)
          - 7. Elizabeth SUTTIE (b.24 Jun 1861-Brechin,Angus,Scotland)
          - 7. Jane SUTTIE (b.18 Feb 1863-St. Cyrus,Kincardine,Scotland)
          - 7. David SUTTIE (b.11 Apr 1871-St. Cyrus,Kincardine,Scotland)
             sp: Jeanie MCGREGOR (b.~1875;m.3 Apr 1896)

Descendants of James GRAHAM(E)

```
├─ 6. Alexander GRAHAM (b.1835-Arbuthnott,Kincardineshire,Scotland)
├─ 6. William GRAHAM (b.15 Aug 1837-Arbuthnott,Kincardineshire,Scotland;d.6 Oct 1907-Montrose,Angus,Scotland)
│     sp: Margaret LAWRENCE (b.26 Jan 1845-L,K,Scotland;m.25 Nov 1880;d.7 May 1887-Brechin,Angus,Scotland)
└─ 6. John Thomson GRAHAM (b.7 Aug 1841-Arbuthnott,Kincardine,Scotland;d.15 May 1857-St. Cyrus,K,Scotland)
─ 5. Isobelle GRAHAM (b.9 Jun 1805-Montrose,Angus,Scotland;d.11 Jan 1822-St. Cyrus,Kincardine,Scotland)
─ 5. Jean GRAHAM (b.15 Oct 1807-Montrose,Angus,Scotland;d.24 Oct 1867-St. Cyrus,Kincardineshire,Scotland)
└─ 5. Janet GRAHAM (b.4 Feb 1813-St. Cyrus,Kincardine,Scotland;d.3 Nov 1824-St. Cyrus,Kincardine,Scotland)
─ 4. Margaret GRAHAM (c.18 Jun 1777-St. Cyrus,Kincardineshire,Scotland;d.Bef 1780)
─ 4. Robert GRAHAM (c.11 Jun 1778-St. Cyrus,Kincardine,Scotland)
   sp: Mary NICOL (m.Not married)
      ─ 5. Alexander GRAHAM (b.Feb/Mar 1797-Marykirk,Kincardine,Scotland;d.17 Jun 1871-Dundee,Angus,Scotland)
         sp: Elisabeth SHARP (m.Not married)
            ─ 6. Margaret Nicholson GRAHAM (b.8 May 1821-Marykirk,Kincardine,Scotland;d.28 Jan 1897-Ceres,Fife,Scotland)
               sp: Charles WATT (b.1822-Montrose,Angus,Scotland;m.27 Dec 1846)
               └─ 7. John WATT (b.1847-Montrose,Angus,Scotland;d.26 Dec 1925-Cupar,Fife,Scotland)
                     sp: Mary Ann ANDERSON (b.29 Jan 1850-Marykirk,Kincardine,Scotland)
                        ─ 8. David Faulkner WATT (b.18 Apr 1875-Ceres,Fife,Scotland)
                        ─ 8. Mary WATT (b.1877-Dundee,Angus,Scotland)
                        ─ 8. John WATT (b.1880-Dundee,Angus,Scotland;d.19 Oct 1958-Cupar,Fife,Scotland)
                           sp: Jane Malcolm STEWART (b.~1872-Alyth,Perth,Scotland;m.20 Jul 1900)
                           └─ 9. John WATT (b.29 Jul 1906-Tarvit Mill,Ceres,Fife,Scotland)
                        ─ 8. Fred WATT (b.1885-Dundee,Angus,Scotland)
                        └─ 8. Isabella WATT (b.1886-Cupar,Fife,Scotland)
         sp: Christian DOIG (c.10 Jan 1784-Glamis,Angus,Scotland;m.Not married;d.27 Dec 1847-Glamis,Angus,Scotland)
            ─ 6. James Campbell GRAHAM (b.1822-Glamis,Angus,Scotland;d.18 Dec 1865-Dundee,Angus,Scotland)
               sp: Catherine WILKIE (c.1 Feb 1826-Forfar,A,Scotland;m.9 Jul 1848;d.21 Feb 1898-Dundee,Angus,Scotland)
                  ─ 7. David Alma GRAHAM (b.1 May 1854-Stirling,Stirlingshire Scotland;d.21 Oct 1933-Hollis,Queens,NY,USA)
                     sp: Agnes Robb CUTHBERT (b.6 May 1857-Dundee,Angus,Scotland;m.20 Aug 1885;d.14 Nov 1922-)
                        ─ 8. Jennie Francis GRAHAM (b.11 Jun 1886-Brooklyn,NY;d.30 Dec 1969-Brooklyn,NY)
                        ─ 8. David Alma GRAHAM (b.26 Jan 1888-Brooklyn,Kings,NY,USA;d.18 Aug 1955-Ridgewood,Q,NY,USA)
                           sp: Emma Frances SCHWARZ (b.3 Aug 1893-Brooklyn,NY,USA;m.25 Nov 1914;d.21 Apr 1978-)
                              ─ 9. Robert David GRAHAM (b.6 Jan 1921-Ridgewood,Q,NY,USA;d.16 Oct 2004-C,Norfolk,Virginia)
                                 sp: Dorothy E. BACHMAN (b.4 Mar 1922-Bridgeport,CT;m.16 Oct 1943;d.21 May 1994-)
                                    ─ 10. Linda Carol GRAHAM (b.13 May 1948-Bridgeport,CT)
                                       sp: Thomas BRADLEY (m.14 Jun 1969)
                                       └─ 11. Kenneth BRADLEY (b.25 Feb 1973-Norwood,NJ)
                                             sp: Michele Ann TOMICICH (b.24 Jan 1969-Pueblo,CO;m.12 Dec 1998)
                                             └─ 12. Taylor Nicole BRADLEY (b.3 Mar 2004-Denver,Adam,Colorado)
```

Grahams o' the Mearns

Descendants of James GRAHAM(E)

```
            └─ 10. Barbara Lee GRAHAM (b.7 Apr 1952-Bridgeport,CT)
                  sp: William Terry PATE (b.20 Oct 1957-Conway,SC;m.28 May 1993)
         └─ 9. Charles James GRAHAM (b.12 May 1929-Brooklyn,NY;d.12 Nov 1990-Marietta,GA)
               sp: Marilyn Louise LAFRANCE (b.8 Aug 1928-Schnectady,NY;m.9 Jun 1951)
               ├─ 10. David Lee GRAHAM (b.4 Oct 1956-Pittsfield,MA)
               │     sp: Jane Ellen HARBAUGH (b.12 Nov 1957-New York,NY;m.10 Sep 1983)
               │     ├─ 11. Connor David GRAHAM (b.7 Aug 1989-Seattle,WA)
               │     └─ 11. Charles James GRAHAM (b.23 Jul 1991-Seattle,WA)
               └─ 10. Nancy Lynn GRAHAM (b.14 Mar 1961-Pittsfield,MA)
                     sp: Richard Brian BARKER (b.14 Feb 1954-Detroit,MI;m.24 Sep 1994(Div))
                     ├─ 11. Chase Riley BARKER (b.10 Sep 1998-Atlanta,GA)
                     ├─ 11. Kyle Danic BARKER (b.10 Sep 1998-Atlanta,GA)
                     sp: Robert HAMILTON (m.16 Oct 2008)
   ├─ 8. Alexander J GRAHAM (b.1 Jan 1889-Brooklyn,Kings,NY;d.2 Apr 1889-Brooklyn,Kings,NY,USA)
   ├─ 8. Agnes Cuthbert GRAHAM (b.25 Jan 1890-Brooklyn,NY;d.15 Nov 1955-Forest Hills,NY)
   ├─ 8. George Forbes GRAHAM (b.7 Aug 1892-Brooklyn,NY;d.17 Jun 1972-Hempstead,Nassau,NY)
   │     sp: Lenora WIRTH (b.31 Jan 1896-Liberty PA;m.5 Jun 1920;d.15 Aug 1971-Centereach,S,NY,USA)
   │     ├─ 9. George Charles GRAHAM MD (b.9 May 1921-Brooklyn NY;d.8 Oct 1996-Hempstead Nassau NY)
   │     │     sp: Muriel Elsie HUENE MD (b.19 Sep 1921-Lakeview,N,NY;m.23 Jun 1945;d.22 Oct 2005-)
   │     │     ├─ 10. Heather GRAHAM (b.19 Apr 1950-Mineola,NY;d.5 Aug 1982-West Hempstead,NY,USA)
   │     │     ├─ 10. Lorna Nancy GRAHAM (b.18 Apr 1954-Mineola,NY)
   │     │     │     sp: Kenneth Jonathon BROPHY (b.30 May 1951-Rahway,NJ,USA;m.Not married)
   │     │     │     └─ 11. Connor George GRAHAM (b.25 Oct 1997-Scranton,PA,USA)
   │     │     └─ 10. George Charles GRAHAM (b.1 Jul 1957-Mineola,NY)
   │     └─ 9. Ruth Lenora GRAHAM (b.27 Jul 1925-Woodhaven,Q,NY;d.12 Sep 2010-Leesburg,FL)
   │           sp: Edmund FULLER (b.6 Jun 1923-Brooklyn NY;m.11 Nov 1944;d.27 May 1997-Tampa,FL)
   │           ├─ 10. Diane FULLER (b.11 Oct 1945-Jamaica Queens,Queens NY)
   │           │     sp: Neil LAMPARTER (m.25 Jul 1965(Div))
   │           │     └─ 11. Neil Roger LAMPARTER (b.5 May 1966-Bethpage,NY)
   │           └─ 10. Jean FULLER (b.29 Aug 1947-Queens Village,Queens NY)
   │                 sp: William LAMPARTER (m.30 May 1971)
   │                 ├─ 11. Sean LAMPARTER (b.29 Dec 1975-Syosset,NY)
   │                 └─ 11. Dana LAMPARTER (b.18 Jun 1979-Syosset,NY)
   │                       sp: UNKNOWN
   │                       └─ 12. Lilly (b.Sep 2009)
   └─ 8. Charles James GRAHAM (b.Apr 1899-Brooklyn NY;d.~18 Jun 1904-Brooklyn,Kings NY)
├─ 7. James Talford GRAHAM (b.28 Mar 1856-Govan,Lanark Scotland)
├─ 7. Charles Iconaclast Bradlauch GRAHAM (b.10 Aug 1861-New Monkland,Lanark Scotland;d.15 Dec 1945-)
```

Descendants of James GRAHAM(E)

sp: Agnes Small CANDOW (b.17 Feb 1863-Longforgan,Perth Scotland;m.28 Dec 1886;d.7 Jul 1891-)

- 8. Charles George GRAHAM (b.5 Oct 1887-Dundee,Angus Scotland;d.29 Nov 1892-D,Angus Scotland)
- 8. William Melville GRAHAM (b.14 Apr 1889-Dundee,Angus Scotland;d.30 Jan 1961-Thornhill,D,Scotland)
  - sp: Helen Kilpatrick LYON (b.1882;m.4 Nov 1910;d.25 Mar 1976-Lanark,Lanark,Scotland)
    - 9. Charles Lord GRAHAM (b.6 Sep 1911-Lanark,Lanark,Scotland;d.5 May 2000-Lanark,L,Scotland)
      - sp: Elizabeth Ethel ECCLESTON (b.10 Oct 1914-G,L,Scotland;m.29 Apr 1938;d.17 May 2006-)
        - 10. Agnes Helen GRAHAM (b.24 Jul 1940-Thornhill,Dumfries & Galloway,Scotland)
          - sp: Frederick Harvey SMAIL (m.2 Oct 1964(Div))
            - 11. Michael Charles SMAIL (b.2 Nov 1966-Jersey,Channel Islands,England)
              - sp: Amanda WRIGHT (m.31 Dec 2004)
                - 12. Georgia SMAIL (b.18 Apr 2007)
            - 11. Jonathan William SMAIL (b.7 May 1968-Jersey,Channel Islands,England)
              - sp: Julia BARNES (m.Aug 1996(Div))
                - 12. Jake Charles SMAIL (b.27 Jan 1998)
              - sp: Mairi BROWN (m.5 Sep 2004)
                - 12. Finlay SMAIL (b.15 Jan 2007)
                - 12. Billy SMAIL (b.3 Jun 2008)
            - 11. Peter Graham SMAIL (b.28 Nov 1975)
          - sp: John HOLROYD (m.6 Oct 1991)
        - 10. Jean Arthur GRAHAM (b.27 Aug 1946)
          - sp: Nikolas TOMBRAS (m.27 Jul 1984)
- 8. Agnes Minnie GRAHAM (b.18 Mar 1891-Dundee,Angus Scotland;d.4 Aug 1891-Dundee,A,Scotland)

sp: Agnes Dickson SOUTAR (b.19 Aug 1859-Errol,Perth,Scotland;m.27 Apr 1892;d.14 Dec 1943-)

- 8. David Soutar GRAHAM (b.24 Jan 1893-Dundee,Angus Scotland;d.19 May 1965-Arrochar,A,Scotland)
  - sp: Margaret Gardiner BRAND (b.29 May 1890-Arbroath,A,Scotland;m.15 Apr 1916;d.15 Jan 1965-)
    - 9. Kenneth McGregor GRAHAM (b.1920-ASV,Angus,Scotland;d.3 Jan 2007-Sale,Cheshire,England)
      - sp: Pam ????
        - 10. Stewart Richard GRAHAM (b.1950-Salford,Cheshire,England)
          - sp: Audrey ????? (m.16 Jun 1979)
  - sp: Grace Coupar WINTER (b.12 Jan 1912-Coupar Angus,A,Scotland;m.Not married;d.25 Feb 2002-)
    - 9. Donald Malcolm GRAHAM (b.6 Apr 1938-Dundee,Angus,Scotland)
      - sp: Melinda LEE (m.3 May 1974(Div))
        - 10. Nicole Choei-Lin GRAHAM (b.23 Feb 1984-Vancouver,BC,Canada)
      - sp: Mary Louise WILSON (m.11 May 1992(Div))
- 8. George Albert GRAHAM (b.Feb 1894-Dundee,Angus,Scotland;d.7 Oct 1896-Dundee,Angus,Scotland)
- 8. Charles GRAHAM (b.10 Nov 1895-Dundee,Angus Scotland;d.20 Sep 1979-Dundee,Angus,Scotland)
  - sp: Mary Constance FOX (m.7 Jul 1924)
    - 9. Sheila GRAHAM (b.19 Jul 1926-Maidstone,Kent,England)

Descendants of James GRAHAM(E)

```
                    sp: Ronald RATTRAY (b.8 Apr 1927-Carnoustie,Angus,Scotland;m.11 Oct 1951)
                      ├─ 10. Rosalyn Mary RATTRAY (b.16 Jul 1953-Horsforth,Yorkshire,England)
                           sp: Kenneth Stewart BARCLAY (b.14 Jan 1952-Glasgow,Lanark Scotland;m.14 Feb 1975)
                           └─ 11. Rona Margaret BARCLAY (b.10 Jan 1980-Glasgow,Lanark Scotland)
                                sp: UNKNOWN
                                └─ 12. Craig Kenneth BARCLAY (b.8 Apr 1996-Rutherglen,Lanark,Scotland)
                      ├─ 10. Joy Alexandra RATTRAY (b.20 Apr 1956-Dumfries,Scotland)
                           sp: William Wishart CAMPBELL (b.24 May 1954-Helensburgh,D,Scotland;m.5 Aug 1978)
                           ├─ 11. Rachel Mary CAMPBELL (b.26 Aug 1983-Glasgow,Lanark Scotland)
                           └─ 11. Sonia Helen CAMPBELL (b.2 May 1986-Glasgow,Lanark Scotland)
                      └─ 10. Howard John Charles RATTRAY (b.10 Nov 1961-Dumfries,Dumfriesshire,Scotland)
                           sp: Angela MASTERSON (m.16 Aug 1990)
                           ├─ 11. Georgia Amy RATTRAY (b.25 Sep 1997-Falkirk,Stirlingshire,Scotland)
                           └─ 11. Gavin Alexander RATTRAY (b.19 May 2000-Falkirk,Stirlingshire,Scotland)
                 ├─ 9. Gordon Richard Bradlaw GRAHAM (b.1930;d.31 Aug 1932-Dundee,Angus,Scotland)
                 ├─ 9. Maureen GRAHAM (b.30 Dec 1933-Dundee,Angus,Scotland)
                 └─ 9. Donald Charles GRAHAM (b.15 Jul 1938)
                      sp: Wilma Breathwood GIBB (b.25 Aug 1943-Dundee,Angus,Scotland;m.19 Dec 1964)
                      ├─ 10. Laura GRAHAM (b.27 Oct 1965-Dundee,Angus,Scotland)
                           sp: Scott WITCHALLS (m.1 Jun 1990)
                           ├─ 11. Molly Hannah WITCHALLS (b.9 Jan 1995-Reading,England)
                           ├─ 11. Alice Rose WITCHALLS (b.28 Dec 1996-Reading,England)
                           └─ 11. Grace Mary WITCHALLS (b.11 Jan 2003-Reading,England)
                      ├─ 10. Jane GRAHAM (b.5 Jan 1967-Dundee,Angus,Scotland)
                           sp: Anthony CARACCIOLO (m.22 Jun 2008)
                           ├─ 11. Cruz CARACCIOLA (b.20 Dec 2009-Reading,Berkshire,England)
                           └─ 11. Lola CARACCIOLA (b.20 Dec 2009-Reading,Berkshire,England)
                      ├─ 10. Kirstin GRAHAM (b.25 Jul 1970-Perth,Perthshire,Scotland)
                      └─ 10. Claire GRAHAM (b.29 Mar 1977-Bellshill,Lanark,Scotland)
                           sp: Steven SIMON (m.14 Aug 2004)
                           ├─ 11. Lily Eve SIMON (b.26 Apr 2007-Edinburgh,Midlothian,Scotland)
                           └─ 11. Brodie SIMON (b.1 Jan 2011-Edinburgh,Midlothian,Scotland)
            └─ 8. Agnes GRAHAM (b.24 May 1897-Dundee,Angus Scotland;d.~1960s)
                 sp: Frank Howard FAIRWEATHER (b.1891-Forgan,Fife,Scotland;m.5 Nov 1949;d.1971)
       └─ 7. George Heron GRAHAM (b.6 Sep 1864-Dundee,Angus Scotland)
  sp: Ann LINDSAY (b.btw 1791-1796-Angus,Scotland;m.22 Sep 1821;d.btw 1841-1848)
  ├─ 6. Alexander GRAHAM (b.3 Nov 1821-Marykirk,Kincardine,Scotland;d.4 Jun 1843-Marykirk,Kincardineshire,SCT)
  ├─ 6. Mary Ann GRAHAM (b.20 Dec 1822-Marykirk,Kincardine,Scotland;d.26 May 1902-Fetteresso,K,Scotland)
```

Grahams o' the Mearns

Descendants of James GRAHAM(E)

```
            sp: John DOIG (b.1828-Montrose,Angus,Scotland;m.Not married;d.1897-Montrose,Angus,Scotland)
             ─ 7. Elizabeth DOIG (b.~May 1850-Montrose,Angus,Scotland;d.23 Apr 1893-Cupar,Fife,Scotland)
                sp: UNKNOWN
                └ 8. Mary Ann DOIG (b.7 Feb 1874-Dundee,Angus,Scotland;d.2 Jul 1874-Kinnaber Mills,M,Angus,Scotland)
            sp: James Sime SMITH (m.Not married)
             ─ 7. Renwick GRAHAM (b.3 Aug 1856-Dundee,Angus,Scotland;d.6 May 1858-Dundee,Angus,Scotland)
         sp: Thomas FALCONER (b.1823-Dundee,A,Scotland;m.16 Jan 1864;d.18 Feb 1895-Logie Pert,A,Scotland)
    ─ 6. John GRAHAM (b.Abt 1824-Marykirk,Kincardineshire,Scotland;d.5 Jun 1905-Brisbane,Queensland,Australia)
      sp: Mary MILNE (b.8 Sep 1824-Logie-Pert,A,Scotland;m.Not married;d.25 Mar 1910-Logie-Pert,A,Scotland)
       ─ 7. Mary Ann GRAHAM (b.1 Dec 1844-Logie-Pert,Angus,Scotland;d.13 Aug 1938-Wellington,New Zealand)
          sp: Joseph Blyth GRAHAM (b.1852-Dunblane,P,Scotland;m.27 Jun 1871;d.24 Dec 1915-W,New Zealand)
           ─ 8. Mary Ann GRAHAM (b.27 Nov 1873-Montrose,Angus,Scotland;d.30 Jul 1955-C,New Zealand)
              sp: Decimus ROWE (b.27 Aug 1875-Christchurch,New Zealand;m.23 Mar 1899;d.21 Sep 1946-)
               ─ 9. Ethel Inez ROWE (b.2 Mar 1900-New Zealand;d.27 Jul 1980-Masterton,New Zealand)
                  sp: Albert John SIDEY (b.1884;m.26 Dec 1923;d.11 Jan 1935-Lyall Bay,Wellington,New Zealand)
                   ─ 10. Denzel Molly SIDEY (b.1924-New Zealand)
                      sp: Percy MILLAR
                       ─ 11. Kenneth Albert MILLAR (b.May 1945)
                      sp: Frank PAYNE (b.Abt 1915-Lower Hutt,New Zealand;d.2000-Lower Hutt,New Zealand)
                   ─ 10. Rodney Graham SIDEY (b.18 Feb 1926-W,New Zealand;d.2000-Papamoa,BOP,New Zealand)
                      sp: Mary Angela BYRON-WOOD (b.9 Jun 1921;m.(Div);d.19 Feb 1983-Waihake Island,A,NZ)
                       ─ 11. Sharon Gail SIDEY (b.21 Jan 1945)
                       ─ 11. Kevin Graham SIDEY (b.25 Oct 1947-Lower Hutt,New Zealand;d.1979)
                       ─ 11. Rodney Desmond SIDEY (b.11 Dec 1950-Lower Hutt,New Zealand)
                       ─ 11. Michael Dennis SIDEY (b.1 Jul 1951-Lower Hutt,New Zealand)
                       ─ 11. Geoffrey Colin SIDEY (b.28 Jan 1954-Lower Hutt,New Zealand)
                       └ 11. Keith Robert SIDEY (b.25 Aug 1961-Lower Hutt,New Zealand)
                   └ 10. Yvonne Ngaire SIDEY (b.31 Oct 1930-W,New Zealand;d.1 Jun 1987-Greytown,New Zealand)
                      sp: Gordon Alister PAYNE (b.28 Aug 1924-Lower Hutt,New Zealand;d.23 Jun 1996-)
                       ─ 11. Stuart John PAYNE (b.25 Mar 1949-Lower Hutt,New Zealand)
                          sp: Cynthia Marrion ROBERTS (b.26 Jun 1948-Australia;m.11 Jul 1970(Div))
                       ─ 11. Sandra Alice PAYNE (b.17 May 1950-Lower Hutt,New Zealand)
                          sp: Ian Barry BLAKE (b.6 Jun 1951-Caterton,New Zealand;m.15 Nov 1975)
                           ─ 12. Nicola Lee BLAKE (b.30 Aug 1978-Masterton,NZ)
                           ─ 12. Kieran James BLAKE (b.1 Feb 1981-Masterton,NZ)
                              sp: Sarah-Jane Nesta CAMERON (b.24 Feb 1981-M,New Zealand;m.14 Mar 2009)
                           └ 12. Brendan Michael BLAKE (b.3 Apr 1983-Masterton,NZ)
                       ─ 11. Susan Decima PAYNE (b.17 May 1950-Lower Hutt,New Zealand;d.23 May 1950-)
```

Grahams o' the Mearns

Descendants of James GRAHAM(E)

```
                        ├─ 11. Heather Laureen PAYNE (b.12 Dec 1951-Lower Hutt,New Zealand)
                        │    sp: John William BOWNESS (b.13 Apr 1950;m.7 Mar 1970)
                        └─ 11. Dean Alistair PAYNE (b.1954-Lower Hutt,New Zealand)
              ├─ 9. Charles Francis ROWE (b.10 Mar 1901-New Zealand;d.25 Oct 1994-Upper Hutt,New Zealand)
              │    sp: Marjorie Rowsell WAINWRIGHT (b.Abt 1901;m.1926;d.3 Oct 1995-Upper Hutt,New Zealand)
              │    ├─ 10. Cynthia Graham ROWE (b.30 May 1928-Lower Hutt,New Zealand)
              │    │    sp: Hugh Hector NANKIVELL
              │    ├─ 10. Marion ROWE
              │    └─ 10. Suzie ROWE
              ├─ 9. Henry Graham ROWE (b.7 Nov 1904-New Zealand;d.1 Sep 1977-New Zealand)
              │    sp: Greta Mary HOPPER (b.21 Feb 1909-W,New Zealand;d.20 Aug 1988-A,New Zealand)
              │    ├─ 10. Clive ROWE (b.27 Dec 1934-Wellington,New Zealand)
              │    │    sp: Faye BRANDON (b.1938;m.1964)
              │    │    ├─ 11. Michael Berry ROWE (b.1962-New Zealand)
              │    │    ├─ 11. Perry Martin ROWE (b.1964-New Zealand)
              │    │    ├─ 11. Quentin Wayne ROWE (b.1966-New Zealand)
              │    │    ├─ 11. Steve Manu Clive ROWE (b.1969-New Zealand)
              │    │    └─ 11. Karina Faye ROWE (b.13 Nov 1970-New Zealand)
              │    ├─ 10. Dale Irene ROWE (b.23 Oct 1936-Wellington,New Zealand)
              │    │    sp: Clifford BRANIGAN
              │    ├─ 10. Trevor ROWE (b.Jan 1938-Wellington,New Zealand)
              │    │    sp: Elizabeth GRAY
              │    └─ 10. Linda Kathryn ROWE (b.26 Dec 1950-Wellington,New Zealand)
              ├─ 9. Sidney Eric ROWE (b.21 Dec 1911-Wellington,New Zealand;d.3 Jul 1997-Dunedin,O,New Zealand)
              │    sp: Ethel Friday MCKAY (b.Abt 1916-D,O,New Zealand;d.29 Nov 1994-Dunedin,O,New Zealand)
              └─ 9. Lottie Joan ROWE (b.1913-New Zealand)
    ├─ 8. Charles Riper GRAHAM (b.31 Jan 1876-RIL,New Zealand;d.18 May 1931-Wellington,New Zealand)
    │    sp: Edith Emma Margaret SPENCER (b.Abt 1897;m.1919)
    │    ├─ 9. Joyce GRAHAM (b.Abt 1919-New Zealand)
    │    └─ 9. Charles GRAHAM (b.Abt 1922-New Zealand)
    ├─ 8. John Harland GRAHAM (b.1881-Dunedin,New Zealand;d.17 Jul 1952-Palmerston North,New Zealand)
    │    sp: Annie Elizabeth BURKETT (b.20 Nov 1887;d.21 Jun 1984-Palmerston North,New Zealand)
    ├─ 8. Ernest GRAHAM (b.1885-New Zealand;d.Apr 1917-Wellington,New Zealand)
    ├─ 8. Edwin Allen GRAHAM (b.27 Oct 1886-Dunedin,New Zealand;d.17 Apr 1975-Dannevirke,New Zealand)
    ├─ 8. Joseph Ivon GRAHAM (b.Aft Apr 1888-New Zealand;d.5 Apr 1908-Palmerston North,New Zealand)
    ├─ 8. Herbert Rowell GRAHAM (b.1890-Dunedin,New Zealand;d.26 May 1947-PN,New Zealand)
    │    sp: Clarice Mary Claire MCALINDON (b.Abt 1892;m.1925;d.9 Nov 1959-PN,New Zealand)
    │    ├─ 9. ???? GRAHAM (b.Abt 1927-Palmerston North,New Zealand)
```

Descendants of James GRAHAM(E)

```
└─ 9. ???? GRAHAM (b.Abt 1928-Palmerston North,New Zealand)
   8. Alice Elizabeth GRAHAM (b.14 Aug 1892-New Zealand;d.1988-New Zealand)
      sp: Reginald Lewis HULSTON (m.1914)
7. Amelia GRAHAM (b.2 Aug 1848-Logie-Pert,Angus,Scotland;d.4 Aug 1917-Wanganui,New Zealand)
   sp: Robert William Oswald STEWART (b.Abt 1845-Dumfries,D,Scotland;m.7 Jun 1872;d.30 Jun 1927-)
      8. Wilhelmina GRAHAM (b.23 Apr 1869-Dundee,Angus,Scotland)
      8. Robert William Oswald STEWART (b.30 Jun 1873-Partick,L,Scotland;d.20 Oct 1873-Partick,L,Scotland)
      8. George STEWART (b.1876-New Zealand)
      8. Amelia Gillespie STEWART (b.1878-New Zealand)
      8. John Taylor STEWART (b.1879-New Zealand;d.1941-New Zealand)
         sp: Florence Jane THOMSON (m.1918)
      8. Mary Eleanor STEWART (b.22 Jul 1880-H,Otago,New Zealand;d.11 Feb 1934-Hurstville,NSW,Australia)
         sp: Charles Arthur BOWEN (b.5 Dec 1877-Kaipoi,New Zealand;m.24 Apr 1900;d.5 May 1948-)
            9. Gwendoline BOWEN (b.22 Dec 1901-Wanganui,New Zealand;d.1973-Blacktown,Australia)
               sp: Alfred WRIGHT (b.14 Dec 1897;m.12 May 1923;d.1980-Sydney,NSW Australia)
                  10. Robert WRIGHT (b.25 May 1924-Lidcombe,NSW,Australia)
                  10. Helena WRIGHT (b.14 Oct 1926-Sydney,NSW,Australia)
                  10. Maxwell Stewart WRIGHT (b.29 Jul 1927-Sydney,NSW,Australia;d.1993)
                  10. Margaret WRIGHT (b.1936-Sydney,NSW,Australia)
            9. Charles BOWEN (b.30 Nov 1905-Wanganui,New Zealand;d.1937-Botany Bay,Sydney,N,Australia)
            9. Maxwell BOWEN (b.25 Jun 1911-Willoughby,NSW Australia;d.1958-Sydney,NSW Australia)
      8. Jessie Anna STEWART (b.1882-New Zealand;d.1885-New Zealand)
      8. Andrew Duncan STEWART (b.1883-New Zealand;d.1911-New Zealand)
      8. James Sinclair STEWART (b.1885-New Zealand)
      8. Louisa Carter STEWART (b.1887-New Zealand;d.1945-New Zealand)
         sp: John DALZELL (m.22 May 1906)
            9. Howard DALZELL (b.4 Aug 1906-Wanganui,New Zealand;d.6 Oct 1981-Hamilton,New Zealand)
               sp: Grace Elizabeth GWYNN (b.21 Feb 1902-Ilford,London,UK;d.17 Jul 1965-W,New Zealand)
                  10. Margaret Priscilla DALZELL (b.13 Jun 1946-Wanganui,New Zealand)
      8. Elizabeth Florence Maude STEWART (b.1890-New Zealand;d.1978-??,Victoria,Australia)
         sp: Frederick BYRON (m.1929)
      8. Ruby Valerie Castlemaine Ballance STEWART (b.1895-New Zealand;d.1973-New Zealand)
         sp: Norman Herbert MCEWEN (m.1918)
6. Andrew GRAHAM (b.1828-Marykirk,Kincardine,Scotland;d.1 Jan 1902-Little Dunkeld,Perth,Scotland)
   sp: Ann BLYTHE (b.~1830-Dugary,Tyrone,Ireland;m.4 Jan 1851;d.27 Feb 1886-Dunblane,Perth,Scotland)
      7. Joseph Blyth GRAHAM (b.1852-Dunblane,Perth,Scotland;d.24 Dec 1915-Wellington,New Zealand)
         sp: Mary Ann GRAHAM (b.1 Dec 1844-Logie-Pert,Angus,Scotland;m.27 Jun 1871;d.13 Aug 1938-)
            8. Mary Ann GRAHAM (b.27 Nov 1873-Montrose,Angus,Scotland;d.30 Jul 1955-) ** Printed on Page 6 **
```

Grahams o' the Mearns

Descendants of James GRAHAM(E)

```
            ├── 8. Charles Riper GRAHAM (b.31 Jan 1876-RIL,New Zealand;d.18 May 1931-) ** Printed on Page 7 **
            ├── 8. John Harland GRAHAM (b.1881-Dunedin,New Zealand;d.17 Jul 1952-) ** Printed on Page 7 **
            ├── 8. Ernest GRAHAM (b.1885-New Zealand;d.Apr 1917-Wellington,New Zealand) ** Printed on Page 7 **
            ├── 8. Edwin Allen GRAHAM (b.27 Oct 1886-Dunedin,New Zealand;d.17 Apr 1975-) ** Printed on Page 7 **
            ├── 8. Joseph Ivon GRAHAM (b.Aft Apr 1888-New Zealand;d.5 Apr 1908-,New Zealand) ** Printed on Page 7 **
            ├── 8. Herbert Rowell GRAHAM (b.1890-Dunedin,New Zealand;d.26 May 1947-) ** Printed on Page 7 **
            └── 8. Alice Elizabeth GRAHAM (b.14 Aug 1892-New Zealand;d.1988-New Zealand) ** Printed on Page 8 **
        ├── 7. John Blyth GRAHAM (b.1854-Dunblane,Perth,Scotland;d.27 Dec 1942-Auchterarder,Perth,Scotland)
        │    sp: Janet MCINTYRE (b.9 May 1857-Dunblane,P,Scotland;m.26 Jul 1878;d.23 Nov 1937-A,P,Scotland)
        │       ├── 8. Andrew Herbert Francis GRAHAM (b.19 May 1879-Dunblane,P,Scotland;d.26 Dec 1896-D,P,Scotland)
        │       ├── 8. Duncan Henry Malcolm GRAHAM (b.1883-Dunblane,P,Scotland;d.15 May 1942-Renfrew,R,Scotland)
        │       │    sp: Edith HOLLYER (b.1878-Colaba,Bombay,India;m.1 Aug 1915;d.Aft 1942)
        │       ├── 8. Mary Anne GRAHAM (b.24 Mar 1887-Dunblane,Perth,Scotland)
        │       ├── 8. John Alexander GRAHAM (b.24 Jan 1891-Dunblane,P,Scotland;d.22 Mar 1891-Dunblane,S,Scotland)
        │       └── 8. John GRAHAM (b.5 Apr 1892-Dunblane,Stirling,Scotland;d.20 Jul 1983-Larbert,Stirling,Scotland)
        │            sp: Ann HENDERSON (b.27 Apr 1884-Stirling,Stirling,Scotland;m.7 Jan 1921;d.28 Jun 1948-)
        ├── 7. James GRAHAM (b.25 Feb 1855-Dunblane,Perth,Scotland;d.20 Mar 1856-Dunblane,Perth,Scotland)
        ├── 7. Jessie GRAHAM (b.6 Dec 1856-Dunblane,Perth,Scotland;d.24 Jun 1898-Saline,Fife,Scotland)
        │    sp: William ROBERTSON (b.14 Nov 1848-Keith,Banffshire,Scotland;m.25 Jan 1878)
        │       ├── 8. Jessie Ann ROBERTSON (b.18 Feb 1880-Dunblane,Perth,Scotland)
        │       ├── 8. Mary Jane Cameron ROBERTSON (b.22 Oct 1881-Saline,Fife,Scotland)
        │       ├── 8. James Graham ROBERTSON (b.9 Jun 1884-Saline,Fife,Scotland)
        │       ├── 8. William Blyth ROBERTSON (b.6 Aug 1886-Saline,Fife,Scotland;d.1971-Parramatta,NSW,Australia)
        │       └── 8. Andrew ROBERTSON (b.24 Dec 1888-Saline,Fife,Scotland)
        ├── 7. Andrew GRAHAM (b.13 May 1859-Dunblane,Perth,Scotland;d.16 Apr 1860-Dunblane,Perth,Scotland)
        └── 7. Mary Anne GRAHAM (b.22 Feb 1861-Dunblane,Perth,Scotland;d.15 Aug 1862-Dunblane,Perth,Scotland)
    ├── 6. Renwick GRAHAM (b.1830-Marykirk,Kincardine,Scotland;d.28 Jun 1904-Dundee,Angus,Scotland)
    │    sp: Mary PETRIE (b.31 Oct 1819-Forfar,Angus,Scotland;m.28 Jun 1858;d.6 Feb 1886-Dundee,A,Scotland)
    │    sp: Barbara TAYLOR (b.1833-Dundee,Angus,Scotland;m.19 Nov 1886;d.29 Mar 1904-Dundee,A,Scotland)
    ├── 6. Elizabeth GRAHAM (b.1832-Marykirk,Kincardine,Scotland)
    │    sp: John Barrie WHITTON (b.31 Mar 1832-Montrose,Angus,Scotland;m.28 Sep 1853)
    │       ├── 7. Mary Ann WHITTON (b.Abt 1855-Perth,Perth,Scotland)
    │       ├── 7. William WHITTON (b.11 Oct 1858-Montrose,Angus,Scotland;d.18 Apr 1901-Bay of Bengal)
    │       ├── 7. Susan WHITTON (b.17 Feb 1861-Montrose,Angus,Scotland;d.16 Sep 1861-Montrose,Angus,Scotland)
    │       └── 7. John Barry WHITTON (b.15 Oct 1866-Dundee,Angus,Scotland)
  sp: Barbara FETTES (b.1828-PSV,Angus Scotland;m.31 Dec 1848;d.21 Jun 1869-Dundee,Angus,Scotland)
 sp: Henrietta LAW (m.14 Jul 1798)
    ├── 5. Archibald Douglas GRAHAM (b.10 Apr 1799-Kilmarnock,Ayr,Scotland)
```

Descendants of James GRAHAM(E)

```
            sp: Elizabeth GOVE (c.20 Jul 1795-Craig,Angus,Scotland;m.13 Dec 1829)
              ├─ 5. Elizabeth Graham or MACKENZIE (b.1826-Craig,Angus,Scotland;d.1 Jan 1906-Craig,Angus,Scotland)
              │    sp: Michael WHYTE (b.30 Aug 1818-Dun,Angus,Scotland;m.21 Dec 1845;d.7 Oct 1888-Craig,Angus,Scotland)
              │     └─ 6. Elizabeth Nicol WHITE OR WHYTE (b.12 Apr 1849-Montrose,A,Scotland;d.25 Jun 1892-Craig,Angus,Scotland)
              └─ 5. Robert GRAHAM (b.10 Nov 1833-Craig,Angus,Scotland)
         ├─ 4. William GRAHAM (c.15 Dec 1779-St. Cyrus,Kincardine,Scotland)
         ├─ 4. Margaret GRAHAM (c.25 Aug 1781-St. Cyrus,Kincardine,Scotland)
         └─ 4. Helen GRAHAM (c.26 Jun 1783-St. Cyrus,Kincardine,Scotland)
              sp: David MOUAT OR MOWAT (c.3 Aug 1783-Kinneff & Catterline,Kincardine,Scoltand;m.20 Apr 1805)
              ├─ 5. Anne MOUAT (b.28 Oct 1805-St. Cyrus,Kincardine,Scotland)
              ├─ 5. David MOWAT (b.17 Sep 1807-Kinneff & Catterline,Kincardineshire,Scotland)
              ├─ 5. Margaret MOWAT (b.27 Aug 1809-Kinneff & Catterline,Kincardineshire,Scotland)
              ├─ 5. John MOWAT (b.4 Jun 1811-Kinneff & Catterline,Kincardineshire,Scotland)
              ├─ 5. Robert MOWAT (b.11 Aug 1813-Kinneff & Catterline,Kincardineshire,Scotland)
              ├─ 5. Elizabeth MOWAT (c.11 Mar 1819-Kinneff & Catterline,Kincardineshire,Scotland)
              ├─ 5. Alexander MOWAT (b.3 Sep 1821-Kinneff & Catterline,Kincardineshire,Scotland)
              └─ 5. David MOWAT (b.7 Nov 1823-Kinneff & Catterline,Kincardine,Scoltand)
    ├─ 3. Ann GRAHAM (c.7 Apr 1745-St. Cyrus,Kincardine,Scotland)
    ├─ 3. James GRAHAM (c.17 Feb 1748-St. Cyrus,Kincardine,Scotland)
    ├─ 3. Mary GRAHAM (c.1 Apr 1750-St. Cyrus,Kincardine,Scotland)
    ├─ 3. Margaret GRAHAM (c.21 Jun 1752-St. Cyrus,Kincardine,Scotland)
    ├─ 3. John GRAHAM (c.2 Jun 1754-St. Cyrus,Kincardine,Scotland)
    ├─ 3. Helen GRAHAM (c.27 Jun 1756-St. Cyrus,Kincardine,Scotland)
    ├─ 3. Andrew GRAHAM (c.17 Feb 1760-Benholm,Kincardine,Scotland)
    └─ 3. Jean GRAHAM (b.16 May 1762-St. Cyrus,Kincardine,Scotland)
└─ 2. Alexander GRAHAM (c.23 Jul 1710-St. Cyrus,Kincardine,Scotland)
    sp: Mart. SMITH (m.25 Jun 1749)
    ├─ 3. Jean GRAHAM (c.23 Jul 1749-St. Cyrus,Kincardine,Scotland)
    ├─ 3. Janet GRAHAM (c.21 May 1750-St. Cyrus,Kincardine,Scotland)
    ├─ 3. Helen GRAHAM (c.13 Oct 1751-St. Cyrus,Kincardine,Scotland)
    ├─ 3. Charles GRAHAM (c.26 Apr 1752-St. Cyrus,Kincardine,Scotland)
    ├─ 3. Ann GRAHAM (c.28 May 1754-St. Cyrus,Kincardine,Scotland)
    └─ 3. Alexander GRAHAM (c.14 Jul 1754-St. Cyrus,Kincardine,Scotland;d.btw 1841 - 1851-St. Cyrus,Kincardine,Scotland)
         sp: Isobel YOUNG (c.14 Apr 1766-Kinneff & Catterline,K,Scotland;m.11 Nov 1787;d.Aft 1841-St. Cyrus,K,Scotland)
         └─ 4. Janet GRAHAM (c.29 Sep 1788-St. Cyrus,Kincardine,Scotland;d.29 Dec 1839-Guthrie,Angus,Scotland)
              sp: Alexander STRACHAN (b.1781;m.25 Nov 1815;d.14 Feb 1864-Guthrie,Angus,Scotland)
              ├─ 5. James STRACHAN (b.14 Jul 1817-St. Cyrus,Kincardine,Scotland)
              ├─ 5. Alexander STRACHAN (b.12 Jan 1821-St. Cyrus,Kincardine,Scotland)
```

Grahams o' the Mearns

Descendants of James GRAHAM(E)

```
└─ 5. Jean STRACHAN (b.17 Jan 1823-St. Cyrus,Kincardine,Scotland)
─ 4. Aikman GRAHAM (b.20 Jul 1790-St. Cyrus,Kincardine,Scotland;d.2 Apr 1878-Inverallan,Grantown,Aberdeen,Scotland)
   sp: Susan GOW (m.23 Dec 1821;d.Bef 1878)
   ├─ 5. May GRAHAM (b.1 Oct 1822-Kettins,Angus,Scotland)
   │   sp: Burnet GORDON (m.28 May 1841)
   │   ├─ 6. David Graham GORDON (b.5 Sep 1857-Banchory Devenick,Kincardine,Scotland)
   │   └─ 6. Lewis GORDON (b.13 Dec 1861-Fetteresso,Kincardineshire,Scotland)
   ├─ 5. Aikman GRAHAM (c.27 Oct 1824-Kettins,Angus,Scotland)
   ├─ 5. Phanuel GRAHAM (c.29 Sep 1826-Kettins,Angus,Scotland)
   └─ 5. Isabella GRAHAM (b.17 Jun 1828-Kettins,Angus,Scotland)
       sp: William GIBSON (m.1 Jun 1852)
       ├─ 6. William GIBSON (b.29 Jun 1855-Edinburgh,Midlothian,Scotland)
       ├─ 6. Aikman Graham GIBSON (b.14 Jun 1857-Edinburgh,Midlothian,Scotland)
       ├─ 6. Grant Bowie GIBSON (b.17 Dec 1859-Edinburgh,Midlothian,Scotland)
       ├─ 6. Agnes Henry GIBSON (b.27 Apr 1862-Edinburgh,Midlothian,Scotland)
       ├─ 6. Isabella Graham GIBSON (b.22 Jun 1866-Edinburgh,Midlothian,Scotland)
       ├─ 6. Alexander GIBSON (b.28 Apr 1864-Edinburgh,Midlothian,Scotland)
       ├─ 6. Thomas Finlayson GIBSON (b.28 Aug 1868-Edinburgh,Midlothian,Scotland)
       └─ 6. Mary Lang GIBSON (b.31 Oct 1871-Edinburgh,Midlothian,Scotland)
─ 4. James GRAHAM (c.26 Jul 1792-St. Cyrus,Kincardine,Scotland;d.6 May 1881-St. Cyrus,Kincardine,Scotland)
   sp: Mary JACK (c.5 Aug 1795-Logie-Pert,Angus,Scotland;m.21 May 1820;d.17 Jan 1862-St. Cyrus,Kincardine,Scotland)
   ├─ 5. William GRAHAM (c.25 Mar 1821-St. Cyrus,Kincardine,Scotland)
   ├─ 5. John GRAHAM (c.6 Jul 1823-St. Cyrus,Kincardine,Scotland;d.20 Dec 1889-Edinburgh,Midlothian,Scotland)
   │   sp: Jean or Jane OFFICER (b.4 May 1823-Dundee,Angus,Scotland;m.15 Jun 1851;d.1896-Edinburgh,M,Scotland)
   │   ├─ 6. Julia Ann GRAHAM (b.28 Jun 1857-Edinburgh,Midlothian,Scotland)
   │   ├─ 6. William Officer GRAHAM (b.1 Jun 1860-Edinburgh,Midlothian,Scotland;d.Bef 1881-Edinburgh,M,Scotland)
   │   ├─ 6. Helen GRAHAM (b.1 Sep 1862-Edinburgh,Midlothian,Scotland)
   │   ├─ 6. James GRAHAM (b.Abt 1865-Edinburgh,Midlothian,Scotland)
   │   └─ 6. Mary Jane GRAHAM (b.4 Nov 1867-Edinburgh,Midlothian,Scotland;d.Bef 1881-Edinburgh,Midlothian,Scotland)
   ├─ 5. Mary GRAHAM (c.4 Sep 1825-St. Cyrus,Kincardine,Scotland)
   ├─ 5. Charlotte GRAHAM (c.4 Feb 1827-St. Cyrus,Kincardine,Scotland)
   │   sp: Robert JOHNSTON (m.9 Oct 1861)
   │   ├─ 6. Hugh JOHNSTON (b.2 Jul 1862-Longside,Aberdeen,Scotland)
   │   ├─ 6. Graeme JOHNSTON (b.16 Mar 1864-Oyne,Aberdeen,Scotland)
   │   ├─ 6. William JOHNSTON (b.18 Jul 1867-Oyne,Aberdeen,Scotland)
   │   └─ 6. Mary Jane JOHNSTON (b.29 Apr 1870-Oyne,Aberdeen,Scotland)
   ├─ 5. Ann GRAHAM (b.11 Mar 1829-St. Cyrus,Kincardine,Scotland)
   │   sp: George WYNESS (b.17 Feb 1823-Aboyne,Aberdeen,Scotland;m.23 Dec 1855)
```

Grahams o' the Mearns

Descendants of James GRAHAM(E)

```
            ├─ 6. Alexander WYNESS (b.23 Oct 1856-Craig by Montrose,Angus,Scotland)
            ├─ 6. Ann WYNESS (b.18 May 1858-Craig by Montrose,Angus,Scotland)
            ├─ 6. Jane WYNESS (b.12 Jan 1861-Craig by Montrose,Angus,Scotland)
            ├─ 6. George WYNESS (b.5 Aug 1863-Craig by Montrose,Angus,Scotland)
            └─ 6. Julia WYNESS (b.21 Jan 1872-Craig by Montrose,Angus,Scotland)
         ├─ 5. Julia GRAHAM (b.1831-St. Cyrus,Kincardine,Scotland)
         ├─ 5. Janet GRAHAM (b.12 Aug 1839-St. Cyrus,Kincardine,Scotland)
         └─ 5. Isabella GRAHAM (b.12 Aug 1839-St. Cyrus,Kincardine,Scotland)
      ├─ 4. William GRAHAM (c.12 Jul 1795-St. Cyrus,Kincardine,Scotland)
      ├─ 4. Susan GRAHAM (c.28 May 1797-St. Cyrus,Kincardine,Scotland)
      │     sp: Phanuel DUNCAN (c.15 Oct 1792-Benholm,Kincardine,Scotland;m.11 Jun 1820)
      │        ├─ 5. Alexander DUNCAN (b.11 Apr 1821-St. Cyrus,Kincardine,Scotland)
      │        ├─ 5. Phanuel DUNCAN (b.10 Nov 1822-St. Cyrus,Kincardine,Scotland)
      │        ├─ 5. Isobel DUNCAN (b.14 Jul 1824-St. Cyrus,Kincardine,Scotland)
      │        ├─ 5. Aikman DUNCAN (b.23 Mar 1826-St. Cyrus,Kincardine,Scotland)
      │        ├─ 5. Anna DUNCAN (b.24 Jan 1828-St. Cyrus,Kincardine,Scotland)
      │        ├─ 5. William DUNCAN (b.14 Mar 1830-St. Cyrus,Kincardine,Scotland)
      │        ├─ 5. John DUNCAN (b.23 Nov 1831-St. Cyrus,Kincardine,Scotland)
      │        ├─ 5. Anne DUNCAN (b.19 Dec 1833-St. Cyrus,Kincardine,Scotland)
      │        ├─ 5. George DUNCAN (b.20 Mar 1836-Montrose,Angus,Scotland)
      │        ├─ 5. Susan DUNCAN (b.13 May 1838-Montrose,Angus,Scotland)
      │        ├─ 5. David Foote DUNCAN (b.13 May 1838-Montrose,Angus,Scotland)
      │        └─ 5. Christina DUNCAN (b.18 Oct 1841-Montrose,Angus,Scotland)
      └─ 4. Anne GRAHAM (c.4 Mar 1804-St. Cyrus,Kincardine,Scotland)
   ├─ 3. Mary GRAHAM (c.17 Apr 1757-St. Cyrus,Kincardine,Scotland)
   └─ 3. William GRAHAM (c.13 Jun 1762-St. Cyrus,Kincardine,Scotland)
```

Odds and Ends

Table of All Grahams Baptised in St. Cyrus, Old Parish Registries 1696-1852

italics mean speculative, regular font means known or proven

Name1	Surname	Chr Date	BrthDate	Father	Mother	Parish	Location
Robert	Grahame	8/30/1696		James Grahame		St. Cyrus	Wardropertoun
Helin	Grahame	2/25/1697		John Graham		St. Cyrus	Craigie
James	Grahame	4/21/1698		James Grahame	*Isoble HILL*	St. Cyrus	Wardropertoun
Robert	Grahame	12/24/1700		Robert Grahame		St. Cyrus	Bridgtoun
John	Grahame	9/15/1700		James Grahame	*Isoble HILL*	St. Cyrus	Wardropertoun
Margaret	Grahame	3/9/1701		John Graham		St. Cyrus	Craigie
Janet	Grahame	9/20/1702		James Grahame	*Isoble HILL*	St. Cyrus	Wardropertoun
David	Grahame	2/11/1703		Robert Grahame		St. Cyrus	Bridgtoun
Francis	Grahame	10/16/1703		John Graham		St. Cyrus	Craigie
James	Grahame	10/8/1704		James Grahame	*Isoble HILL*	St. Cyrus	Wardropertoun
Robert	**Grahame**	**12/14/1707**		**James Grahame**	***Isoble HILL***	**St. Cyrus**	**Wardropertoun**
Alexr	Grahame	7/23/1710		James Grahame	*Isoble HILL*	St. Cyrus	Wardropertoun
Ann	Grahame	6/16/1710		David Graham	Mary Smith	St. Cyrus	
Margaret	Grahame	7/18/1714		John Graham		St. Cyrus	Little Woodstoun
Jean	Graham	8/28/1715		John Graham		St. Cyrus	Little Woodstoun
Janet	Graham	3/17/1717		John Graham		St. Cyrus	Scotstoun
Mary	Graham	10/16/1719		John Graham		St. Cyrus	Burnhead
William	Graham	12/13/1719		John Graham		St. Cyrus	Burnhead
Anna	Graham	3/12/1720		Robt Graham		St. Cyrus	Nenlands
Margaret	Graham	2/16/1721		John Graham		St. Cyrus	Burnhead
Robert	Graham	2/24/1722		Robert Graham		St. Cyrus	Nenlands
Elizabeth	Graham	5/27/1722		John Graham		St. Cyrus	Burnhead of Scotstoun
Joseph	Graham	7/16/1723		John Graham		St. Cyrus	Burnhead
Elizabeth	Graham	4/5/1724		Robert Graham		St. Cyrus	Nenlands
Cicil	Graham	3/16/1727		Robert Graham		St. Cyrus	Nenlands
Jean	Graham	5/27/1729		Robert Graham		St. Cyrus	Nenlands
Janet	Graham	4/20/1730		John Graham		St. Cyrus	sometimes in Ober Cre
Francis	Graham	11/24/1732		Robert Graham		St. Cyrus	Muirhead
James	Graham	5/23/1735		James Graham	*Isobell Nicoll*	St. Cyrus	Green (Morphie)
Margaret	Graham	3/13/1737		James Graham	*Isobell Nicoll*	St. Cyrus	Green (Morphie)
Mary	Graham	8/5/1739		James Graham	*Isobell Nicoll*	St. Cyrus	Green (Morphie)
Robert	Graham	3/30/1740		Robert Graham	*Janet White*	St. Cyrus	Wardropertoun

Name1	Surname	Chr Date	BrthDate	Father	Mother	Parish	Location
John	Graham	6/5/1742		James Graham	*Isobell Nicoll*	St. Cyrus	Upper Creigie
Alexander	**Graham**	**5/28/1743**		**Robert Graham**	***Janet White***	**St. Cyrus**	**Upper Wardropertoun**
Alexander	Graham	7/15/1744		James Graham	*Isobell Nicoll*	St. Cyrus	Pitbidlie
Ann	Graham	4/7/1745		Robert Graham	*Janet White*	St. Cyrus	Wardropertoun
David	Graham	10/18/1747		James Graham	*Isobell Nicoll*	St. Cyrus	Pitbidlie
James	Graham	2/17/1748		Robert Graham	*Janet White*	St. Cyrus	Little Woodstoun
Jean	Graham	7/23/1749		Alxr Graham		St. Cyrus	Maither??
Mary	Graham	4/1/1750		Rot Graham	*Janet White*	St. Cyrus	cotterman in ??
Janet	Graham	5/21/1750		Alexander	*Mart Smith*	St. Cyrus	cotterman in Morphie
Helen	Graham	10/13/1751		Alexander Graham		St. Cyrus	cotterman in Eastoun of West
Charles	Graham	4/26/1752		Alex Graham	*Mart Smith*	St. Cyrus	cotterman in Morphie
Margaret	Graham	6/21/1752		Robert Graham	*Janet White*	St. Cyrus	cotterman in Morphie
Alexander	Graham	7/14/1754		Alexr Graham	*Mart Smith*	St. Cyrus	cotterman to Kirkside
John	Graham	6/2/1754		Robert Graham	*Janet White*	St. Cyrus	subtenant in Morphie
Ann	Graham	5/28/1754		Alexr Graham	*Mart Smith*	St. Cyrus	subtenant in Morphie
Helen	Graham	10/27/1754		James Graham	*Ann Dorrat*	St. Cyrus	weaver in Nether Wardroptoun
Helen	Graham	6/27/1756		Robert Graham	*Janet White*	St. Cyrus	in Morphy
Mary	Graham	4/17/1757		Alexr Graham		St. Cyrus	in Morphy
Ann	Graham	9/14/1757		Alexr Graham		St. Cyrus	in Whitehill
John	Graham	3/4/1759		James Graham	*Ann Dorrat*	St. Cyrus	Nether Wardroptoun
James	Graeme	6/29/1760		Alexander		St. Cyrus	Kirkside
William	Graham	6/13/1762		Alexr Graham		St. Cyrus	Whitehill
Jean	Graham	5/16/1762		Robert Graham		St. Cyrus	Glenhankin
Arthur	Graham	4/14/1765		Alexr Graham		St. Cyrus	Whitehill
Janet	Graeme	9/3/1769		Alexander	*Jane/Jean Mitchel*	St. Cyrus	Pitbidlie
Mary	Graeme	3/11/1771		Alexander	*Jane/Jean Mitchel*	St. Cyrus	Pitbidlie
Anne	Graeme	10/4/1772		Alexander	*Jane/Jean Mitchel*	St. Cyrus	Pitbidlie
Alexander	Graham	9/26/1773		Alexr Graham	*Jane/Jean Mitchel*	St. Cyrus	Pitbidlie
Margaret	Graham	6/18/1777		Alexr Graham	*Jane/Jean Mitchel*	St. Cyrus	Pitbidlie
Robert	**Graham**	**6/11/1778**		**Alexr Graham**	***Jane/Jean Mitchel***	**St. Cyrus**	**Hill of Morphie**
William	Graeme	12/15/1779		Alexander	*Jane/Jean Mitchel*	St. Cyrus	Hill of Morphie
Anne	Graham	3/28/1779		John Graham		St. Cyrus	Milltown
Margaret	Graeme	8/25/1781		Alexander	*Jane/Jean Mitchel*	St. Cyrus	Hill of Morphie

Name1	Surname	Chr Date	BrthDate	Father	Mother	Parish	Location
James	Graham	1/3/1781		John Graham		St. Cyrus	Milltown
Helen	Graham	6/26/1783		Alexander	Jane/Jean Mitchel	St. Cyrus	Hill of Morphie
Janet	Graham	9/29/1788		Alexander	Isobel Young	St. Cyrus	Kirkside
Aikman	Graham	8/8/1790		Alexander	Isobel Young	St. Cyrus	Kirkside
James	Graham	7/26/1792		Alexander	Isobel Young	St. Cyrus	Kirkside
Alexander	Graham	5/31/1795		William Graham	Helen Reid	St. Cyrus	
William	Graham	7/12/1795		Alexander	Isobel Young	St. Cyrus	
Susan	Graham	5/28/1797		Alexander	Isobel Young	St. Cyrus	Lochside
Anne	Graham	6/4/1804		Alexander	Isobel Young	St. Cyrus	Lochside
Alexander	Graham	4/29/1810		William Graham	Isabel Brown	St. Cyrus	
Charles	Graham	12/15/1811		William Graham	Isabel Brown	St. Cyrus	
Mary	Graham	12/6/1812		John Graham	Mary Clark	St. Cyrus	illegitimate
Janet	Graham	2/14/1813		Alexander	Jane Black	St. Cyrus	Brownhill
Elizabeth	Graham	10/22/1815		William Graham	Isabel Brown	St. Cyrus	Snowden
William	Graham	3/25/1821		James Graham	Mary Jack	St. Cyrus	
John	Graham	7/6/1823		James Graham	Mary Jack	St. Cyrus	
Mary	Graham	9/4/1825		James Graham	Mary Jack	St. Cyrus	
Charlotte	Graham	2/4/1827		James Graham	Mary Jack	St. Cyrus	
Ann	Graham	3/11/1829		James Graham	Mary Jack	St. Cyrus	
Janet	Graham	8/12/1839		James Graham	Mary Jack	St. Cyrus	
Isabella	Graham	8/12/1839		James Graham	Mary Jack	St. Cyrus	
Jane Howie	Graham	2/17/1841		James Graham	Ann Hutchison	St. Cyrus	
Alexander	Graham		4/20/1844	John Graham	Mary Todd	Marykirk	
Ann	Graham		10/25/1845	John Graham	Mary Todd	Marykirk	
John	Graham	7/16/1847	6/25/1847	John Graham	Mary Todd	St. Cyrus	
Betsy	Graham	7/16/1847	6/25/1847	John Graham	Mary Todd	St. Cyrus	
Isabella	Graham	8/18/1849	7/23/1849	John Graham	Mary Todd	St. Cyrus	
James	Graham	2/29/1852	2/11/1852	John Graham	Mary Todd	St. Cyrus	

List of Grahams

Sorted Individuals List

RIN	Name	Born/Chr	Died/Bur	MRIN		Spouse, Parent or Child
1084	GRAHAM(E), Elizabeth	1834	7 Mar 1878	557	S	Alexander GOVE
1167	GRAHAM(E), James			405	S	Isoble HILL
771	GRAHAM, Agnes	24 May 1897	~1960s	902	S	Frank H FAIRWEATHER
19	GRAHAM, Agnes Cuthbert	25 Jan 1890	15 Nov 1955	3	P	David Alma GRAHAM
2228	GRAHAM, Agnes Helen	24 Jul 1940		897	S	Frederick Harvey SMAIL
30	GRAHAM, Agnes Minnie	18 Mar 1891	4 Aug 1891	9	P	Charles I B GRAHAM
1028	GRAHAM, Aikman	27 Oct 1824		963	P	Aikman GRAHAM
1976	GRAHAM, Aikman	20 Jul 1790	2 Apr 1878	963	S	Susan GOW
2394	GRAHAM, Alexander	1835		431	P	William GRAHAME
1602	GRAHAM, Alexander	26 Sep 1773	8 Apr 1840	375	S	Jean BLACK
1319	GRAHAM, Alexander	15 Jul 1744		380	P	James GRAHAM
2441	GRAHAM, Alexander	14 Jul 1754	btw 1841 - 1851	852	S	Isobel YOUNG
1699	GRAHAM, Alexander	23 Jul 1710		1432	S	Mart. SMITH
499	GRAHAM, Alexander	20 Apr 1810		436	P	William GRAHAM
2172	GRAHAM, Alexander	3 Nov 1821	4 Jun 1843	294	P	Alexander GRAHAM
908	GRAHAM, Alexander	28 May 1743		985	S	Jean or Jane MITCHEL
21	GRAHAM, Alexander	Feb/Mar 1797	17 Jun 1871	336	S	Elisabeth SHARP
1637	GRAHAM, Alexander J	1 Jan 1889	2 Apr 1889	3	P	David Alma GRAHAM
1169	GRAHAM, Alice Elizabeth	14 Aug 1892	1988	644	S	Reginald Lewis HULSTON
2059	GRAHAM, Amelia	2 Aug 1848	4 Aug 1917	1117	S	Robert William O STEWART
1857	GRAHAM, Andrew	13 May 1859	16 Apr 1860	826	P	Andrew GRAHAM
936	GRAHAM, Andrew	1828	1 Jan 1902	826	S	Ann BLYTHE
1096	GRAHAM, Andrew	17 Feb 1760		448	P	Robert GRAHAM
2478	GRAHAM, Andrew Herbert Francis	19 May 1879	26 Dec 1896	817	P	John Blyth GRAHAM
1547	GRAHAM, Ann	21 Sep 1801	7 Jan 1824	375	P	Alexander GRAHAM
1024	GRAHAM, Ann	7 Apr 1745		448	P	Robert GRAHAM
2497	GRAHAM, Ann	28 May 1754		1432	P	Alexander GRAHAM
2525	GRAHAM, Ann	11 Mar 1829		959	S	George WYNESS
2529	GRAHAM, Anne	4 Mar 1804		852	P	Alexander GRAHAM
932	GRAHAM, Anne	4 Oct 1772		985	P	Alexander GRAHAM
1392	GRAHAM, Archibald Douglas	10 Apr 1799		643	P	Robert GRAHAM
118	GRAHAM, Barbara Lee	7 Apr 1952		75	S	William Terry PATE
2387	GRAHAM, Betty	11 Nov 1799	17 Oct 1866	375	P	Alexander GRAHAM

RIN	Name	/Chr	/Bur	MRIN	Spouse, Parent or Child	
2060	GRAHAM, Charles	Abt 1922		1094	P	Charles Riper GRAHAM
1326	GRAHAM, Charles	29 Nov 1811		436	P	William GRAHAM
2504	GRAHAM, Charles	26 Apr 1752		1432	P	Alexander GRAHAM
688	GRAHAM, Charles	10 Nov 1895	20 Sep 1979	343	S	Mary Constance FOX
28	GRAHAM, Charles George	5 Oct 1887	29 Nov 1892	9	P	Charles I B GRAHAM
16	GRAHAM, Charles I B	10 Aug 1861	15 Dec 1945	9	S	Agnes Small CANDOW
329	GRAHAM, Charles James	Apr 1899	~18 Jun 1904	3	P	David Alma GRAHAM
9	GRAHAM, Charles James	23 Jul 1991		238	P	David Lee GRAHAM
2	GRAHAM, Charles James	12 May 1929	12 Nov 1990	1	S	Marilyn Louise LAFRANCE
962	GRAHAM, Charles Lord	6 Sep 1911	5 May 2000	884	S	Elizabeth Ethel ECCLESTON
1552	GRAHAM, Charles Riper	31 Jan 1876	May 1931	1094	S	Edith Emma M SPENCER
2520	GRAHAM, Charlotte	4 Feb 1827		991	S	Robert JOHNSTON
927	GRAHAM, Claire	29 Mar 1977		522	S	Steven SIMON
8	GRAHAM, Connor David	7 Aug 1989		238	P	David Lee GRAHAM
1577	GRAHAM, Connor George	25 Oct 1997		358	P	Kenneth Jonathon BROPHY
2330	GRAHAM, David	18 Oct 1747	17 Sep 1820	442	S	Mary BRAND
6	GRAHAM, David Alma	1 May 1854	21 Oct 1933	3	S	Agnes Robb CUTHBERT
4	GRAHAM, David Alma	26 Jan 1888	18 Aug 1955	2	S	Emma Frances SCHWARZ
1	GRAHAM, David Lee	4 Oct 1956		238	S	Jane Ellen HARBAUGH
687	GRAHAM, David Soutar	24 Jan 1893	19 May 1965	280	S	Margaret Gardiner BRAND
913	GRAHAM, Donald Charles	15 Jul 1938		345	S	Wilma Breathwood GIBB
158	GRAHAM, Donald Malcolm	6 Apr 1938		726	S	Melinda LEE
1405	GRAHAM, Duncan Henry Malcolm	1883	15 May 1942	869	S	Edith HOLLYER
2585	GRAHAM, Edwin Allen	27 Oct 1886	17 Apr 1975	1133	P	Joseph Blyth GRAHAM
1895	GRAHAM, Elizabeth	1832		954	S	John Barrie WHITTON
1275	GRAHAM, Elizabeth	17 Oct 1815		989	S	William BOATH
2199	GRAHAM, Ernest	1885	Apr 1917	1133	P	Joseph Blyth GRAHAM
1942	GRAHAM, George Albert	Feb 1894	7 Oct 1896	279	P	Charles I B GRAHAM
338	GRAHAM, George Charles	1 Jul 1957		102	P	George Charles GRAHAM M
327	GRAHAM, George Charles MD	9 May 1921	8 Oct 1996	102	S	Muriel Elsie HUENE MD
18	GRAHAM, George Forbes	7 Aug 1892	17 Jun 1972	99	S	Lenora WIRTH
17	GRAHAM, George Heron	6 Sep 1864		5	P	James Campbell GRAHAM
959	GRAHAM, Gordon Richard Bradlaw	1930	31 Aug 1932	343	P	Charles GRAHAM
336	GRAHAM, Heather	19 Apr 1950	5 Aug 1982	102	P	George Charles GRAHAM M
1959	GRAHAM, Helen	1 Sep 1862		883	P	John GRAHAM
1258	GRAHAM, Helen	27 Oct 1754		421	P	James GRAHAM
1470	GRAHAM, Helen	26 Jun 1783		78	S	David MOUAT OR MOWAT
		Born	**Died**			

RIN	Name	/Chr	/Bur	MRIN	Spouse, Parent or Child	
2465	GRAHAM, Helen	13 Oct 1751		1432	P	Alexander GRAHAM
1095	GRAHAM, Helen	27 Jun 1756		448	P	Robert GRAHAM
2571	GRAHAM, Herbert Rowell	1890	1947	750	S	Clarice Mary C McALINDON
2522	GRAHAM, Isabella	12 Aug 1839		960	P	James GRAHAM
1635	GRAHAM, Isabella	17 Jun 1828		480	S	William GIBSON
2435	GRAHAM, Isobelle	9 Jun 1805	11 Jan 1822	375	P	Alexander GRAHAM
2238	GRAHAM, James	Abt 1865		883	P	John GRAHAM
2457	GRAHAM, James	25 Feb 1855		826	P	Andrew GRAHAM
503	GRAHAM, James	23 May 1735		421	S	Ann DORRAT
1152	GRAHAM, James	17 Feb 1748		448	P	Robert GRAHAM
1266	GRAHAM, James	26 Jul 1792	6 May 1881	960	S	Mary JACK
1617	GRAHAM, James	8 Oct 1704	27 Feb 1785	380	S	Isobell NICOLL
13	GRAHAM, James Campbell	1822	18 Dec 1865	5	S	Catherine WILKIE
15	GRAHAM, James Talford	28 Mar 1856		5	P	James Campbell GRAHAM
925	GRAHAM, Jane	5 Jan 1967		1165	S	Anthony CARACCIOLA
1015	GRAHAM, Janet	4 Feb 1813	3 Nov 1824	375	P	Alexander GRAHAM
1073	GRAHAM, Janet	21 May 1750		1432	P	Alexander GRAHAM
2521	GRAHAM, Janet	12 Aug 1839		960	P	James GRAHAM
1613	GRAHAM, Janet	29 Sep 1788	29 Dec 1839	512	S	Alexander STRACHAN
2135	GRAHAM, Janet	20 Sep 1702		405	P	James GRAHAM(E)
930	GRAHAM, Janet	3 Sep 1769		985	P	Alexander GRAHAM
2418	GRAHAM, Jean	15 Oct 1807	24 Oct 1867	375	P	Alexander GRAHAM
2415	GRAHAM, Jean	23 Jul 1749		1432	P	Alexander GRAHAM
1495	GRAHAM, Jean	30 Nov 1833	1914	982	S	David SUTTIE
1030	GRAHAM, Jean	16 May 1762		448	P	Robert GRAHAM
2090	GRAHAM, Jean Arthur	27 Aug 1946		168	S	Nikolas TOMBRAS
20	GRAHAM, Jennie Francis	11 Jun 1886	30 Dec 1969	3	P	David Alma GRAHAM
2142	GRAHAM, Jessie	6 Dec 1856		826	P	Andrew GRAHAM
1876	GRAHAM, John	Abt 1824	1905	1131	S	Mary MILNE
316	GRAHAM, John	4 Mar 1759		421	P	James GRAHAM
495	GRAHAM, John	5 Jun 1742		380	P	James GRAHAM
2236	GRAHAM, John	6 Jul 1823	20 Dec 1889	883	S	Jean or Jane OFFICER
1053	GRAHAM, John	15 Sep 1700		412	S	Margaret NICOLL
1094	GRAHAM, John	2 Jun 1754		448	P	Robert GRAHAM
2572	GRAHAM, John Alexander	5 Apr 1892	Aft 1948	1140	S	Ann HENDERSON
2534	GRAHAM, John Blyth	1854	27 Dec 1942	817	S	Janet MCINTYRE
2439	GRAHAM, John Harland	1881	17 Jul 1952	1141	S	Annie Elizabeth ?
		Born	**Died**			

RIN	Name	/Chr	/Bur	MRIN	Spouse, Parent or Child	
1660	GRAHAM, John Thomson	7 Aug 1841	15 May 1857	431	P	William GRAHAME
2004	GRAHAM, Joseph Blyth	1852	24 Dec 1915	1133	S	Mary Ann GRAHAM
2587	GRAHAM, Joseph Ivon	Aft Apr 1888	5 Apr 1908	1133	P	Joseph Blyth GRAHAM
1508	GRAHAM, Joyce	Abt 1919		1094	P	Charles Riper GRAHAM
2703	GRAHAM, Julia	1831		960	P	James GRAHAM
1281	GRAHAM, Julia Ann	28 Jun 1857		883	P	John GRAHAM
126	GRAHAM, Kenneth McGregor	1920	3 Jan 2007	631	S	Pam ????
926	GRAHAM, Kirstin	25 Jul 1970		345	P	Donald Charles GRAHAM
924	GRAHAM, Laura	27 Oct 1965		351	S	Scott WITCHALLS
117	GRAHAM, Linda Carol	13 May 1948		36	S	Thomas BRADLEY
984	GRAHAM, Lorna Nancy	18 Apr 1954		358	S	Kenneth Jonathon BROPHY
1071	GRAHAM, Margaret	13 Mar 1737		380	P	James GRAHAM
1092	GRAHAM, Margaret	25 Aug 1781		985	P	Alexander GRAHAM
1097	GRAHAM, Margaret	21 Jun 1752		448	P	Robert GRAHAM
934	GRAHAM, Margaret	18 Jun 1777	Bef 1780	985	P	Alexander GRAHAM
886	GRAHAM, Margaret Nicholson	8 May 1821	28 Jan 1897	331	S	Charles WATT
1485	GRAHAM, Mary	5 Aug 1739		380	P	James GRAHAM
2491	GRAHAM, Mary	17 Apr 1757		1432	P	Alexander GRAHAM
1294	GRAHAM, Mary	4 Sep 1825		960	P	James GRAHAM
1093	GRAHAM, Mary	1 Apr 1750		448	P	Robert GRAHAM
931	GRAHAM, Mary	11 Mar 1771		985	P	Alexander GRAHAM
1580	GRAHAM, Mary Ann	27 Nov 1873	30 Jul 1955	1249	S	Decimus ROWE
1730	GRAHAM, Mary Ann	1 Dec 1844	Aug 1938	1133	S	Joseph Blyth GRAHAM
752	GRAHAM, Mary Ann	20 Dec 1822	26 May 1902	121	S	John DOIG
2702	GRAHAM, Mary Anne	24 Mar 1887		817	P	John Blyth GRAHAM
220	GRAHAM, Mary Anne	22 Feb 1861	15 Aug 1862	826	P	Andrew GRAHAM
2069	GRAHAM, Mary Jane	4 Nov 1867	Bef 1881	883	P	John GRAHAM
912	GRAHAM, Maureen	30 Dec 1933		343	P	Charles GRAHAM
1453	GRAHAM, May	1 Oct 1822		474	S	Burnet GORDON
11	GRAHAM, Nancy Lynn	14 Mar 1961		37	S	Richard Brian BARKER
2538	GRAHAM, Nicole Choei-Lin	23 Feb 1984		726	P	Donald Malcolm GRAHAM
1674	GRAHAM, Phanuel	29 Sep 1826		963	P	Aikman GRAHAM
1748	GRAHAM, Renwick	3 Aug 1856	6 May 1858	1067	P	James Sime SMITH
1195	GRAHAM, Renwick	1830	28 Jun 1904	420	S	Mary PETRIE
1804	GRAHAM, Robert	30 Aug 1696		405	P	James GRAHAM(E)
1459	GRAHAM, Robert	10 Nov 1833		641	P	Robert GRAHAM
1400	GRAHAM, Robert	30 Mar 1740		448	P	Robert GRAHAM
1643	GRAHAM, Robert	14 Dec 1707		448	S	Janet WHITE

RIN	Name	Born/Chr	Died/Bur	MRIN		Spouse, Parent or Child
828	GRAHAM, Robert	11 Jun 1778		310	S	Mary NICOL
12	GRAHAM, Robert David	6 Jan 1921	16 Oct 2004	35	S	Dorothy E. BACHMAN
328	GRAHAM, Ruth Lenora	27 Jul 1925		103	S	Edmund FULLER
911	GRAHAM, Sheila	19 Jul 1926		344	S	Ronald RATTRAY
726	GRAHAM, Stewart Richard	1950		631	P	Kenneth McGregor GRAHAM
1057	GRAHAM, Susan	28 May 1797		990	S	Phanuel DUNCAN
2548	GRAHAM, William	15 Aug 1837	6 Oct 1907	1334	S	Margaret LAWRENCE
979	GRAHAM, William	15 Dec 1779		985	P	Alexander GRAHAM
2500	GRAHAM, William	13 Jun 1762		1432	P	Alexander GRAHAM
1348	GRAHAM, William	25 Mar 1821		960	P	James GRAHAM
1476	GRAHAM, William	12 Jul 1795		852	P	Alexander GRAHAM
935	GRAHAM, William			436	S	Isobel BROWN
29	GRAHAM, William Melville	14 Apr 1889	30 Jan 1961	333	S	Helen Kilpatrick LYON
1837	GRAHAM, William Officer	1 Jun 1860	Bef 1881	883	P	John GRAHAM
1153	GRAHAME, Ann	21 Sep 1801	1824			
2251	GRAHAME, Betty	11 Nov 1799				
1328	GRAHAME, Janet	20 Sep 1702				
1404	GRAHAME, Jean	15 Oct 1807				
1466	GRAHAME, John	15 Sep 1700				
1336	GRAHAME, William	11 Aug 1803	14 Apr 1881	431	S	Jean DONALD

Most Popular Given Names

Charles	11
Alexander	10
John	10
James	8
William	8
Ann/Anne	6
Jean	6
David	5
Mary Ann	5

Online Resources – Places I've Posted

1. http://wc.rootsweb.ancestry.com/ database name gsgroup; public
2. www.genesreunited.co.uk (subscription service)
3. http://www.myheritage.com/site-122829612/graham (subscription service)
4. www.scotlandspeoples.gov.uk (cost per downloaded image) contact me via email and I will provide ID and password so that you can see all the images I've collected.

Selected Maternal Lines

The Wilkies

For those of us Grahams connected to James Campbell Graham, it is fitting to explore, albeit more briefly the Wilkie family for it was James' wife Catherine Wilkie that bore him four sons.

Catherine WILKIE was christened 1 Feb 1826 in Forfar, Forfarshire. She was the third of six children born to David WILKIE and Margaret McLEAN. This couple had the following children, all christened in Forfar where David was a flesher or butcher:

Agnes	11 Apr 1820
Margaret	18 Sep 1824
Catherine	1 Feb 1826
Betty	6 Jan 1828
David	26 Dec 1831
James	27 Jul 1834

The 1841 census entry indicated that the family lived on Castle Street in Forfar and that Agnes (already married to James Nicoll) and Catherine were not living at home. However, granddaughter Margaret Nicoll having been born 11 Nov 1838 in Dundee was living in the household.

By the 1851 census, the household was still located at 12 Castle Street in Forfar but now comprised David, his wife Margaret, his remaining daughter Betty or Betsy, his sons David (listed as tinsmith, journeyman) and James (listed as flesher, journeyman). Each of the elder daughters had by now been married.

David Wilkie's wife Margaret died and was buried in the Forfar cemetery on 19 Sep 1852. This must have been difficult for him as he died 29 Dec 1856 also in Forfar. His brother Alexander was witness on the death registration.

Despite my best efforts to trace the remaining children of David and Margaret WILKIE, I was unable to find any clues as to what happened to Betsy, David and James. However, with the help of a Forfar based family history researcher, I was able to learn that David, wife Margaret and their daughter Margaret

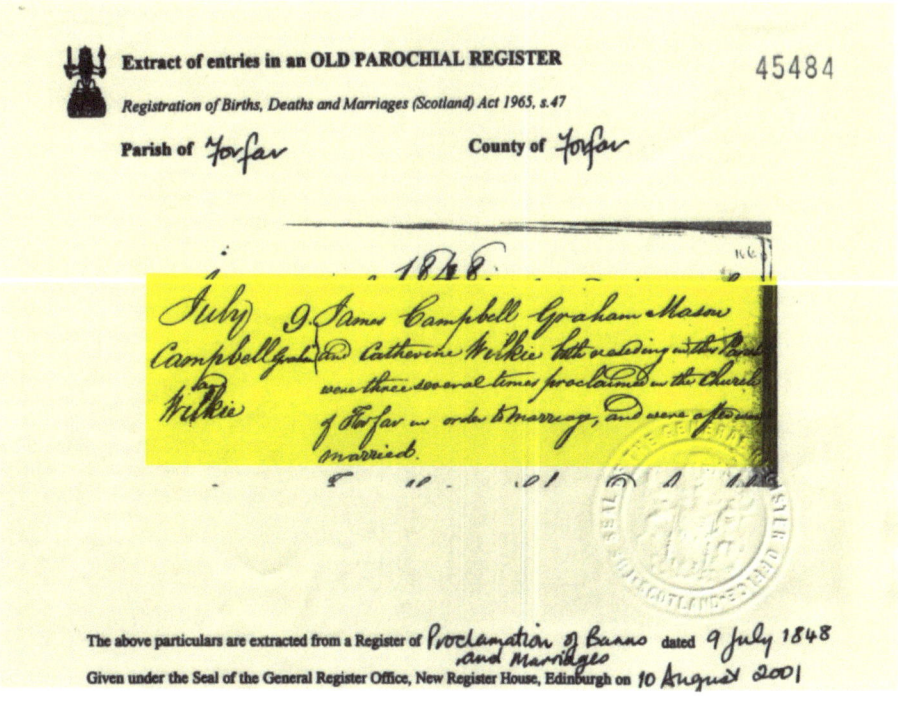

(Wilkie) McNab and her husband Robert McNab were all buried in a family plot in the Forfar cemetery. Though the eldest daughter Agnes married James Nicoll 21 Jan 1838 in Forfar all of their nine children were born in Dundee. Ultimately, it is not clear from the records whether the WILKIE family was particularly close to one another though it seems reasonable to assume that they maintained contact within Dundee and between it and Forfar, a distance of less than fifteen miles.

On the following page, I can be certain that David Wilkie was born 1794 to Alexander Wilkie and Elizabeth Brown but Alexander's lineage is less certain.

Descendants of William Wilkie

1. William Wilkie
  sp: UNKNOWN
  └─ 2. James Wilkie
       sp: Eliza Samson (m.25 Jun 1715)
       └─ 3. James Wilkie
            sp: Isabel Ormond (m.28 Apr 1739)
            ├─ 4. Isabel Wilkie (c.23 May 1747-Forfar,Angus Scotland)
            ├─ 4. Jean Wilkie (c.1 May 1750-Forfar,Angus Scotland)
            └─ 4. Alexander Wilkie (c.3 Jun 1751-Forfar,Angus,Scotland;d.Prob bef 1836-Forfar,Angus,Scotland)
                 sp: Elizabeth Brown (b.~1760;m.8 Feb 1783;d.10 Jun 1836-Forfar,Angus,Scotland)
                 ├─ 5. Margaret Wilkie (b.16 Jun 1784-Forfar,Angus Scotland)
                 ├─ 5. George Wilkie (b.7 Jul 1786-Forfar,Angus Scotland)
                 ├─ 5. Andrew Wilkie (b.15 Sep 1788-Forfar,Angus Scotland)
                 ├─ 5. Betty Wilkie (b.14 Aug 1791-Forfar,Angus Scotland)
                 ├─ 5. David Wilkie (b.2 Jan 1794-Forfar,Angus Scotland;d.29 Dec 1856-Forfar,Angus Scotland)
                 │   sp: Margaret McLean (b.1797-Kirriemuir,Angus Scotland;m.31 Oct 1819;d.19 Sep 1852-Forfar,Angus Scotland)
                 │   ├─ 6. Agnes Wilkie (c.11 Apr 1820-Forfar,Angus Scotland)
                 │   │   sp: James Nicoll (m.21 Jan 1838)
                 │   ├─ 6. Margaret Wilkie (c.18 Sep 1824-Forfar,Angus Scotland;b.8 Aug 1874-Forfar Cemetery,Forfar,Angus)
                 │   │   sp: Robert McNab (b.1825;m.8 Dec 1844;d.15 Apr 1875-Forfar,Angus,Scotland)
                 │   ├─ 6. Catherine Wilkie (c.1 Feb 1826-Forfar,Angus,Scotland;d.21 Feb 1898-Dundee,Angus,Scotland)
                 │   │   sp: James Campbell Graham (b.1822-Glamis,A,Scotland;m.9 Jul 1848;d.18 Dec 1865-Dundee,A,Scotland)
                 │   │   sp: James Watson (b.12 Feb 1800-Dundee,A,Scotland;m.22 May 1867;d.20 Oct 1875-D,Angus Scotland)
                 │   ├─ 6. Betty Wilkie (c.6 Jan 1828-Forfar,Angus Scotland)
                 │   ├─ 6. David Wilkie (c.26 Dec 1831-Forfar,Angus Scotland)
                 │   └─ 6. James Wilkie (c.27 Jul 1834-Forfar,Angus Scotland)
                 ├─ 5. John Wilkie (b.23 Nov 1796-Forfar,Angus Scotland)
                 │   sp: Barbara McKay (m.13 Mar 1824)
                 │   ├─ 6. Charles Wilkie (b.9 Jul 1827-Dundee,Angus,Scotland)
                 │   ├─ 6. Jean Wilkie (b.29 Sep 1829-Dundee,Angus,Scotland)
                 │   ├─ 6. John Wilkie (b.25 Sep 1834-Dundee,Angus,Scotland)
                 │   ├─ 6. Catherine Wilkie (b.11 Jul 1839-Dundee,Angus,Scotland)
                 │   └─ 6. James Wilkie (b.18 Mar 1842-Dundee,Angus,Scotland)
                 │   sp: Elizabeth Jenkins
                 ├─ 5. Alexander Wilkie (b.16 May 1799-Forfar,Angus Scotland)
                 └─ 5. Jean Wilkie (b.12 Oct 1803-Forfar,Angus Scotland)

The Cuthberts

David Alma Graham, the oldest son of James and Catherine married Agnes Robb Cuthbert on 20 Aug 1885 at 14 Barrack St. in Dundee, Agnes' home. David was listed as a 31 year old gasfitter; Agnes a 27 year old spinster. Witnesses were Charles IB Graham and Agnes Candow (his future first wife). Agnes Robb Cuthbert was born to George Cuthbert and Agnes Kidd on 6 May 1857 at Shepard's Close, Dundee. Her father was listed as a coachbuilder, a fact with many intriguing implications. Agnes Kidd's mother was Agnes Robb, so the daughter was one of three Agnes' in succession. Agnes R. Cuthbert was the middle child between older brother George (born roughly 1855 in Dundee as no birth record exists) and younger brother James (b. 21 Jan 1860). But tragedy struck the Cuthberts when father George died of a stroke at age 39 on 17 Oct 1861 in Dundee. George's oldest brother, Thomas Cuthbert (born to John Cuthbert and Jane Sharp in Perth and christened 6 Dec 1801) was in control of the Cuthbert Coachbuilder business and witnessed his brother's death registration. But the relationship between brothers and their families must not have been close as the widow Agnes Cuthbert and her three children experienced life in the Dundee Poorhouse on two different occasions, once in 1863 and another in 1865. By the time of the 1871 census, widow Agnes along with George and Agnes were living at 8 Park Street, Lochee. Mother Agnes' occupation was housekeeper, George was listed as coachbuilder and Agnes was a power loom weaver. Young James may have been farmed out to a relative or apprenticed to a tradesman's family in the area.

So while it is true that the Cuthberts were successful coach manufacturers, the control, wealth and power associated with factory ownership was not equally shared amongst the descendents of John Cuthbert and his first wife Jane Sharp. I can only guess that family members were welcomed into the firm as laborers but were expected to live according to their means, and in the event of tragic consequences, well, too bad. Life for the family of George Cuthbert must have been hard following his death. Widow Agnes died 17 Nov 1896 at Dundee Parochial Hospital listed as Pauper, Widow of George Cuthbert Coachbuilder. Her oldest child George married Jessie Taylor, daughter of a coachpainter, in 1883 in Dundee. But George, like his father, died at a young age of 43 in Kelvin Lanark. James married Margaret Moran at age 38 in 1898 but died of colon cancer two years later. He was listed as a small wares hawker.

That Agnes would meet, marry and migrate to America with David A. Graham makes her story the most successful of her immediate family. Though there was some family folklore that the Cuthberts looked down upon the marriage, my guess is that David and Agnes committed to immigrating to the USA well before their marriage. They probably had to save carefully to book passage for the New World and the hope of a brighter future. Were their dreams realized in Brooklyn? We have no firsthand knowledge but they lived there from Sep 1885 until their respective deaths in 1922 (hers) and 1933 (his). They had six children, four of whom survived childhood. From these limited datapoints, we can only assume that life proved good enough to keep them in Brooklyn for nearly 50 years.

What of the other Cuthberts? The patriarch John Cuthbert (b. 1775 Panbride, Angus; d. 1 Mar 1853 Dundee) left his oldest son Thomas in charge. Thomas was born in 1801 and died 21 Feb 1892 at home on Dudhope Street in Dundee. He had eight children by his first wife Mary Hutchison and remarried Jane Mudie after being widowed in 1850. Of the eight offspring, three were boys and though the oldest one – Thomas – died at age thirteen, it was the youngest son and youngest child, George that succeeded him in the coach building business. Interestingly, my research led to connections with relations of the middle son John Cuthbert who now live in Australia.

THOMAS CUTHBERT.
DUNDEE YEAR BOOK, 1892

Mr Cuthbert, who had enjoyed good health during his long life, was taken ill about a fortnight before his death, and so recently as the 9th February he was able to be about. A slight cold afterwards confined him to the house, and although he suffered from no bodily ailment he gradually became weaker, and died at his residence in Dudhope Place on Sunday, 21st February. The deceased gentleman was a native of Perth, where he was born 90 years ago. He learned the trade of a coachbuilder in Perth, and upwards of half a century ago he came to Dundee, where he started on his own account in premises on a site which now forms part of Bank Street. About 43 years since he removed to the building at the corner of Constitution Road and Meadowside, where until twelve years ago, when he retired from business in favour of his son George, he uninterruptedly carried on a large coachbuilding establishment. One of the reasons for his removal from Barrack Street to Meadowside was to obtain sufficient accommodation to construct railway carriages. Mr Cuthbert was the first in Scotland to undertake this class of work, and he carried it on, with the most satisfactory results, until the large Railway Companies began to build for themselves. Among other railway lines which he supplied with rolling stock was the Dundee and Newtyle line and the Glasgow and Ayr line. When this branch of his trade was given up Mr Cuthbert set himself to the extension of the coachbuilding department, and in this, as in the construction of railway carriages, he was eminently successful. So well known did the firm become for the excellent workmanship produced that Mr Cuthbert had many orders from the South and even from abroad, and this connection has always been maintained, so that at the present moment the business is the largest of its kind in this district. In the course of his lifetime Mr Cuthbert frequently took part in public affairs. He was induced to enter the Town Council, and discharged his duties so efficiently that his colleagues raised him to the Magistracy. He also held office for many years as a Governor of the Morgan Hospital, to which he was elected at the opening of that institution, and from the opening of the Kinaird Hall till his death he was a Director of the Corn Exchange and Public Hall Association. Mr Cuthbert was also a member of the Hammermen Trade, and acted as Deacon of that body for a time. Deceased was connected with the Free Church, and was one of the oldest members of Willison congregation. He is survived by two sons and two daughters.

But one final note on George Cuthbert (born 1844 Dundee, died 8 Aug 1934 Richmond, England). He married Christian Soote Sime 9 Mar 1882 and together they had two daughters, Margaret Jane Mudie Cuthbert (b. 10 Jan 1883, Dundee) and Catherine Maude Cuthbert (b. 4 May 1889, Dundee). Margaret took a very atypical path in life for her times; she became a doctor, practicing in Richmond outside of London. She never married. Her sister Catherine married a Church of Scotland minister – John Ford McLeod in Dundee 1920. Young pastor McLeod was leading a congregation in Craigrownie, a small town west of Glasgow on the Firth of Clyde. But he must have been recognized as a fine pastor as he would go on to lead the Tron Kirk in Edinburgh by the mid-1930's. Due to privacy restrictions, I have not been able to determine if the McLeod's had children but I did learn that John McLeod died in Newington, Midlothian in 1960 and Catherine (Cuthbert) McLeod died in the same place in 1962.

Let me add that some of the information about the Cuthberts came to me via Isobel (Cuthbert) Martin who was born in Dundee but immigrated to Australia in the fifties at age eleven with her parents and two older sisters. Isobel and I have been active email correspondents for nearly two years. She was enthused to find out what I had discovered on the Dundee Cuthberts and, likewise, I have been pleased to learn about her lineage and stories of her family in Australia.

WEDNESDAY, AUGUST 8, 1934

DEATH OF NOTED DUNDEE CITIZEN

Mr George Cuthbert

A venerable citizen of Dundee, greatly esteemed by all who knew him, has been removed by the death of Mr George Cuthbert, which occurred yesterday at the residence of his daughter in Richmond.

In many ways the life of Mr Cuthbert was similar to that of his father, Mr George Cuthbert, who died in 1892. Both were oldest members of the Nine Incorporated Trades of Dundee, and both served as deacon of the Hammermen Trade. Each died in his 91st year.

Mr Cuthbert belonged to a family of coachbuilders. His father, who was born in Perth, came to Dundee as a young man, and rapidly extended the business of Thos. Cuthbert & Son, which his father had founded.

He feued from the town nearly a quarter of an acre of the Meadows, where he erected the most extensive coach works in the North-East of Scotland.

Built Rail Carriages

He was the first man in Scotland to build railway carriages. In this enterprise he was so successful that he erected a new establishment in Meadowside for this special purpose.

He built carriages for the Dundee and Newtyle Railway, the Glasgow and Ayr, Dundee and Arbroath, and Dundee and Perth railways.

In 1880 his son, whose death has now occurred, was transferred to the Meadowside establishment. He later took part in the negotiations for the transfer of the coach works property to the Government.

The site was acquired for the General Post Office, and Messrs Cuthbert removed to premises in Ward Road.

Amongst the members of the Nine Incorporated Trades Mr Cuthbert was an extremely popular personality. He had held the offices of deacon and assessor, and even in advanced years he worthily played his part in the social gatherings of that body.

Skilled Musician

He was a skilled musician in his younger days, playing the violin well and possessing a sweet tenor voice. When he had long passed the allotted span he used to delight the members of the Nine Trades at their social functions with his rendering of "The Dear Little Shamrock."

He was also a keen angler.

Mr Cuthbert, who retired from business a considerable time ago, was for long connected with Willison-Bell Church. Predeceased by his wife, he is survived by two daughters. One is a doctor in Richmond, and the other is the wife of Rev. J. Ford M'Leod, Tron Church, Edinburgh.

Mr Cuthbert formerly resided at Gartlands, Stratharn Road, Broughty Ferry.

Descendants of William CUTHBERT

1. William CUTHBERT
  sp: Ann CHIELD (c.5 Nov 1746-Panbride,Angus,Scotland;m.10 Dec 1774)
- 2. John CUTHBERT (c.2 Sep 1775-Panbride,Angus,Scotland;d.1 Mar 1853-Dundee,Angus,Scotland)
    sp: Jean or Jane SHARP (c.8 Nov 1779-Perth,Perth,Scotland;m.28 Nov 1800;d.Bef 1826)
    - 3. Thomas CUTHBERT (c.6 Dec 1801-Perth,Perth,Scotland;d.21 Feb 1892-Dundee,Angus,Scotland)
        sp: Mary HUTCHISON (b.~1805-Perth,Perth Scotland;m.25 Jun 1823;d.15 Jun 1850-Dundee,Angus Scotland)
        - 4. Margaret Wallace CUTHBERT (c.23 May 1824-Perth,Perth,Scotland;d.29 Nov 1850-Dundee,Angus,Scotland)
        - 4. Jane CUTHBERT (c.25 Dec 1825-Perth,Perth,Scotland;d.11 Sep 1872-Dundee,Angus,Scotland)
            sp: William Butchart WALKER (c.29 May 1825-D,Angus Scotland;m.31 Dec 1846;d.27 Sep 1866-D,Angus Scotland)
        - 4. Mary CUTHBERT (c.22 May 1828-Perth,Perth,Scotland;d.24 Jun 1872-Dundee,Angus,Scotland)
        - 4. Jean CUTHBERT (c.16 Mar 1830-Dundee,Angus Scotland)
            sp: Andrew STEWART (m.10 Jun 1858)
            - 5. Mary Cuthbert STEWART (b.Jun 1859-Dundee,Angus Scotland;d.31 Dec 1859-Dundee,Angus Scotland)
        - 4. Elizabeth CUTHBERT (b.~1832-Dundee,Angus,Scotland;d.17 Feb 1919-Forthill,Angus,Scotland)
            sp: Robert MALCOLM (b.Abt 1828;m.27 Apr 1858;d.7 Jul 1893-Callendar,Perth,Scotland)
            - 5. Thomas Cuthbert MALCOLM (b.18 Aug 1859-Dundee,Angus,Scotland)
            - 5. Frederick James MALCOLM (b.30 Dec 1860-Dundee,Angus,Scotland;d.24 Nov 1924)
            - 5. Margaret Cuthbert MALCOLM (b.20 Jul 1862-Dundee,Angus,Scotland;d.12 Apr 1896-London,England)
                sp: ROBERTSON
            - 5. Norman Johnston MALCOLM (b.4 Jan 1865-Dundee,Angus,Scotland;d.24 Jul 1932-Kirriemuir,Angus,Scotland)
            - 5. Elizabeth Mary MALCOLM (b.28 Oct 1866-Dundee,Angus,Scotland;d.5 Nov 1917-Forthill,Angus,Scotland)
            - 5. Florence MALCOLM (b.28 Apr 1869-Dundee,Angus,Scotland)
            - 5. Herbert MALCOLM (b.22 Apr 1872-Monifieth,Angus,Scotland)
        - 4. Thomas CUTHBERT (c.23 Aug 1834-Dundee,Angus,Scotland;d.18 Sep 1847-Perth,Perth,Scotland)
        - 4. Helen CUTHBERT (b.Abt 1838-Dundee,Angus,Scotland;d.17 Dec 1876-Dundee,Angus,Scotland)
        - 4. John CUTHBERT (c.17 Dec 1839-Dundee,Angus Scotland;d.28 Dec 1914-Dundee,Angus,Scotland)
            sp: Mary Ann BIRD (b.1849-Stockton-on-Tees,Durham,England;m.19 Jul 1869;d.18 Jun 1901-Dundee,Angus,Scotland)
            - 5. Frederick CUTHBERT (b.1870-Middlesborough,England)
            - 5. Edith CUTHBERT (b.1871-Wolviston,Durham,England)
            - 5. Jane CUTHBERT (b.1875-Middlesborough,Yorkshire,England)
            - 5. John CUTHBERT (b.1876-Middlesborough,Yorkshire,England)
            - 5. George CUTHBERT (b.1877-Jarrow,Durham,England;d.Abt 1937)
                sp: Margaret Scott Lynch (b.1886-Fife,Scotland;m.6 Jan 1915;d.3 Nov 1943-Edinburgh,Midlothian,Scotland)
                - 6. George CUTHBERT (b.Abt 1900;d.Abt 1950-Wales,England)
                - 6. Frederick CUTHBERT (b.24 Aug 1907-Wemyss,Fife,Scotland;d.26 Mar 1973-NSW,Australia)
                    sp: Jemima Peebles (b.6 Aug 1911-Tayport,Fife,Scotland;m.18 May 1936;d.4 Dec 2009-Berry,NSW,Australia)
                    - 7. Elizabeth Jemima CUTHBERT (b.4 Oct 1936;d.13 Oct 1993-Wollongong,NSW Australia)
                        sp: William CRAIG (b.Abt 1934)

Descendants of William CUTHBERT

```
                    └─ 8. Freda Cuthbert CRAIG (b.21 Jul 1955-Dundee,Angus,Scotland)
                 ─ 7. Margaret Catherine CUTHBERT (b.7 Sep 1939-Dundee,Angus,Scotland)
                    sp: Matthew ROBERTSON (b.5 Dec 1928;m.18 Dec 1958;d.17 Jul 2000-Wollongong,NSW,Australia)
                    ├─ 8. Deborah Anne ROBERTSON (b.11 Jan 1960-Wollongong,NSW,Australia)
                    ├─ 8. Alan Dale ROBERTSON (b.26 Jun 1963-Wollongong,NSW,Australia)
                    ├─ 8. Christina ROBERTSON (b.4 Dec 1968-Wollongong,NSW,Australia)
                    └─ 8. Heather ROBERTSON (b.31 May 1971-Wollongong,NSW,Australia)
                 └─ 7. Isobel Ann CUTHBERT (b.19 Mar 1944-Dundee,Angus,Scotland)
                    sp: Matthew George PATTERSON (b.2 Oct 1941-Wollongong,NSW,Australia;m.1960(Div))
                    ├─ 8. Mark PATTERSON (b.1 Aug 1961-Wollongong,NSW,Australia)
                    │    sp: UNKNOWN
                    │    ├─ 9. Georgia PATTERSON (b.~1990-Australia)
                    │    ├─ 9. Sarina PATTERSON (b.~1995-Australia)
                    │    └─ 9. Olivia PATTERSON (b.~1998-Australia)
                    ├─ 8. Allison Margart PATTERSON (b.9 Jul 1963-Wollongong,NSW,Australia)
                    │    sp: UNKNOWN
                    │    ├─ 9. Lauren  (b.~1997-Australia)
                    │    └─ 9. Sarah  (b.~2004-Australia)
                    └─ 8. Luke Anthony PATTERSON (b.5 Jul 1965-Wollongong,N,Australia;d.17 Jun 1980-Australia)
                    sp: Roger Wyckoff MARTIN (m.8 Jun 1974;d.30 Jul 2003-Berry,NSW,Australia)
              ├─ 6. John CUTHBERT (b.26 Sep 1911-Wemyss,Fife,Scotland)
              ├─ 6. Nan CUTHBERT (b.Abt 1909-Wemyss,Fife,Scotland)
              └─ 6. Alice Maud CUTHBERT (b.19 Jul 1914-Wemyss,Fife,Scotland)
           ├─ 5. Thomas CUTHBERT (b.1879-Middlesborough,Yorkshire,England)
           ├─ 5. Florence CUTHBERT (b.1884-Inverness,Inverness,Scotland)
           ├─ 5. Elizabeth CUTHBERT (b.1881-Middlesborough,Yorkshire,England)
           ├─ 5. Edward CUTHBERT (b.1887-Inverness,Scotland)
           └─ 5. Alice CUTHBERT (b.1890-England)
      ─ 4. George CUTHBERT (b.~1844-Dundee,Angus,Scotland;d.8 Aug 1934-Richmond,Surrey,England)
         sp: Christian Soote SIME (b.25 Aug 1855-Flisk,Fife,Scotland;m.9 Mar 1882;d.18 Sep 1914-Dundee,Angus,Scotland)
         ├─ 5. Margaret Jane Mudie CUTHBERT (b.10 Jan 1883-Dundee,Angus,Scotland)
         ├─ 5. George CUTHBERT (b.Jan 1885-Dundee,Angus,Scotland;d.4 Nov 1887-Dundee,Angus,Scotland)
         └─ 5. Catherine Maud(e) CUTHBERT (b.4 May 1889-Dundee,Angus,Scotland;d.1962-Newington,Midlothian,Scotland)
              sp: John Ford MCLEOD (b.1889;m.21 Sep 1920;d.1960-Newington,Midlothian,Scotland)
      sp: Jane MUDIE (b.16 Feb 1812-Dundee,Angus,Scotland;d.Bef 1891-Dundee,Angus,Scotland)
─ 3. Mary CUTHBERT (c.22 May 1803-Perth,Perth Scotland;b.21 Jul 1848-Howff Cemetery,Dundee,Angus,Scotland)
   sp: Peter CAMPBELL (m.Jun 1827)
   └─ 4. Thomas Bruce CAMPBELL (b.26 Dec 1837-Dundee,Angus,Scotland)
```

Grahams o' the Mearns

Descendants of William CUTHBERT

- 3. Ann CUTHBERT (c.16 Jun 1805-Perth,Perth Scotland;d.16 Jan 1872-Dundee,Angus,Scotland)
  - sp: John DOWNIE (b.23 Jun 1806-Dundee,Angus,Scotland;m.3 Jan 1831)
    - 4. Jean DOWNIE (b.15 Jun 1831-Dundee,Angus,Scotland)
    - 4. Ann DOWNIE (b.Mar 1833-Dundee,Angus,Scotland)
    - 4. Isabella (Bella) DOWNIE (b.1835-Dundee,Angus,Scotland)
    - 4. James DOWNIE (b.10 Feb 1837-Dundee,Angus,Scotland)
    - 4. Anne (Annie) DOWNIE (b.1839-Dundee,Angus,Scotland)
    - 4. John Cuthbert DOWNIE (b.1844-Dundee,Angus,Scotland)
    - 4. William Cuthbert DOWNIE (b.1845-Dundee,Angus,Scotland)
- 3. John CUTHBERT (c.3 May 1807-Perth,Perth Scotland;d.26 Jan 1862-Dundee,Angus,Scotland)
  - sp: Jean COCHRAN (b.4 Jun 1809-Perth,Perth,Scotland;m.2 Mar 1830;d.9 Jan 1836-Dundee,Angus,Scotland)
    - 4. John CUTHBERT (b.2 Apr 1832-Perth,Perth Scotland)
    - 4. James CUTHBERT (b.10 Jun 1834-Perth,Perth Scotland;d.13 Jan 1870-Dundee,Angus,Scotland)
  - sp: Elizabeth LAMB (b.31 Dec 1809-Dundee,Angus,Scotland;m.22 Jun 1837;d.10 Apr 1888-Dundee,Angus,Scotland)
    - 4. Mary CUTHBERT (b.11 Aug 1838-Dundee,Angus,Scotland;d.11 Jan 1843-Dundee,Angus,Scotland)
    - 4. Thomas CUTHBERT (b.1842-Dundee,Angus,Scotland;d.9 Jul 1908-Dundee,Angus,Scotland)
      - sp: Catherine LAIRD (b.1841-Dundee,Angus,Scotland;m.26 Jun 1863)
        - 5. Elizabeth Lamb CUTHBERT (b.27 Jun 1864-Dundee,Angus,Scotland)
        - 5. Mary Isabella CUTHBERT (b.5 Jun 1866-Dundee,Angus,Scotland)
        - 5. John William CUTHBERT (b.11 Mar 1874-Dundee,Angus,Scotland;d.1936-Dundee,Angus,Scotland)
          - sp: Maggie BROWN (m.1906)
            - 6. Thomas CUTHBERT
            - 6. Flora Lamb CUTHBERT (b.9 Oct 1915)
            - 6. Catherine CUTHBERT
    - 4. Mary CUTHBERT (b.1846-Dundee,Angus,Scotland;b.18 Jan 1851-Howff Cemetery,Dundee,Angus,Scotland)
    - 4. David CUTHBERT (b.20 Jun 1857-Dundee,Angus,Scotland)
- 3. William CUTHBERT (c.16 Jul 1809-Perth,Perth,Scotland;d.1846-Dundee,Angus,Scotland)
- 3. Amelia Ann CUTHBERT (b.10 Jan 1812-Perth,Perth,Scotland;d.Bef 1850)
  - sp: John LINDSAY (m.3 Jan 1831)
- 3. James CUTHBERT (c.26 Mar 1815-Perth,Perth,Scotland;d.2 Jan 1840-Dundee,Angus,Scotland)
- 3. Jean CUTHBERT (c.20 Jul 1817-Perth,Perth Scotland)
  - sp: Alexander MOON (b.~1798;m.22 Dec 1840)
    - 4. Charles MOON (b.18 Jan 1843-Dundee,Angus Scotland;d.19 Apr 1917-Dundee,Angus,Scotland)
      - sp: Eva CRAMMOND (b.~1855-Milton of Crags,Angus,Scotland;m.13 Jun 1877)
        - 5. Charles John Cuthbert MOON (b.11 Sep 1878-Dundee,Angus Scotland;d.13 Nov 1953-Dundee,Angus,Scotland)
        - 5. Alice Anne MOON (b.12 Mar 1880-Dundee,Angus Scotland;d.15 Jun 1881-Dundee,Angus,Scotland)
        - 5. Eva MOON (b.9 Sep 1881-Dundee,Angus,Scotland)
          - sp: John THORNTON (b.31 Aug 1868-Arbroath,Angus,Scotland;m.12 Dec 1906)

Descendants of William CUTHBERT

- 5. Patrick Murison MOON (b.27 Jun 1883-Dundee,Angus,Scotland)
- 5. George Crammond MOON (b.2 Feb 1885-Dundee,Angus,Scotland;d.5 Nov 1944-Dundee,Angus,Scotland)
- 5. James Stocks MOON (b.30 Nov 1886-Dundee,Angus,Scotland)
- 5. Frederick William MOON (b.30 Jun 1888-Dundee,Angus,Scotland)
- 5. Alexander W MOON (b.1894-Dundee,Angus,Scotland)
- 4. Jean MOON (b.29 May 1844-Dundee,Angus Scotland)
- 4. Margaret MOON (b.30 Dec 1848-Dundee,Angus,Scotland)
- 4. John Cuthbert MOON (b.7 Oct 1853-Dundee,Angus Scotland)
- 4. MOON (d.8 Oct 1841-Dundee,Angus Scotland)
- 3. George CUTHBERT (b.17 Mar 1822-Perth,Perth,Scotland;d.17 Oct 1861-Dundee,Angus,Scotland)
  - sp: Agnes KIDD (b.29 Jul 1823-Dundee,Angus,Scotland;m.20 Dec 1851;d.17 Nov 1896-Dundee,Angus,Scotland)
  - 4. George CUTHBERT (b.1855-Dundee,Angus,Scotland;d.12 Jun 1898-Kelvin,Glasgow,Lanark,Scotland)
    - sp: Jessie TAYLOR (b.13 Apr 1856-Edinburgh,Midlothian,Scotland;m.17 Jul 1883)
  - 4. Agnes Robb CUTHBERT (b.6 May 1857-Dundee,Angus,Scotland;d.14 Nov 1922-Brooklyn,NY,USA)
    - sp: David Alma GRAHAM (b.1 May 1854-S,Stirlingshire Scotland;m.20 Aug 1885;d.21 Oct 1933-Hollis,Queens,NY,USA)
    - 5. Jennie Francis GRAHAM (b.11 Jun 1886-Brooklyn,NY;d.30 Dec 1969-Brooklyn,NY)
    - 5. David Alma GRAHAM (b.26 Jan 1888-Brooklyn,Kings,NY,USA;d.18 Aug 1955-Ridgewood,Queens,NY,USA)
      - sp: Emma Frances SCHWARZ (b.3 Aug 1893-Brooklyn,NY,USA;m.25 Nov 1914;d.21 Apr 1978-Ridgewood,N,USA)
      - 6. Robert David GRAHAM (b.6 Jan 1921-Ridgewood,Queens,NY,USA;d.16 Oct 2004-Chesapeake,Norfolk,Virginia)
        - sp: Dorothy E. BACHMAN (b.4 Mar 1922-Bridgeport,CT;m.16 Oct 1943;d.21 May 1994-Virginia Beach,VA)
        - 7. Linda Carol GRAHAM (b.13 May 1948-Bridgeport,CT)
          - sp: Thomas BRADLEY (m.14 Jun 1969)
          - 8. Kenneth BRADLEY (b.25 Feb 1973-Norwood,NJ)
            - sp: Michele Ann TOMICICH (b.24 Jan 1969-Pueblo,CO;m.12 Dec 1998)
            - 9. Taylor Nicole BRADLEY (b.3 Mar 2004-Denver,Adam,Colorado)
        - 7. Barbara Lee GRAHAM (b.7 Apr 1952-Bridgeport,CT)
          - sp: William Terry PATE (b.20 Oct 1957-Conway,SC;m.28 May 1993)
      - 6. Charles James GRAHAM (b.12 May 1929-Brooklyn,NY;d.12 Nov 1990-Marietta,GA)
        - sp: Marilyn Louise LAFRANCE (b.8 Aug 1928-Schnectady,NY;m.9 Jun 1951)
        - 7. David Lee GRAHAM (b.4 Oct 1956-Pittsfield,MA)
          - sp: Jane Ellen HARBAUGH (b.12 Nov 1957-New York,NY;m.10 Sep 1983)
          - 8. Connor David GRAHAM (b.7 Aug 1989-Seattle,WA)
          - 8. Charles James GRAHAM (b.23 Jul 1991-Seattle,WA)
        - 7. Nancy Lynn GRAHAM (b.14 Mar 1961-Pittsfield,MA)
          - sp: Richard Brian BARKER (b.14 Feb 1954-Detroit,MI;m.24 Sep 1994(Div))
          - 8. Chase Riley BARKER (b.10 Sep 1998-Atlanta,GA)
          - 8. Kyle Danic BARKER (b.10 Sep 1998-Atlanta,GA)
          - sp: Robert HAMILTON (m.16 Oct 2008)

Descendants of William CUTHBERT

```
        ├─ 5. Alexander J GRAHAM (b.1 Jan 1889-Brooklyn,Kings,NY;d.2 Apr 1889-Brooklyn,Kings,NY,USA)
        ├─ 5. Agnes Cuthbert GRAHAM (b.25 Jan 1890-Brooklyn,NY;d.15 Nov 1955-Forest Hills,NY)
        ├─ 5. George Forbes GRAHAM (b.7 Aug 1892-Brooklyn,NY;d.17 Jun 1972-Hempstead,Nassau,NY)
        │    sp: Lenora WIRTH (b.31 Jan 1896-Liberty PA;m.5 Jun 1920;d.15 Aug 1971-Centereach,Suffolk,New York,USA)
        │    ├─ 6. George Charles GRAHAM MD (b.9 May 1921-Brooklyn NY;d.8 Oct 1996-Hempstead Nassau NY)
        │    │    sp: Muriel Elsie HUENE MD (b.19 Sep 1921-Lakeview,Nassau,NY;m.23 Jun 1945;d.22 Oct 2005-C,NY)
        │    │    ├─ 7. Heather GRAHAM (b.19 Apr 1950-Mineola,NY;d.5 Aug 1982-West Hempstead,NY,USA)
        │    │    ├─ 7. Lorna Nancy GRAHAM (b.18 Apr 1954-Mineola,NY)
        │    │    │    sp: Kenneth Jonathon BROPHY (b.30 May 1951-Rahway,NJ,USA;m.Not married)
        │    │    │    └─ 8. Connor George GRAHAM (b.25 Oct 1997-Scranton,PA,USA)
        │    │    └─ 7. George Charles GRAHAM (b.1 Jul 1957-Mineola,NY)
        │    └─ 6. Ruth Lenora GRAHAM (b.27 Jul 1925-Woodhaven,Queens,NY;d.12 Sep 2010-Leesburg,FL)
        │         sp: Edmund FULLER (b.6 Jun 1923-Brooklyn NY;m.11 Nov 1944;d.27 May 1997-Tampa,FL)
        │         ├─ 7. Diane FULLER (b.11 Oct 1945-Jamaica Queens,Queens NY)
        │         │    sp: Neil LAMPARTER (m.25 Jul 1965(Div))
        │         │    └─ 8. Neil Roger LAMPARTER (b.5 May 1966-Bethpage,NY)
        │         └─ 7. Jean FULLER (b.29 Aug 1947-Queens Village,Queens NY)
        │              sp: William LAMPARTER (m.30 May 1971)
        │              ├─ 8. Sean LAMPARTER (b.29 Dec 1975-Syosset,NY)
        │              └─ 8. Dana LAMPARTER (b.18 Jun 1979-Syosset,NY)
        │                   sp: UNKNOWN
        │                   └─ 9. Lilly  (b.Sep 2009)
        └─ 5. Charles James GRAHAM (b.Apr 1899-Brooklyn NY;d.~18 Jun 1904-Brooklyn,Kings NY)
   └─ 4. James CUTHBERT (b.21 Jan 1860-Dundee Angus Scotland;d.1 Dec 1900-Dundee,Angus,Scotland)
        sp: Margaret MORAN (b.~1870;m.22 Jul 1898)
   sp: Ann TAYLOR (b.20 Jun 1787-Newburgh,Fife Scotland;m.14 Nov 1826;d.4 May 1853-Dundee,Angus Scotland)
   ├─ 3. Elisabeth CUTHBERT (c.10 Sep 1827-Perth,Perth,Scotland)
   ├─ 3. Helen CUTHBERT (c.17 Dec 1829-Dundee,Angus,Scotland;d.1 Dec 1853-Dundee,Angus,Scotland)
   └─ 3. Isabell CUTHBERT (b.1832-Dundee,Angus Scotland)
├─ 2. Mary CUTHBERT (c.10 May 1777-Panbride Angus,Scotland)
├─ 2. James CULBERT OR CUTHBERT (c.14 Apr 1779-Panbride Angus,Scotland)
├─ 2. William CUTHBERT (b.6 Jun 1781-Dun,Angus,Scotland)
└─ 2. Isabell CUTHBERT (c.2 May 1784-Dundee,Angus,Scotland)
```

On Fevers, Fate and Family History
By David Graham (No. 4096)

[Authors Note: this essay was submitted to the Tay Valley Family History Society in the spring of 2005 and was published in a more edited form in the Tay Valley Family History Journal in October 2005. It reflected what I knew at the time and the passionate hobby it had become for me.]

This tale is not simply one of family history, but one of relationships – relationship to the past, to ancestors unknown, to a country and culture, to other researchers that share ideas and information and occasionally find common ancestors, and finally to blood relatives near and far. It is also a story still unfolding, a work in progress still being created even as I write this. My tale of family history research is not unfamiliar to members of the genealogy set as it contains exciting early discoveries, brickwalls and blind alleys, extensive time reviewing microfilms and surfing the internet and within the past year, a discovery, or more properly, a rediscovery of living Scottish relatives. And this last breakthrough could not have been made without the help and assistance of TVFHS members! Here is my tale.

I liken family history research to a virulent bug. If never exposed, a person can proceed through life blissfully ignorant of one's ancestry and quite happy I'm sure. Four years ago I counted myself in this group, faintly aware of my Scots ancestry and that the Graham name was one of the renowned Scottish clans. But I knew little else until I took my family on a trip to Scotland and spent part of a day perusing my family history in the General Registry Office in Edinburgh. Within hours, I discovered detailed information about three generations of Graham ancestors that little had been known about or passed down. I had been exposed, and in my case the family history bug was indeed an infectious strain.

In 2000, I was in my mid-forties, self-employed, happily married with two pre-teen sons. My dad passed away from an untimely heart attack at the age of 61. His father, a first generation American of Scot parents, survived a heart attack at 62 but couldn't beat the next one at 67. As I began to contemplate my own mortality I also began to gain a curiosity about my roots, just what stock was I derived from? Coincidentally, I have been a life-long golfer and had a small but burgeoning interest in single malt scotches. Genetics or fate, but whatever the reason I got my wife and family interested in a trip to Scotland and off we headed. After a few days in London, we took the train to Edinburgh and began a five night stay there. In researching our trip beforehand, I became aware of the General Registry Office and its extensive archives so on a mizzly Friday morning I left my wife and kids and headed over. Paying my entrance fee (which seemed a bit steep at the time), I walked into on of the rooms expecting a few people and not much else. Was I surprised! Even at 9:30 in the morning, the cubicles were nearly full with folks of all types busily scanning computer screens, fiches and films. A kindly docent got me started and off I went.

My knowledge of my Graham relations was limited. I had one surviving 80 year old uncle who passed along what little he knew about his grandparents that arrived in the US in the mid-1880's. The information was sketchy. He did not know birth or marriage dates, locations or even when they immigrated before landing in Brooklyn, New York. Looking back now, I represented the classic genealogy newcomer walking in with a few notes on a page uncertain as to what he might find and having modest hopes and expectations. Yet within minutes I uncovered more information than I ever thought possible! With each discovery of documented birth, marriage and death information my excitement rose. I was recapturing information that had been lost over time. My plan to stay an hour or so became two, then three, then three and a half. My wife arrived because we had agreed to meet for lunch. With our boys we grabbed a bite to eat and managed to tour the National Gallery for another hour and half but then I excused myself to go back to the New Registry House for one final push. I had been exposed and the infection has yet to subside.

My great grandfather David Alma GRAHAM was born 1 May 1854 in Stirling to James Campbell GRAHAM and Catherine WILKIE. David, a tinsmith, married Agnes CUTHBERT on 20 Aug 1885 in Dundee where they both resided. I knew that their first child, Jennie GRAHAM was born in Brooklyn in June 1886 so they must have immigrated sometime between that August and the following June. Next I found the marriage listing for James Campbell and Catherine – they married in Forfar 9 Jul 1848. These, my 2X great grandparents, had four sons:

- David Alma GRAHAM, b. 1 May 1854, Stirling, Stirling
- James Talford GRAHAM, b. 28 Mar 1856, Govan, Lanark
- Charles Iconaclast Bradlauch GRAHAM, b. 10 Aug 1861, New Monkland, Lanark
- George Heron GRAHAM, b. 6 Sep 1864, Dundee, Angus

At the time, I did not appreciate the unusual middle names, but more on that later. Minutes later, I found that James Campbell GRAHAM, a mason, died 18 Dec 1865 of typhus at the untimely age of 43 in Dundee. His parents were listed as Alexander GRAHAM, tailor and Christina Graham, m.s. Doig (deceased). Subsequent searching however did not locate a birth record for James Campbell or a marriage record for Alexander and Christina DOIG. Little did I realize in these first exciting moments that I had quickly uncovered a 'brickwall.' I did manage to find the death certificate for Catherine Wilkie and 1881 census data for her and two of her Graham sons as well as two young daughters named WATSON giving clues about a subsequent marriage for the widow Catherine. Having accomplished far more than I ever expected, I walked out of the stately New Register House elated, fascinated and intrigued. My excitement was palpable. Adding to my effusive mood, the clouds broke, the sun came out and I rejoined my family for a walk over to Calton Hill and then on up Arthurs' Seat that gave us a spectacular view of greater Edinburgh.

The very next day we left Edinburgh for a counterclockwise driving tour of the Highlands. Having arranged accommodations in Banchory we headed there via an extended tour of the southern coast of Fife and several hours in St. Andrews. In a bit of tragic irony, we did not stop in Dundee, Forfar or other areas of Angus that have proven to be the stomping grounds for my Graham ancestors though we did spend a Sunday driving back to Montrose and up the coast to Dunnotar. The rest of our trip was wonderful in every way though we had hoped for better weather on Skye and the western side of this stunning and starkly beautiful country.

Once back home, I found the internet and the worldwide web to be a fantastic tool. Determined to explore my Scots heritage and pursue my Graham lineage, I began spending countless hours on the LDS site, Rootsweb, ScotsOrigins (now ScotlandsPeople.gov.uk) and many others. By the fall of 2001 I learned about the Tay Valley Family History Society and became a member. Using the Society's Yahoo Groups site, I found numerous postings and soon created electronic friendships with others holding useful data such as Memorial Inscriptions and census indices. Of course, I also hoped to find living relatives with relations to my Graham ancestors but none emerged. And I couldn't overcome my 'brickwall' 3X GGF Alexander Graham, tailor.

Allow me to interject one thought. As one of two Graham males of my generation, I have always felt the subtle pressure of carrying on the Graham line, at least as it has existed in the American branch. We were blessed with two sons who, now in their teen years, could care less about dad's fascination with family history. Nonetheless, I have been particularly keen to extend my knowledge of our Graham ancestry. Like many, I had hoped to uncover some royal or noble lineage. Family history work raised questions that many of us face – what was life like back then? How did people work and live? What were their politics, religious practices and other interests? And for me, why did the oldest son immigrate to the US shortly after marrying at age 31? Unable to answer these questions specifically, I began to read more and more Scottish history. Just recently I read Buchan's biography of James Graham, first Marquis of Montrose which only reinforced my keen interest in our surname.

Now that 'genie' fever was rampant, I began to study all the Alexander Grahams and Christina Doigs in the time period. The LDS site proved very helpful as I catalogued all the possibilities in Angus. Online, I located birth, marriage and death entries for possible relatives. I even ordered up certificates of things that I had found during that fateful day in June 2001. Checking for Christina Doigs, I found one born in Maryton-by-Montrose in 1774 to James DOIG and Mary CAMPBELL and thought that an illegitimate birth might have led to the unusual naming James Campbell Graham. After all, history would tell us that Grahams and Campbells are not clans or surnames often seen together. This supposition ultimately proved to be a blind alley, but not before I traced back this Doig family two more generations. My web searching located a site dedicated to Doigs (www.doig.net) and I corresponded several times with its creator.

By mid-autumn 2001 I located and wrote for a death certificate for a Christina Graham who died in Dundee in 1856 but she was listed as single, another blind alley. At the same time I ordered up a death certificate for an Alexander GRAHAM that died in St. Peter, Dundee in 1871. Imagine my surprise when it arrived with the others some weeks later.

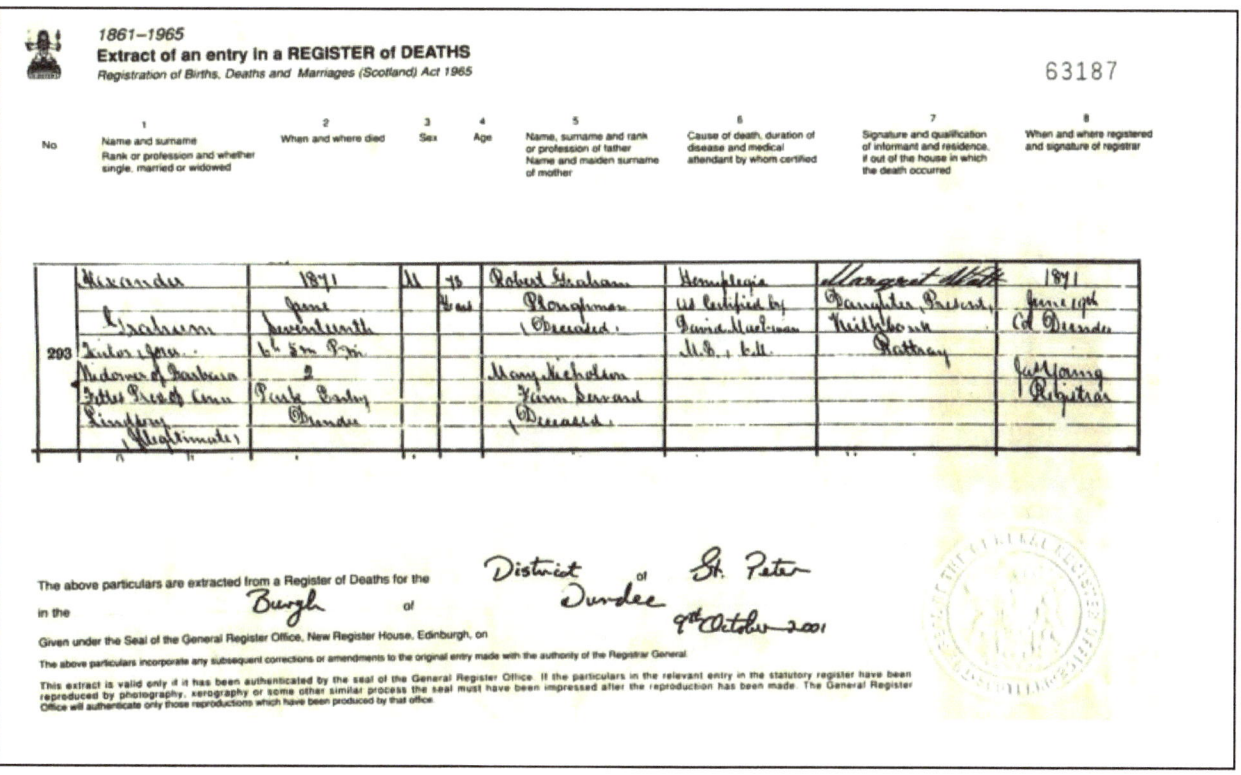

This Alexander GRAHAM was a tailor (journeyman) born in 1798 in St. Cyrus, the illegitimate son of Robert GRAHAM, ploughman and Mary NICHOLSON, farm servant. It indicated that he was married first to Ann LINDSAY and again to Barbara FETTES. These marriages were confirmed in the International Genealogical Index at www.familysearch.org. This Alexander had two children by his first wife (an Alexander GRAHAM b. 3 Nov 1821 Marykirk, Kincardineshire and a Mary Ann

GRAHAM, b. 20 Dec 1822, Marykirk, Kincardineshire) but none to his second wife. His death certificate was witnessed by Margaret WATT, daughter from Keithbank Rattray.

This intriguing finding did not provide the confirmation I had hoped, but it did offer several new clues and avenues to pursue. It opened my eyes to Kincardineshire Grahams, an area that I wasn't familiar with and had not thought to check early on. Also, I couldn't quite figure out the daughter Margaret. I uncovered a marriage between Charles WATT and Margaret GRAHAM in Montrose Dec 1846 and my first thought was that Mary Ann changed her name to Margaret later in life. I created a matrix of all Alexander GRAHAMs born in the counties of Fife, Perth, Angus, Kincardineshire and Aberdeenshire between 1775 and 1800. ScotsOrigin evolved into the ScotlandsPeople website, where I downloaded and reviewed death certificates for Alexander Grahams that died between 1865 and 1890 in the Tay Valley region. The only one listed as a tailor is the very first one I obtained in the fall of 2001.

Like many family history hobbyists, my efforts waxed and waned - the 'genie' bug would grow dormant followed by flare-ups. In early 2003, I learned about the UK's Public Records Office and located military service discharge papers for Robert GRAHAM (born 11 Jun 1778 St. Cyrus to an Alexander GRAHAM no mother listed), the father of Alexander Graham (the tailor). Robert proved to be a 21 year veteran of Wellington's second Battalion of the Royal Regiment of Artillery. His discharge papers from May 1824 indicated that *"He is about 45 years of age, is, Five Feet Ten Inches in height, Light hair, Grey eyes, Fresh complexion; and by Trade or Occupation a Laborer. Was given sum of One pound Two shillings being thirty three days Marching Money at /8 (18?)d per diem (the difference between his Pension and 1/8d per diem) allowed by His Majesty's Regulations to carry him from Dublin to Aberdeen the place of his original Enlistment, and that he has received Five Shillings Passage Money from Donaghadee to Port Patrick."* Efforts to see if he was at Waterloo have thus far proven fruitless. Nor have I been able to locate him back in Scotland after his discharge. *[Note: I did ultimately learn that Robert Graham returned to the Montrose area, remarried and had at least one more child.]*

Cuthbert Coachbuilders factory at Meadowside in the 1870's.

Meanwhile, I continued using the internet to explore my maternal lines and found that my maternal grandmother's maiden name McWITHEY could be traced to a Scot captured at the Battle of Worcester in 1650 and sent to the Massachusetts colony for seven years of servitude. Investigations of the CUTHBERT family led me to an email exchange with Margaret Mill from the TVFHS and though we determined that there was no direct relationship she was kind enough to supply census and Memorial Inscription (MI) data that helped me realize that my Cuthbert's were part of the coachbuilder family. The Dundee Archives site has photos of the business in the early 1880's where it was located at Meadowside and Constitution Road. On my wife's side, her maternal line had links back to a John BURNETT b. 1611

Aberdeen who subsequently immigrated to the Virginia Colony. My knowledge of our family's Scots heritage was growing by leaps and bounds. It was great fun to fill in other lines and continue to be part of the electronic genealogy community. Yet, my desire to overcome my brickwall and push back my Graham lineage remained.

When researchers don't make progress going backward in time, understandably, they move in other directions. From Day 1, I had known that Catherine WILKIE had died in 1898 due to burns of the head, neck and extremities. The witness was her son Charles ('the Iconaclast'). Thus I was able to find that he married first Agnes Small CANDOW (m. 28 Dec 1886, Dundee) and had three children by her. An 1891 census record showed the children whose births were confirmed on ScotlandsPeople. Yet interestingly, the 1901 census showed his wife Agnes with a different age and now four children. It didn't take long to figure out that his first wife had died and he married another Agnes – Agnes Dickson SOUTAR and had three children by her. Two of his children by his first wife had died in the early 1890's. Charles Iconoclast Bradlauch Graham died 18 Dec 1945 witnessed by his son Charles GRAHAM with an address at Hill Street, Monifieth. I sat on this fact for quite awhile, but it seemed reasonable that some Graham relations might still be in Scotland. But would they be in the Dundee area and could I locate them?

By now, it was January 2004 and I had been conducting family history research for two and a half years. The issue of locating living relations became the itch that I couldn't scratch. How would I access them given the privacy restrictions on the ScotlandsPeople site? First, I posted a general inquiry on the use of paid researchers on our Tay Valley Bridges message board on Yahoo. I then followed up with a query on how to go about finding living relatives assuming that other members had crossed this issue themselves. Several folks suggested placing ads in local papers. That seemed daunting and, frankly, not very productive. Though prepared to move in that direction, I had one further thought. I posted again, but this time put forward specific information directed to any members in the Dundee area, specifically that I was looking for living relations to Charles Graham, son of Charles I.B. Graham who had lived in Monifieth in the 1940's. Now, it was the kindness of TVFHSers that came to the fore. Barrie Jack went to a directory and posted a reply listing what he had found about a Charles Graham, insurance agent and town councilor. Once more, I responded but the next event was one of those moments that make family history research special.

One afternoon in February 2004 I was at my desk speaking with my business partner when an email arrived from a second cousin once removed living in Broughty Ferry. I could barely contain myself. Again, I had Barrie Jack to thank as he placed a phone call to my cousin asking if she was related to the Charles GRAHAM in question and upon hearing affirmatively, gave her my email information and explained that she had an American cousin looking for relatives. In a strange twist of fate, my newly discovered second cousin had just been in touch with her older sister who was about to join the TVFHS in hopes of finding other Graham relatives! We began a series of (dare I say 'feverish') email exchanges and shared information about our respective branches of the Graham family. Unfortunately, the Scots side had no more information about our brickwall than I did. But we have exchanged copies of photos and letters that make our particular family history really come alive. Together, we have had a chuckle about our aspirations of noble links only to discover that our common ancestor James Campbell GRAHAM was illegitimate as, most likely, was his father Alexander. Clearly, the promise of the internet making this a global community had been realized once again and it would not have happened without the support from many TVFHS members.

While this connection to living relatives occurred, I used advice from several posters on the Tay Valley Bridges site and simultaneously hired a local researcher. This person quickly found an 1861 census entry for James Campbell GRAHAM and family giving his birth location as Glamis. Next an 1841 Glamis census entry showed a William MUIR (45), Christina DOIG (55) and James GRAHAM (15).

Finally a review of kirk session minutes yielded another amusing nugget in an entry for Glamis kirk dated 2 Dec 1821:

> *Christian Doig appeared and acknowledged herself to be guilty of a relapse in fornication. She declared that she was with child to Alexr Graham who lately removed from this place & was now residing in Aberdeen. The woman promised to get a letter from him to the Kirk Session acknowledging him to be the father of her child, which would serve till he returned to make his confession before the Kirk Session. Christian Doig after being warned of her danger & suitably chastised was dismissed for the present.*
>
> *L.N. (?) Closed with prayer*

Armed with this new information, I was finally able to ascertain that Christina DOIG had been born to Robert DOIG and Isabella NEAVE in Glamis 10 Jan 1784. Again, www.Doig.net proved helpful as I found out that she had a previous illegitimate son by a William Donaldson which explained the 'relapse in fornication'. But again, it did not close the linkage to Alexander GRAHAM. I rechecked records for Aberdeenshire but nothing seemed to fit. However, I next found an entry for a Margaret Nicholson GRAHAM born to Alexander GRAHAM and Elizabeth SHARP 8 May 1821 Marykirk, Kincardineshire. This proved to be the Margaret that witnessed her father's death certificate in 1871.

In another twist of fate, I found an entry on Doig.net for an Elizabeth DOIG, illegitimate daughter of a John DOIG and Mary Ann GRAHAM residing in the household of Charles and Margaret WATT. Back in 2001 upon finding the death certificate of the tailor Alexander Graham, I did find the marriage between Charles WATT and Margaret GRAHAM. Yet I had overlooked the significance of this finding until this new and randomly acquired census entry. Wanting to see this for myself I ordered a copy of the 1851 census on microfilm. Already, I had spent many hours at a local LDS church Family History Center reviewing microfilm of census data – laborious work and tough on the eyes but this time I knew an entry existed making the task a bit easier. So it appeared that Margaret Nicholson Graham married Charles Watt and was close enough to her 'legitimate' sister Mary Ann to take in her illegitimate daughter Elizabeth Doig. Once found and copied, the Watt census entry yielded another interesting finding. In the household was an Elizabeth GRAHAM (age 17, flaxspinner) listed as "good sister." Though no birth information can be found on the IGI, my pursuits led me to an Elizabeth Graham that married an Alexander GOVE in Arbuthnott 22 Dec 1866 but her death certificate in 1873 listed her father as Alexander Graham, laborer rather than tailor. This too may be a blind alley. *[It was.]*

Though our common ancestor James Campbell was a mason that moved about quite a bit in the 1850's (refer back to the varying birth locations of his four sons), he must have been politically aware and perhaps a bit sardonic. His first son David Alma Graham (my GGF) was born in May 1854 and christened in May 1855. We surmise that the middle name Alma was derived from Britain's victory over the Russians in the Crimean War at the Battle of Alma which occurred 20 Sep 1854. Likewise, Charles Iconaclast Bradlauch Graham was named for Charles Bradlaugh, an atheist and founder of the National Secular Society who wrote under the pseudonym 'Iconoclast.' I cannot help but laugh when thinking of the poor registrar faithfully transcribing James' thick Scots pronunciation of the unusual name for his new born son. As to James Talford Graham and George Heron Graham, we are left to speculate about their middle names as these two disappeared from view after the 1881 census. At one time, I thought I had found a connection between the Wilkies and the Heron family. This precipitated a pleasant exchange of letters with Mr. Ian McKenzie who kindly provided cemetery information about

Wilkies buried in Forfar which added more knowledge to my WILKIE line, but alas the suspected Wilkie-Heron connection could not be proven. I wonder if James Campbell had enough wit to use the middle name Heron because the Graham family crest shows a heron being attacked by an eagle?

2004 proved to be a very fruitful year for me and my family history research. I located long lost cousins, found the mysterious Christina DOIG, answered questions about Margaret Graham Watt and her apparent close relationship with her father and half-sisters Mary Ann and Elizabeth, and I even found the ship's manifest for my great grandparent's arrival in New York on 18 Sep 1885 just a month after their marriage. We still speculate as to why this couple came to the USA though family folklore suggests that the CUTBHERT family was none too pleased by the union. After exchanging information with cousins on both sides of the Atlantic, I prepared a complete treatise on all that I suspected, collected, or knew about our Graham lineage. Presently, I believe that the Alexander GRAHAM, tailor from Dundee is our 3X GGF though this cannot be proven absolutely. He was probably raised by his mother Mary Nicholson and thought fondly enough of her that he would name his first (illegitimate) child Margaret Nicholson Graham, who also remained close enough to her father that she would be witness to his death in Dundee despite residing in Rattray at the time. Alexander was himself illegitimate but appears to be derived from GRAHAMs with 18th century roots in St. Cyrus and lower Kincardineshire. I have contemplated conducting a one name study like Ken Doig and Sheila Gerner but find that hurdle too great as yet.

As I write this, the fever has subsided, at least temporarily. From that very first day in the GROS I have experienced all the pleasures and pitfalls of genealogy and family history research -- brickwalls and blind alleys, countless hours in front of a computer or microfilm reader, the use of paid research and many more payments to ScotlandsPeoples, but most especially the joy of community with other researchers (particularly through the TVFHS) that led to the discovery of living relations and the desire to learn more about Scotland and my own heritage. Yet I cannot be cured. The itch will return, the fever will take hold again and off I will go to order microfilms, peruse message boards, and look for more clues regarding the whereabouts of yet to be discovered ancestors. When do I resign myself to the prospect that no more information is available, that no further progress can be gained? This lesson may be better addressed by other more experienced researchers than I. But this would represent a 'cure' and signal the end of those glorious moments when new findings arise, new discoveries are made, and I get that indescribable sense of pushing back the curtains of time on the mystery of my Graham family history.

Chuck feeding grandson Connor with dad Dave looking on, Sep 1989

Epilogue

"For that is the mark of the Scot of all classes: that he stands in an attitude towards the past unthinkable to Englishmen, and remembers and cherishes the memory of his forebears, good and bad; and there burns alive in him a sense of identity with the dead even to the twentieth generation."

Robert Louis Stevenson

Sometime during the past ten year family history journey, I came across the above Robert Louis Stevenson quotation. It captures well my strange fascination with our Graham family history. In the spring of 2001 at the age of forty-four, I could never have predicted how much time I would spend or the fun I would have investigating our family history. But what started out as a straightforward investigative exercise to discover early ancestors evolved into something much richer and more valuable than I could have possibly imagined at the outset of this journey. I have truly enjoyed and been blessed by the numerous connections to family members that were unknown to me before beginning this hobby. The visit Nancy and I took to Scotland in June 2006 will forever be a highlight of my life. And I still have ambitions to get back to this land of our forebears so that I may play the great golf courses, bag a Munro, sample more fine whiskys, visit family and share my passion for Scottish and Graham family history. Many others with distant or tenuous links to our Grahams have proven to be delightful correspondents willing to share their own histories and become members in this ever-growing community of family history researchers. More recent connections with distant family in Australia and New Zealand represent the on-going fruits of this peculiar avocation, but I suspect there will be even more to come.

Despite my best efforts, our family history is neither complete nor finished. It can never be finished. The chapter Loose Threads – Mysteries to be Solved lays out some of the most vexing questions about 'lost' ancestral relations. The fall 2009 discovery of Grahams in New Zealand opened avenues for further exploration which I (or my successors) have yet to pursue. I think it highly likely that there are Grahams in various countries of the British Commonwealth that may yet be uncovered someday. I, for one, look forward to such new discoveries and to welcoming any and all that share our Scots heritage and Graham lineage in one fashion or another.

There are no doubt errors and omissions for which I take full responsibility. If I have missed something or mislabeled photos or images, please accept my apology. What has been written represents nearly ten years of research, investigations, emails and exchanges with family members near and far. The amount of data, images, census entries, and websites are astronomical. Though I have tried to be meticulous in recording sources, transcription errors may have occurred. I have not pursued every living relation as fully as possible and there are certainly some gaps. In some instances, I have undoubtedly been guilty of interjecting my own thoughts and opinions in subtle and not-so-subtle ways. Though certainly not my intent, if I have upset any living relative, please accept my apologies. For me, this record has more value to our own ancestors that might be living fifty, one hundred or perhaps even several hundred years from now. Because I have pondered time and again what Alexander Graham or Robert Graham were like, their personalities, values, political and religious beliefs, I realize that this effort is a gift to future generations.

Finally, the astute reader will realize that I did not contribute to the section on remembrances and family stories. I could certainly write a bundle, yet somehow I feel that my thoughts, opinions and experiences are more than sufficiently sprinkled throughout this document already. But let me touch upon one theme that I have come to believe about our earliest recorded Graham ancestors – the bonds of family were neither tight nor overly warm. Why do I say this? Both Alexander the tailor and James Campbell Graham were illegitimate sons who did not appear to have a father figure in their lives. Perhaps it was just a reflection of the times and the challenge of making a living. It may have been some ethnic or genetic component to personality but from Robert Graham until the generations now living, those Grahams did not appear to be close knit families. Fathers left to be in the military, or to be itinerant tailors and tradesmen. Some immigrated abroad, no doubt seeking better economic circumstances. It is not clear from the limited historical records how close the familial bonds were throughout the 1800's. Even into the early twentieth century, World War I defined the young men that fought and survived. Reticence, reserve, and an inability to connect with their own children seemed to be a hallmark of our early Graham ancestors, though I'm sure it wasn't just confined to us Grahams. Admittedly, my sense of our Grahams may be completely off-base. We lack records or stories that would color the basic facts beyond birth, marriage, census and death entries. But thankfully, I believe, that the tide turned with those born in the 1920's and later. I sense that family and children became more important, familial bonds stronger and more solid. Perhaps it was just a sign of the time – more leisure time, less energy needed to scrape out a living allowing us to be together without stress or at least the kind of stress that surely existed in the eighteenth, nineteenth and early twentieth centuries. It may very well be that our earliest ancestors had to work awfully hard to survive, and that when presented with opportunities to move or migrate, they did. Whatever the case, our Graham ancestors did indeed spread across the globe in search of new and better lives.

Looking back upon my immediate family I have been extremely fortunate to come from such loving parents. My father, Chuck Graham, was the kind of man and father any son should aspire to. He was intelligent, optimistic, engaging, faithful and honorable. He was a loving husband and father and a successful business executive throughout his entirely too short 61 years. He was an avid golfer and an excellent athlete. Some of my best memories are playing with or against him on the links, in the squash court or on the paddle tennis platform. I only regret that my sons never knew him or could appreciate how much he would have enjoyed being a grandfather to them. And I know he would have greatly enjoyed participating with me on this family history journey. Those few of you who knew him would pay me a great compliment to say that 'you're just like your dad' or 'you favor your father.'

So let us never forget. Let us never forget who we are and who we descend from. Let us strive to remember to the twentieth generation. Let us continue to seek connections to those in the past, those family members yet to be uncovered in the present, and our descendants yet to come. Share this story with your children and grandchildren. Add to it your own anecdotes, tales and personal histories. Build upon it, expand it, let it grow and flourish. For I guarantee you that someday, one of our Graham descendants will want to know much more about who we were and what we thought. Ne Oublie!

CJ, Jane, Dave and Connor Graham, Oct. 2010

Standing: Agnes "Nan" Graham, Agnes Dickson Soutar Graham, Charles I.B. Graham, David Soutar Graham.
Seated: Charles Graham, David Alma Graham, William Melville Graham. Photo ca 1907 in Dundee Scotland